The Maynard, North, and DeForest Families

The Maynard, North, and DeForest Families

A Story of Immigration, Industry, and Community

Jenifer Kahn Bakkala

with information and guidance from
Holbrook R. Davis (1921–2021)

Genealogy House
Amherst, Massachusetts

Published by Genealogy House,
a division of White River Press, Amherst, Massachusetts
genealogyhouse.net

ISBN: 978-1-887043-92-2

Book and cover design by Lufkin Graphic Designs
Norwich, Vermont 05055
www.LufkinGraphics.com

Library of Congress Cataloging-in-Publication Data

Names: Bakkala, Jenifer Kahn, author. | Davis, Holbrook R. (Holbrook
    Reineman), 1921-2021
Title: The Maynard, North, and DeForest families : a story of immigration,
    industry, and community / Jenifer Kahn Bakkala ; with information and
    guidance from Holbrook R. Davis.
Other titles: Story of immigration, industry, and community
Description: Amherst, Massachusetts : Genealogy House Publishers, [2021] |
    Includes bibliographical references and index. | Summary: "Told in the
    author's narrative style, 'The Maynard, North, and DeForest Families'
    follows the story of Charles North and Isaac Maynard, immigrants who
    arrived in America in 1836 and found success in the early industries of
    upstate New York. Making their homes in Oswego and Utica, the two men's
    descendants came to occupy some of the most prominent seats in New York
    State's booming textiles industry. When North and Maynard's
    grandchildren married each other in 1907, they were at the apex of
    Utica's economic and social stratum and grew to become leaders in their
    thriving community."-- Provided by publisher.
Identifiers: LCCN 2021003631 | ISBN 9781887043922 (hardcover)
Subjects: LCSH: North family. | North, Charles, 1819-1892. | Utica
    (N.Y.)--History--19th century. | Utica (N.Y.)--Genealogy. | Maynard
    family. | Maynard, Isaac, 1815-1885. | De Forest family. | Oswego
    (N.Y.)--Genealogy. | Oswego (N.Y.)--History--19th century. |
    Businessmen--New York (State)--Biography.
Classification: LCC F129.U8 B35 2021 | DDC 929.20973--dc23
LC record available at https://lccn.loc.gov/2021003631

Acknowledgments

THE ONLY TEPID MOMENT in writing this book was the very *first* moment, when Holbrook R. Davis and I wondered whether the characters in this story would be at all interesting. The smallest, initial research findings heated up our enthusiasm rapidly, and warm support for this endeavor flowed in at every point that followed. Many people and institutions gave generously of their time and energy toward the completion of this project. My thanks to all of them.

Holbrook R. Davis (1921–2021) was a thoughtful and ardent partner, pervading this process with his customary wit, curiosity, and charm. His interest in history was insatiable, and his enthusiasm for a well-told story set the tone for this endeavor, as it did for many things that he enjoyed during his near century on earth. He made this book a pleasure to write, blessing its final version before his death. I miss him terribly.

Linda Roghaar, Jean Stone, and all of the other wonderful folks at Genealogy House were capable and ardent supporters from the very beginning. It was a delight to have them, their expertise, and their enthusiasm behind this book. Jean provided a thorough editing of the final manuscript, and her excellent suggestions strengthened the narrative. Janet Blowney was an exceptionally thorough and helpful proofreader, Doug Lufkin created a beautiful design for the pages and the front cover, and Linda Roghaar blessed the project with her customary fortitude, from beginning to end.

Karen Mauer Jones, CG®, FGBS, FUGA, was a shrewd, thoughtful, and careful editor and advisor throughout the writing stage. What I learned from her about genealogical writing will stay with me always.

Kyle Hurst and Kate Bakkala reviewed the almost-final version of the manuscript and offered well-placed, thoughtful suggestions, as well as their customarily warm encouragement. I am grateful that they were willing to be a part of this project.

Maynard K. Davis opened his home and his collection of files and photographs to me, and he and his family were delightful hosts for my visit to their city. Maynard also made a careful and helpful review of the final manuscript.

Mary Kay Stone, David D'Ambrosio, Eva Corradino, and Mark Slosek (all of the Richardson-Bates House and Museum in Oswego, New York), and Oswego County Historian Justin White rolled out the red carpet for my very productive visit to their city. Mary Kay Stone enabled access to many of the photographs that appear in the first chapter.

Christine Gray-Mullen interrupted her travel plans on a day's notice to visit the National Library in Ireland in order to research the "Oswego Letters."

Brian Bakkala provided his usual expert advice regarding word usage, etymology, and handwriting. He and Sarah Sweeney Bakkala solved a vexing handwriting analysis issue in the final hour.

Peter Bakkala, Debra Kilpatrick, and Robert Marchetta reviewed early versions of the manuscript.

Carla Ness of the Cummington Historical Commission, Cummington, Massachusetts, spent the better part of a day providing me with much help and direction regarding her town and its history.

Sheila Perino-Sapienza, Richard Bomford, and Mac Palmer provided invaluable assistance on North family ancestry.

Pamela Holland was an important mentor to me in the area of Irish research.

Pamela Vittorio provided her expertise on canal history and New York newspaper research.

Julie Cahill Tarr helped with Wisconsin newspaper research.

Catherine Becker Wiest Desmarais offered advice and encouragement that helped me move forward at a critical point.

Stella Addo was a delightful facilitator and inspired chef for all the meetings between Holbrook R. Davis and me.

Marilyn Moran provided capable management and support for the completion of the project.

Essential information and help were also provided by: Deborah Seiselmyer and Herb LaGoy of Utica College Library, Utica, New York; the Forest Hill Cemetery Office, Utica; Edgar Manwaring of Riverside Cemetery, Oswego; the Oneida County Historical Society, Utica; Gregory J. Tessier of the Bryant Free Library, Cummington; Carla Swerman of the La Crosse Public Library, La Crosse, Wisconsin; The National Library of Ireland; The New York State Library; Walter Hinchman of the Pomfret School, Pomfret Center, Connecticut; Lauren Friedman-Way of the Baldwin School, Bryn Mawr, Pennsylvania.

Others assisted with field work in Oswego and Utica, providing aid in finding and reading headstones, interpreting maps, locating deeds, and myriad other generosities, large and small. The cities of Oswego and Utica, which grew to become full-fledged characters in this story, I came to appreciate with fondness. I will be ever grateful for the chicken wings at Oswego's Press Box that sustained me, and for the encouragement of Utica's clock tower and its unwavering light, blinking gently in the snow. These and many other blessings moved me—and this book—forward.

Contents

Foreword

Sarah "Sally" DeForest Maynard Davis, about 1938.[1]

SARAH DEFOREST MAYNARD DAVIS, during her life of 93 years, understood that she was the descendant of at least one Mayflower passenger, one congressman, and one Revolutionary War patriot—an ancestry that offers more than ample fodder for a genealogical book about her forebears. Pilgrims, career politicians, and soldiers have traditionally proven to be interesting subjects for historical study time and time again, and they likely will into the future.

This book, however, is not about those ancestors. Instead, this three-generation journey begins with two immigrants in Sarah's family tree, both of whom made contributions to America's heritage as shop owners and businessmen. Like their more noted counterparts, they managed contributions toward progress that mattered and endured. Their efforts and their abilities not only advanced the nation's industrial prowess but also anchored their families for success in future generations.

Sarah DeForest Maynard Davis was an example of the kind of success that her ancestors engendered. Born in Utica, New York in 1922, "Sally" studied music history at Vassar College and lived in Switzerland, Connecticut, and Montreal, Canada, with her husband, Holbrook R. Davis, and their three children—one of whom was named in honor of her Maynard family roots. Sally was active in charity work wherever she went, and she became the president of the Cape Cod Conservatory of Music & Arts when she and her husband retired to Osterville, Massachusetts, later in life.

When Sally died in 2016, she was the matriarch of a family that included seven grandchildren and six great-grandchildren, and she and Holbrook had been married seventy years. A book of black and white portraits and newspaper clippings—given to each of her children—touched lightly on the many gifts that Sally's great-grandfathers Charles North and Isaac Maynard had passed down to her and hers. This book endeavors to paint more vividly the portraits of those many and varied offerings.

Introduction

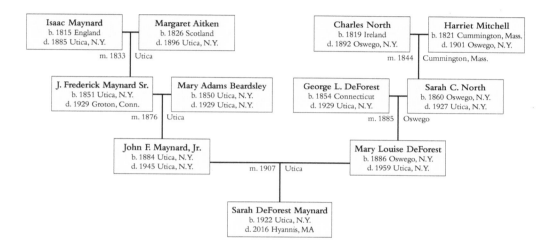

FOR MORE THAN TWO HUNDRED YEARS, men and women had been setting their sights on America in hope of a better life. In the 1830s, that hope was still burning for many inhabitants of the British Isles, as decreasing opportunities for English and Irish second sons inspired young men to look westward over the Atlantic, as so many had done before them. Their leap of faith began with a tenuous walk over a narrow gangplank to a fragile boat about to set sail over a vast ocean. Many had taken that step, and many more would follow, as small sailing vessels grew and developed into larger steamships.

In 1836, although they grew up 500 miles apart, Charles North and Isaac Maynard took this leap almost simultaneously, arriving at the same American port within just three months of each other. Following separate paths into separate cities and businesses, they little suspected a connection to each other that neither would live to see. Seventy years later, their grandchildren would marry each other at a widely celebrated wedding in Utica, New York, where, in one of the most successful industrial cities in the nation, their parents were poised at the top of the social stratum and at the apex of booming industries.

Unlike the story of the pioneers who took their chances in covered wagons to settle America's West, the story of Charles North's and Isaac Maynard's lives happened within a relatively small area. Once they had arrived in the tree-lined hills of the Northeast, both young men leapt at the promise of trade, travel, and industry there. Later, each man succeeded after reimagining his usefulness: Charles took the chance to move to Oswego, where the abundance of trees would support a successful tanning business. Isaac and his friend John Thorn put aside their soap and candle business to rescue and reorganize an ailing railroad.

Their descendants would follow suit. In the next generation, Sarah North's husband, George DeForest, advanced from the salesroom floor to the mill president's office, and Isaac's son J. Fred Maynard abandoned his railroad career and, with little experience in the field, embarked on the management of a major textile firm. Later, J. Fred's son put aside the duties of his career to accept community positions in the face of major crises: the Red Cross during the 1918 flu epidemic, a war chest during World War I, and the search for a missing woman in 1920.

When Charles and Isaac made their leap across the Atlantic, they were atypical as immigrants. Nearly 600,000 people arrived in the United States between 1831 and 1840,[2] but unlike the "huddled masses" who were generally at the bottom of the economic scale, both Charles and Isaac thrived almost immediately. Money, education, skills, and ambition may all have played a role in the successes that they enjoyed compared to their struggling countrymen. Their extended family connections strengthened their chances.

Throughout these same years, America was also in the midst of great changes. In only three generations, the nation advanced from an agrarian and home crafts economy, to small family businesses, to the rise of imposing industrial factories.[3] The Maynard and DeForest families were part of all three stages of this development. Seen in the context of the nation's growth, this transformation represented a relatively rapid change in the lives of its people and in the products that they required and enjoyed.

Like many, Charles and Isaac began with careers that required their hands-on knowledge, using expertise passed down from previous generations. They were both close to their work—Charles would have known the rhythms and the smells of the tannery just as Isaac would have found the heat and the scent of the candle wax in his chandlery a constant companion. Later, their descendants would find that their talents lay in a different kind of skill—the management of larger and larger organizations that were beginning to dominate the industrial scene. Both Charles and Isaac sampled a taste of bigger-business management in their later years; their descendants would make it their specialty.

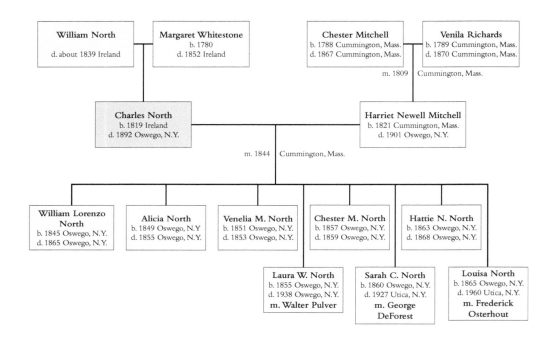

— CHAPTER ONE —

Charles North

CHARLES NORTH was just 16 years old when he made his leap to America in 1836. In the company of his older brother Richard North, 18, he made the voyage from his native Ireland to America aboard the *Pratincole*, which sailed from Galway to New York, arriving on 1 June 1836.[4]

The *Pratincole*, a new brig, had been advertised heavily in Galway-area newspapers that spring. Ads promised a "fast" twenty-two-day journey to the "flourishing city of New York," and offered help in finding work upon arrival.[5] Although the trip took a week longer than advertised, the passengers were pleased. Richard North was among several who signed a certificate attesting to the efficacy of the *Pratincole*:

> [W]e the undersigned Passengers, with the greatest pleasure bear testimony to the very great kindness, good conduct, and prudent management of Captain Rogers, during our voyage, . . . and feel ourselves imperatively called upon to return him our cordial and grateful thanks, for his extreme kindness and uninterrupted attention to all on board, during our voyage of twenty-nine days.[6]

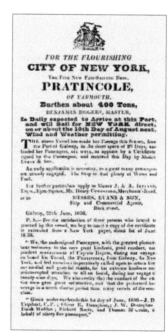

The Galway Patriot's *June 1836 advertisement for the Brig* Pratincole, *headed for New York.*[7]

Charles and his brother Richard were two of the many Irish who comprised the largest immigrant group to the United States between 1820 and 1870. Nearly 2.4 million arrived from Ireland during that period—most of whom came a decade after Charles and Richard in response to the potato famine of 1845–50.[8] Unlike the North brothers, nearly all of the 2.4 million were poor and unskilled. According to historian David J. LaVigne, the men "labored in factories, mines, and docks and for railroad, canal, and construction companies," while the women found employment as "domestic servants, seamstresses, and textile factory hands."[9]

Charles and Richard hailed from fortunate circumstances. Although they were listed as laborers on the *Pratincole's* manifest—as were all of the other passengers on the trip—the brothers had grown up on Northbrook Estate, a "landed estate" in County Galway.[10] Their grandnephew Henry Ringling North later described Northbrook as "an eighteenth century manor house set in wide lawns, shaded by great oaks and copper beeches. . . . The fields of Northbrook spread over some 600 Irish acres, equivalent to 1,500 of ours, and were watered by a small clear stream which ran under a massive single-arch stone bridge."[11] The townland of Northbrook, located between the market towns of Aughrim and Kilconnell, was about 3 miles from the Ballinasloe railroad station.[12]

Although the scene of the North brothers' childhood may have seemed idyllic, Northbrook contained hidden strains that sent the brothers to America. Chief among them was the financial situation in Ireland. Many of the landed estates had become insolvent, encumbered with ancient tithes and crippling mortgages.[13] Unlike England, Ireland had not industrialized, and most residents were forced into agricultural livelihoods—a reality that was only made worse by an increasing population of available workers. These factors sent the Irish economy into a tailspin.[14]

Settling Down

Little is known about Charles's first several years in America. At some point, he reached Ephratah, Fulton County, New York, where he and his brother were in the care of a Mr. or Mrs. Edwards for a time. Ephratah is adjacent to Johnstown, where Richard later settled.[15] Their host was likely linked to Col. William Edwards, who started many tanneries in New York and Massachusetts and was responsible for copious advancements in the tanning processes there.[16]

One of Edwards's tanneries was located in Cummington, Massachusetts, where he partnered with William Hubbard.[17] Here, hides were processed into leather that was used for shoes, clothing, harnesses, blacksmiths' bellows, and bags of all kinds.[18]

Charles and Richard made their way to Cummington by October of 1841. A small "hill town" in the rural western region of that state, most of the inhabitants there were farmers, with a few enclaves of tradesmen operating at the intersections of rivers and roadways.[19] Probably at Edwards's encouragement, the brothers settled in West Cummington—also called "Hubbardville"—where Edwards and Hubbard had operated their tannery since 1804.[20] One of the most successful in the area, in 1832 it produced the highest value of leather for shoe soles in the Connecticut River Valley.[21] Charles and Richard's brother George North may have joined them briefly in Cummington in 1842, apparently having found the money to make his passage to America.[22]

Cummington

Originally called Township No. 5, Cummington was established in 1762 when a few men drew lots and proceeded to settle there. Inhabitants established permanent boundaries in 1788, and by 1790, the town housed 873 residents.[23] When Charles and Richard arrived, it was a growing community of more than 1,800.[24]

Tanning made up the principal industry of Cummington for almost eighty years, and Edwards and Hubbard owned just one of the several tanneries located there.[25] According to Cummington historians Helen H. Foster and William W. Streeter, "inasmuch as the main requirements for the location of successful tanneries depended upon a good source of water and hemlock bark, Cummington was a natural place for this industry to thrive," so much so that a town "leather sealer," responsible for stamping leather with a "seal" of approval for its quality, was elected by town leaders annually.[26]

Ruins of Hubbard Tannery.[27]

The Mitchell Family

Charles, not surprisingly, was called a "tanner" when he married Harriet Mitchell on 8 September 1844. The Rev. Joseph Baldwin, pastor of the West Cummington Congregational Church, performed the double-wedding ceremony for Harriet and Charles—and for Harriet's sister Laura Mitchell and her groom, William H. White—on the same day. Harriet was 24; her sister, 17.[28]

The Mitchell sisters were associated with a tannery on the other side of town from where Charles had settled. Harriet and Laura's grandfather, William Mitchell, had come to Cummington sometime after 3 May 1774, when, as a resident of Bridgewater, Massachusetts, he purchased approximately 90 acres on a hill in the northern section of town with a beautiful view of the valley below.[29] According to Foster and Streeter, William Mitchell built a house there, on the corner of present-day Plainfield and Stage roads. The house served as a public house and tavern, and a portion of it stands today.[30]

The William Mitchell house, Cummington, Massachusetts.[31]

William, described as a "cordwainer"—a maker of leather shoes—came from a family of tanners. His father, Col. Edward Mitchell, was a tanner in East Bridgewater's "Joppa" section, and William's brother Cushing Mitchell eventually inherited most of that business.[32] "[Cushing] was a very celebrated tanner and carried on the business nearly sixty years," according to author Seth Bryant. "He made very excellent leather and carried on an extensive business in the old-fashioned way of tanning by the halves, and either made it into sole or upper leather, as customers chose. He tanned with oak bark[,] and his leather had a great reputation."

According to Bryant, the business was passed down through the family over several generations. "During all these years the old farmers of Plymouth County came up to Joppa, not with offerings, but to get their hides tanned, as bark was plenty there. For 170 years the pilgrims around Joppa crossed over the land with dry feet, well shod."[33]

Apparently William did not inherit his family's business at Joppa, and instead sought his fortune in Cummington.[34] Although his 1774 purchase of land there did not explicitly include the mention of a tannery, in 1779, he was appointed as Cummington's "sealer of leather," and he held that position for many years afterward.[35] William also held a financial interest in a tannery on Mill Brook, just down the road from his house.[36] Whether a business there represented the main source of William's livelihood is not known.

By 1805, 56-year-old William sold about 40 acres of land containing buildings associated with the tannery to his oldest son, Pyam (a 26-year-old tanner). William reserved two-thirds of these buildings for himself. Seven years later, after moving to Delaware County, New York, Pyam sold those 40 acres in Cummington to his younger brother Chester Mitchell—Harriet and Laura's father. This sale included "the dwelling house & barn thereon & one third of the tanyard on the premises & one third of the buildings appertaining to s[ai]d yard."[37]

Charles and Harriet Make Their Move

Beginning their new lives at the same time, it would seem probable that the new Mrs. Charles North and her sister Laura would move forward on similar paths in Cummington. But the young women were no sooner married than they said goodbye to each other. While Laura settled in with her husband in town, Harriet and Charles North set out for a new home more than 200 miles away.[38]

They were not alone in leaving Cummington. This was a time when the community's young people were moving westward. Railroad transportation and the promise of new methods of production fueled the transition from small cottage industries to larger, more productive factories. According to Foster and Streeter, many of the young men from Cummington's larger established families relocated during this period, restless for new opportunity.[39]

The dwindling tree supply motivated young tanners, in particular, to move. The tanning process required great amounts of bark from oak or hemlock trees, and after years of making leather in Massachusetts, forested areas were starting to thin. Many tanners began to look toward New York State and further west in search of untouched forests.[40]

In West Cummington, tannery owner William Hubbard's son—William O. Hubbard—felt the pull. On 15 November 1845, the younger William, (about ten years older than Charles), purchased a tannery in Oswego, New York, "for the purpose of tanning hides & skins and manufacturing leather."[41]

Newlyweds Charles and Harriet North joined William O. Hubbard—and his wife, Czarina, and their five children—in making Oswego their new home.[42] Other Cummington residents later rounded out an extended family group: Czarina's younger brother Rollin Coman and Samuel "Porter" Hubbard, husband of Harriet's sister Venelia.[43] Charles was the foreman of the new business, called Hubbard, Coman & North.[44]

A New Business

About 200 miles northwest of Cummington, Oswego is located at the edge of Lake Ontario and is bisected by the Oswego River, which flows northward into the lake.[45] Oswego was just a small village in 1816 when it became the seat of Oswego County. Growth of settlements in the county proceeded slowly until the Oswego Canal was connected to the larger Erie Canal in 1828. The smaller canal, which ran along the Oswego River, linked the village and the county to the larger canal's myriad of trade opportunities in Syracuse and beyond.

Oswego Harbor in the 1850s.[46]

This new transportation system made relocating to Oswego especially attractive. The Oswego Canal measured 38 miles long, 4 feet deep, and 40 feet wide. Eighteen locks enabled boat traffic to overcome 154 feet in elevation across its distance. More importantly, the canal provided a reliable source of water, and the lease of water rights for use by the tannery was a stipulation of William O. Hubbard's purchase.[47]

The demand for leather, especially shoe leather, had risen during the 1830s, and New York was a key player in the American tanning industry.[48] William Edwards, who had owned the tannery in Cummington, played a major part in the industry's growth. In 1816 he had opened a tannery in Greene County, New York, where he developed new methods and economies of scale that were later adopted by nearby tanners. By the time Charles and Harriet North made their move, Edwards's methods were spreading statewide, and the resulting deforestation of Greene County and the Catskills was making Oswego and the Adirondacks a more attractive location for new tanning ventures.[49]

Unlike the Mitchell's backyard tannery and Cummington's small business tannery, the Oswego tannery held the promise of a large-scale operation. Like others in the Adirondack region, it was likely devoted to the manufacture of leather soles and cattle-hide uppers for boots and shoes.[50]

Tanning in the Adirondacks

The basic steps of tanning had not changed much since colonial times, when the Mitchell family carried it out as a home-based trade. Tanning prevented the rotting of animal hides and skins, creating a material that was strong, pliable, and waterproof. The resulting leather was then used for shoes, boots, harnesses, belts, saddles, and other products.[51]

The process was long and detailed. Animal hides were sometimes salted for preservation and then soaked before entering the multi-step, labor-intensive procedure that turned them into leather. Barbara McMartin describes the process in her book, *Hides, Hemlocks, and Adirondack History*:

> [The hides] were scraped to remove any flesh, blood, or fatty substances . . . [then] placed in warm rooms to sweat, in order to loosen the hair, a tricky process that brought the hides to the point of incipient decomposition. Further soaking in lime solution loosened the hair, and permitted its removal. Liming . . . [also] has a hardening effect, useful in the ultimate production of sole and belt leather.
>
> As part of the [un-hairing] process, hides were usually placed upon a beam—a convex array of boards forming a sort of half barrel and beamed or scraped with a blunt curved knife.
>
> The cleaned hides were washed again, then bated . . . [by] soaking in a fairly strong acid solution. Until the nineteenth century . . . skins were bated by the process of adding dung and animal manure.
>
> In the tanning of heavy hides for sole leather . . . the process was referred to as plumping, which completed the swelling of the cells, distending the pores and rendering the hides ready to absorb the tannin. Plumping was achieved either by washing the lime away or by reducing the alkali by the addition of an acid solution.
>
> [At most tanneries], the cleaned and un-haired sides [were taken] directly to the vats. These vats were large, rectangular wooden boxes sunk into the ground that measured 3 feet by 8 feet by 4 feet deep or larger. Sometimes these vats were filled with alternating layers of ground bark and sides, and then filled with water. The water leached the tannin from the ground bark. As tanning proceeded, bark was added to increase the strength of the tanning liquor.
>
> Vast numbers of vats were required, because of the length of time—upwards of eighteen months in Colonial times, more than six months in the later nineteenth century—that hides had to be soaked in tannin solutions to complete the tanning process. In . . . most early Adirondack tanneries . . . sides were moved from vat to vat, with increasing amounts of bark added to increase the level of acidity. The sides had to be lifted from one vat to the next to make sure that the tanning liquors reached all the parts equally or to advance them into stronger solutions.
>
> While the heavy sides that were to become sole leather could be left in the tanning vats for as little as six months, usually most . . . spent a much longer time in the vats. Temperature played an important role in the rate of tanning, and cool temperatures meant that most Adirondack sides took longer.

In the more modern Adirondack tanneries, tannin was leached from the ground bark in leeches, huge circular tubs filled with ground bark through which heated water was pumped. This tanning liquor was then circulated through the vats in increasingly acidic solutions.

After they were deemed tanned, the sides were hung to dry in huge sheds that were often steam heated. Humidity in these open drying sheds had to be controlled to ensure the proper rate of drying. During the drying process, organic oils were applied to the dry sides: either cod or menhaden oil or paraffin was used. Glucose and other sugars were sometimes added to the sides to give them added weight and stiffness or strength.[52]

Nineteenth-century tanneries required large amounts of water, not only for the tanning process, which needed about 250 gallons for every hide, but also for waterwheels and steam that powered their equipment.[53] Accordingly, the Oswego operation was aptly situated on both the river and the canal, on an island between the two bodies of water. A walking bridge over the canal connected the island to the eastern part of Oswego, where the North, Hubbard, and Coman families made their homes. Eventually, the street on the eastern side of the bridge was called Hubbard Street, as it is today.[54]

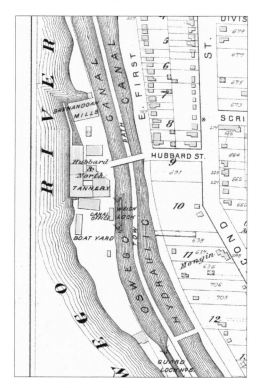

Detail from an 1880 atlas of Oswego.[55]

According to Peter C. Welsh, in an article in the journal *Technology and Culture:*

"[The] technological innovation that marked other American industries was ignored by the leather maker, and the usual generalizations simply do not fit the tanner. For example, the scarcity and high cost of labor in America did not result in the early or widespread application of significant labor-saving machinery to the most burdensome and basic aspects of leather production; nor did the spirit of progress and improvement rampant in the early Republic prove to be stimulating within the confines of the tanyard."[56]

Other historians, however, did mark some notable progress. Leather historian Lucius Ellsworth, in his book *Craft to National Industry in the Nineteenth Century,* points to reduced tanning times, improved chemical processes, and creative water sourcing as helping the industry move forward.[57] Barbara McMartin argues that efficiencies were realized in the management of increasingly larger organizations "by building larger tanneries, dividing the different kinds of labor among different classes of workers, and by designing better factory layouts so the hides could be handled more expeditiously."[58]

The prowess of the tanner was still vitally important to the operation, making whatever education Charles had received in Cummington essential in his new location. "At each step . . . the tanner had to use his best judgment as to whether the step was completed," according to McMartin. "The bating process, the removal of the lime, was considered the 'most delicate and critical operation in the whole range of the manufacture of leather,' because the tanner could only guess at the amount of lime removed. . . . [In the drying process], again, the tanner's judgment was critical, for if a side was dried too quickly, it became brittle, too slowly and it began to mold."[59]

According to Ellsworth, "the appearance, smell, feel, and even taste of the raw material, tanning solutions, and partially prepared leather became guidelines for success. Each man's secret techniques remained a secret to be shared only with associates."[60]

Oswego Grows

In addition to being well situated, the new tannery was part of a flourishing local economy. After recovering from an economic financial panic in 1837, Oswego's small log homes had been replaced by "handsome white farmhouses with green blinds, which rose in every direction," and the boat traffic on Lake Ontario had increased exponentially.[61]

"Oswego, N.Y.," about 1855.[62]

"The appearance of the lake . . . at least in summer, changed with that of the land," according to Oswego historian Crisfield Johnson. "Where once the broad expanse had been broken only by the solitary canoe of the savage, and later by the occasional bateau of the fur-trader, now schooners and sloops and brigs swept in rapid succession before the breeze over the rippling surface, deeply loaded with the grain of Canada and Ohio and Michigan, and of still more distant fields, or bearing in return the manufactures of the east and the immigrant of Europe."[63]

Trade and travel opportunities abounded. In 1847, the Oswego and Syracuse Railroad began work on a line to connect the two communities. They finished the following year, and other railroads followed later, "screaming up and down the west bank of the Oswego." In addition, a "plank road" between Oswego and Syracuse was built in 1848, employing heavy wooden boards that were laid across stringers to create a smooth road surface.[64]

During the 1840s, more than 18,000 new residents had joined the North family in making Oswego County their new home.[65] Charles and Harriet contributed to the population growth directly: their son William L. North was born in 1845, and their daughter Alicia in 1849.[66]

*"Southern view of Oswego," about 1845, which shows a building in the foreground that
was probably part of the tannery. The walking bridge can be seen on the right.*[67]

Famine

While Charles and Harriet were enjoying the prospects and progress of their
new situation, back in Ireland, life had taken a bitter turn for Charles's relatives and
countrymen. Potato crop failures of 1845 and 1846 caused countless peasants to
starve, and near-epidemic disease was fueled by poor sanitation and hygiene. More
than 700,000 people died in Ireland between 1845 and 1849, and 1.75 million people
emigrated from their homeland to other lands—mostly to the United States.[68] Although
the North family in Ireland was presumably insulated from the difficulties gripping the
peasant class, money was tight nonetheless, and the devastation surrounding them was
heartbreaking.

In April 1847, Charles's sister Anne penned a desperate and angry letter to
Charles, begging him for understanding and coming just short of imploring him for
money:

> I regret exceedingly to witness the total want of feeling exhibited in your letter.
>
> You cannot be ignorant of the (at present) lamentable Judgement which has fallen
> on your unhappy native land!!! Disease and famine stalking hand in hand and daily
> dooming hundreds, yea thousands, to death. Not all the exertions of man (and gigantic
> efforts have been made by the benevolent in every country) have been able to stay the
> progress of desolation.
>
> [It was] folly in me ever to have parted with my hard earnings and perhaps the
> time may come—indeed has come—when I bitterly regret having done so.
>
> My mind is so afflicted I cannot write any more—I hope you will tell George I
> will answer his letter if I am spared, shortly. I am glad to hear of your prosperity and
> also of his. I wish I were out of this country. There is very little to comfort in Ireland.[69]

Charles's brother Joseph had inherited the Northbrook estate, and like other estates, it lost money following the economic devastation of the famine. The Encumbered Estates Act of 1849 allowed for the sale of these once-prosperous properties, and by 1850, the North family was prepared to sell. "I have to tell you that Northbrook is to be sold as soon as possible," Anne wrote in May 1850. "A late creditor from whom unfortunate Joseph borrowed £200 has caused proceedings to be taken for that purpose under a new Act of Parliament called the encumbered estates commission." She continued: "[I am] sadly depressed and grieved by the sale of Northbrook, as it will be a sad termination to poor Joseph. . . . Were I to give you a description of the present state of this country you would I am sure say I was exaggerating so I will remain silent on the subject.[70]

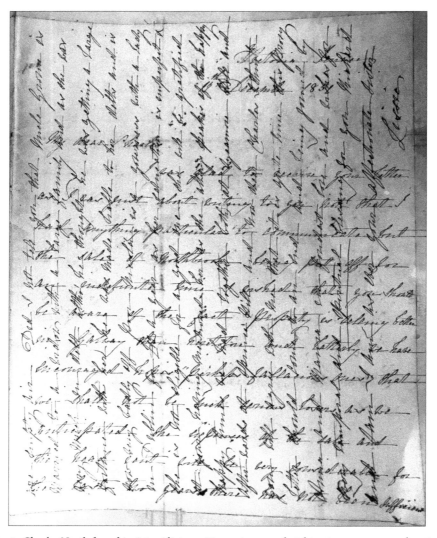

Letter to Charles North from his sister Alicia, written using cross-hatching to save paper and postage.[71]

A year later, the Irish Norths were feeling their economic wounds acutely. Joseph was ejected from the Northbrook estate, even as the sale of the property was postponed indefinitely. "How Joseph will support his wife and children I know not," his sister Alicia lamented in a letter in December 1851. "Anna is just keeping her head above water and [is] thankful for being able to do so. You will not wonder at the falling off in her business when I mention that most of those who patronised at her setting up are now Paupers and their children looking for the lowest situations indeed."[72]

In 1853, Northbrook was placed on the auction block, and "after a very active competition, which was carried on with great spirit between some seven or eight gentlemen," it was sold to Mr. John Rawden Berwick.[73]

Family, Business, and Community Grow

To the degree that life was shrinking for his family in Ireland, it was expanding for Charles North and his extended family in Oswego. In 1847, Joseph B. Hubbard—a probable first cousin of the Cummington Hubbards—moved to town. Joseph was almost certainly the son of Daniel and Asenath Hubbard, who had lived briefly in Worthington, Massachusetts—a town contiguous to Cummington—before moving to Rensselaer County, New York.[74] Although Joseph may have started on the periphery of the North-Hubbard-Coman family group in Oswego, he quickly became an important part of the tannery and hence of Charles North's life.

Other additions to the family came in the form of new babies. The 1850s saw all five of the Oswego families growing. Charles and Harriet were part of this in welcoming their third child, daughter Venelia North, in 1851.[75]

These times were not without sadness, however. Venelia was just 2 years old when she died in 1853.[76] She was the first of five children who would be buried by Charles and Harriet over the course of their marriage. The next death occurred in May 1855, when their oldest daughter, 6-year-old Alicia, succumbed to scarlet fever just a few months after her baby sister, Laura, was born in January.[77]

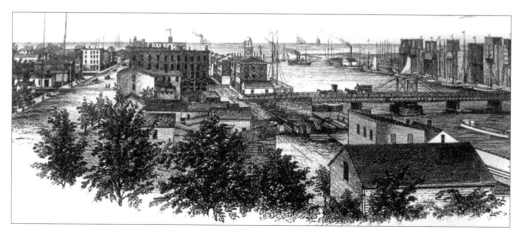

Oswego Harbor, about 1850.[78]

Amidst these joys and sorrows, the Norths had their extended family nearby. At the beginning of the 1850s, the businesses and the residences of the North, Hubbard, and Coman families were situated in a small neighborhood on the east side of Oswego, where many of the streets were numbered in reference to their distance from the canal. The Norths resided on Syracuse Street in the Fourth Ward of the city, probably right next door to William O. and Czarina Hubbard.[79] The value of their two homes indicated that the Norths' frame house was likely dwarfed by the Hubbards' home, which presumably provided ample room for their growing family.[80]

Nearby, Rollin Coman lived on East Albany Street near Sixth Street,[81] Samuel Porter Hubbard resided at 125 East Sixth Street,[82] and newcomer Joseph B. Hubbard was at 161 East Third Street.[83] Their houses were all a short walk from the wooden canal bridge that led to the tannery.

Business boomed. In 1854, a new "reciprocity treaty" between the United States and Great Britain made trade between the two countries more advantageous and represented a major boon to communities along the Oswego Canal.[84] The firm Hubbard, Coman & North became occupied in a significant feat of production. The Oswego city directory described the vastness of it: "This establishment is 200 feet long by 45 wide; added to which are three wings each 75 by 50. It contains 159 vats; and manufactured 40,000 sides of leather during the past year. 50,000 sides of leather can be manufactured at this tannery per annum. There are 25 hands constantly employed in this establishment."[85]

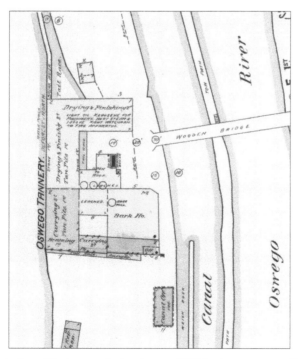

A view of the tannery featured on an 1890 fire insurance map.[86]

The number of workers at Hubbard, Coman & North made it one of the larger tanneries in the Adirondack region.[87] An 1890 insurance map shows what might have existed, or was beginning to exist, by 1854: a bark house with a mill, a leaching room, drying and finishing pits, a beaming area, and currying and tan pits. Two tail races—fast flowing sections of water—suggest the possibility of water wheels but may have simply been locations where waste was emptied into the canal.[88]

William O. Hubbard, the proprietor, probably worked at the tannery each day, as did Charles North and Samuel Porter Hubbard. Joseph B. Hubbard and Rollin Coman, however, appeared to be working off-site as leather dealers, perhaps selling the wares of the manufacturing facility. In 1854, Joseph had a store across the river at 136 West First Street, called "J. B. Hubbard & Co. Leather Dealers."[89] Likely, the tannery supplied a larger market as well. The boot and shoe industry that flourished in Massachusetts obtained most of its heavy leather from New York tanneries during the first half of the nineteenth century. Industrial belts for use in textile mills was a secondary market.[90]

A view of West First Street, between Cayuga and Seneca streets, in about 1848. J. B. Hubbard & Co. Leather Dealers was located on this street several years later.[91]

In addition to their connection to the tannery, the Norths and the Hubbards made inroads into their community. In June 1857, Charles North was among a handful of trustees at the formation of a Congregational Church in town, and in July, Mr. and

Mrs. J. B. Hubbard were among the church's first twenty-eight members. An additional twenty-eight, probably including Charles and Harriet North, joined in August.[92]

The decade ended on a sad note when the North family welcomed, then buried, another child. In 1857, Charles and Harriet's son Chester was born, but he died two years later of consumption.[93] William North, now 15, and little Laura North, 4, remained the only two of Charles and Harriet's five children still living. That soon changed when they welcomed daughters Sarah in 1860 and Hattie in 1863.[94]

The Civil War

Although none of the North-Hubbard-Coman extended family served in the Civil War, their neighbors in Oswego strongly supported the effort. When the conflict broke out in 1861, Oswego distinguished itself as ready responder to the events at hand by being the first to supply volunteers at Elmira, New York, where the 24th Regiment was formed. During the war, the company's long marches and indomitable spirit earned them the title of "The Iron Brigade."[95]

The North-Hubbard-Coman family business—the tannery—most certainly supported the war effort by providing the raw materials for much-needed supplies at the front. Leather was in demand, particularly for shoes, bags, and other Union Army gear. Civil War soldiers' uniforms featured an array of tanned goods. "Shoes were issued to the infantry and were made of leather—uppers, soles, and heels," according to Dorothy Denneen Volo and James M. Volo. "Leather laces were worked through as few as two sets of unreinforced eyelets. . . . Leather or cloth leggings were often buckled on over brogans [shoes] to protect the lower leg.[96]

Perhaps surprisingly, Charles and Harriet's son William, then in his early 20s, did not enlist in the war. He worked as a clerk in 1864, possibly at the tannery.[97] He might have declined to join the Union army because the business needed him, but it is also possible that he suffered from complications of the heart ailment from which he died on 23 October 1865. He was Charles and Harriet's oldest child and their only surviving son—the fourth of their children to die before reaching full adulthood.[98]

Despite the War Between the States, the 1860s was a decade of marked expansion for Oswego. By 1862, the Oswego Canal had been enlarged to 75 feet wide by 7 feet deep, thus allowing for more traffic and bigger boats. From 1860 to 1863, the canal experienced its peak years for total tonnage transported—about a million per year.[99]

Oswego's main business during this period was the milling of wheat into flour. By 1868, the city boasted fifteen flour mills and eleven grain elevators. An expanding network of railroads connected Oswego to neighboring cities, allowing the milled wheat to be transported to a variety of markets. Oswego also contained the largest cornstarch factory in the world.[100]

With the tannery doing well, the Norths moved to a large frame house on Seventh Street, near Church Street,[101] and possibly, the Norths added customized features to this home in honor of Charles's tannery career. Ornamental drawer pulls, which exist on built-in cabinetry in the home today, show engravings of leather belts.[102] Their daughter Louisa was born in this new home in 1865.[103]

One of several ornamental drawer pulls from the North family home, fashioned with the imprint of a leather belt.[104]

The North House, as seen today.[105]

The drawing room at the Richardson-Bates House museum, Oswego. Charles North may have visited this room during his lifetime.[106]

Post-Civil War Oswego

After the war was over, Charles's business partner William O. Hubbard (then in his mid-50s) set his sights on destinations farther west. With his older children all raising families of their own, he and Czarina headed to Grand Rapids, Michigan, with three of their younger children, joining Rollin Coman and his family, who had already made the move. In 1865, Rollin worked as a leather and hide dealer in Grand Rapids.[107] By 1870, William O. Hubbard was working with his son-in-law as a stove manufacturer there.[108]

With both William and Rollin gone, Joseph B. Hubbard, Samuel Porter Hubbard, and Charles North remained to run the Oswego tannery, now renamed Hubbard & North. In 1866, the company produced 200 tons of fine leather and was part of the rapid growth that occurred in Oswego in the post-war era.[109] According to the 1868 city directory:

> The Lake and Canal commerce have increased; the Oswego and Rome Railroad has been completed; the Oswego and Syracuse Railroad and the Northern Transportation Company have been obliged to add to their facilities for the transportation of freight; new Railroads have been initiated; the Water Works have been put in operation; new manufactories have been built, and old establishments have extended their trade. A large number of costly and elegant business edifices, first class dwellings, and public and private buildings, of various descriptions, have been erected, and the population and value of real and personal estate are much larger.[110]

Mayor North

Over the years, Charles had become well known in town, not just because of his work at the tannery. He had twenty-two hounds, which he often walked in the woods, wearing the "high hat" that was his signature article of clothing. He wore this hat at all times; even while shoveling snow in his shirtsleeves.[111]

Charles North's mayoral portrait.[112]

Charles also participated in politics. A Republican, he served as alderman and as city treasurer in town. His world expanded beyond Oswego. He befriended Horace Greeley, whose renowned newspaper—the *New York Tribune*—published outspoken articles on the national political scene and distinctly opposed slavery. Greeley ran against Ulysses S. Grant for president in 1872.[113] Charles also became a friend of Roscoe Conkling, who had risen to political prominence following the Civil War. A Utica resident and a Republican, Conkling often was called the "president-maker" because of his great influence on the national scene.[114]

Charles North's portrait hangs in Oswego's city hall today.[115]

In 1868, although sometimes reluctant to put his hat in the ring, Charles accepted the nomination for mayor of the city of Oswego.[116] He won the title in March 1868 and served as mayor for one year.[117] He managed to preside over heady times. By then, the city had more than 26,000 residents. The new city hall, erected by the federal government, included a customs house, a post office, a courthouse, a jail, an orphan asylum, and a library. Commerce and travelers flowed through the city, connecting the East to the West.[118]

Just as he was savoring his victory, tragedy struck his family again. A few months after his election, 5-year-old daughter Hattie died.[119] Charles and Harriet's three remaining children—13-year-old Laura, 8-year-old Sarah, and 2-year-old Louisa—would thankfully all grow to adulthood.

Meanwhile, Harriet's position as wife of a prominent town figure, coupled with the stress of eight pregnancies and five burials, surely presented more than a trial of wits for her. In spite of what may have been strong emotions on her part, etiquette of the day dictated that she be composed when seen in public. "A lady's conduct is never so entirely at the mercy of critics . . . as when she is in the street," according to *The Ladies' Book of Etiquette,* published in 1876. "Her dress, carriage, walk, will all be exposed to notice; every passer-by will look at her, if it is only for one glance; every unlady-like action will be marked; and in no position will a dignified, lady-like deportment be more certain to command respect. Not only this, but they expose a lady to the most severe misconstruction. Let your conduct be modest and quiet."[120]

A member of the Congregational Church, Harriet might have been one of the many women who volunteered her time and energy there over the years. Women notably took charge of the sanctuary curtains, the embroidered robes of the ministers, carpets, and altar coverings. In addition, they made countless appeals for funding for the church bell, the organ, the mortgage, and the decoration of the lecture room. They also supported the church's missionary work in Turkey, Japan, and India.[121]

Assembly

Charles took a step away from the direction of the tannery to head the Oswego Publishing Company when it launched *The* [Oswego] *Press* in 1870.[122] Still, he remained in politics. In 1876 and again in 1878, he was elected to the New York State Assembly, representing Oswego in Albany.[123] He may not have been as suited for work at the Assembly as he was for other roles. A May 1878 editorial in *The Palladium* offered criticism of his service, even as it praised his popularity and abilities in other spheres:

> Probably no citizen of Oswego bears a better reputation—as a citizen—than Charles North; he has lived long here and is well known to our people. As a business man, he has earned and now enjoys a spotless reputation. The estimation in which he is held among our people has been several times pronounced at the polls where he has been elected alderman, mayor, and finally member of assembly. Whenever the republican party was in a strait; whenever they were hard-pressed for a candidate; whenever a forlorn hope was to be led, they invariably called upon Charles North. He was not a seeker for office. He often declined nominations. He resisted many times the importunities of his friends, and sought rather to evidence his devotion to his party by faithfully working for the advancement of other and more ambitious men. It would have been well for Mr. North if he had adhered to that line of action, and had not been persuaded to deviate from it. In an evil hour he listened to the whisperings of some of the factionists of his party, and took the nomination for member of assembly. He was elected by a splendid majority, and went to Albany to represent an almost enthusiastic constituency. He has served his term; his record is made, and it very properly comes up for fair examination and criticism. What has he done for his district, and how has he done it? Has he been successful as the representative of a district in which there is a large commercial city? To ask these questions is to answer them. To our mind Mr. North has been a complete failure as a member of assembly. He is a striking and forcible illustration of the fact that no matter how honest, how well intentioned, how earnest and willing a man may be, if you put him into a place for which he is not fitted, he will fail. It turns out that Mr. North is not fitted for a legislative position, and that he made a mistake when he took it. He went to Albany on the first of January last,

one of the strongest men, politically, in this district. He came home the 15ᵗʰ of May, without a spot on his integrity, without a charge against his faithfulness and uprightness of purpose, but with a popular reputation for unfitness and inefficiency as a legislator which his warmest friends do not deny, and of which Mr. North himself can not be entirely unconscious.

Mr. North's failure as a member is in no small degree attributable to his amiableness of character—his desire to please everybody, a thing no man has succeeded yet in doing, and which can not be done. Our city was strongly divided on the question of the recently established commissions. In the canvass which preceded Mr. North's election[,] this question was an issue. Mr. North managed to preserve a non-committal position, and the commission favorers voted for him because they were satisfied he would take a reasonable view of the matter; would be in favor of giving the commissions a trial before abolishing them; while the anti-commission men were privately assured— without Mr. North's knowledge or consent, we believe—that he would wipe out the commissions as soon as he got to Albany.

The legislature was convened, and the agitation of the commission question grew hot. Mr. North introduced two bills, one to abolish the appointed board of assessors, and the other to abolish the board of public works. The first of these he got through the assembly, but it was killed in the senate. A strong and numerously signed remonstrance against the passage of the assessors' bill was sent to Albany, but Mr. North suppressed it—thus abrogating and depriving the people of this city the right of petition. But Mr. North was given to understand that this remonstrance must be produced, and it was presented to the senate committee on cities, and the bill was reported adversely and killed.

The board of works bill was introduced to please the anti-commission men. Both are displeased, and both condemn Mr. North's action in the matter. He was badly advised throughout the session and his troubles are all due to this fact. If he had taken a decided stand on one side or the other; if he had been guided by his own cool judgment instead of by the counsel of ring politicians in his part; if he had done what his own sense of right had prompted, he would not have been where he is to-day. If he was satisfied that it would be the best interests of the city to have the commissions abolished, he should have gone right on and abolished them and should not have permitted interference. If he was of the contrary opinion, he should have refused to introduce bills for their repeal, and bravely taken the responsibility. As it is, neither the friends nor opponents of the commissions are satisfied, and Mr. North has the reputation of having failed to carry through local bills which were defeated—one in spite of his best efforts, and the other by his secret consent. Mr. North is not the first man who has left his popularity at Albany, and he probably will not be the last.[124]

If he was daunted by this experience, or by the criticism of it, there is no evidence that it caused Charles to withdraw from the political sphere. He was named a presidential elector in 1880 and mayor again in 1886 and 1887.[125]

Moving On

The First Congregational Church marked its twenty-fifth anniversary in July 1882 with a large celebration. The small congregation had swelled from its original fifty-six to three hundred members by this time, and Harriet North appeared to be active there. She served on the finance committee, and Joseph B. Hubbard's wife taught Sunday school. Joseph himself was the leader of the choir—a position that he had held for the entire history of the organization.[126]

It was quite a blow therefore—for both the church and the tannery—when just three months later, Joseph died on 16 September. The 62-year-old had been Charles's associate for thirty-three years, and his partner for the last sixteen.[127]

After Joseph's death, the tannery was known as Charles North & Company.[128] Although the extended family group of the 1850s had dwindled by the 1880s, a new connection was made into the next generation. In 1885, Charles and Harriet's daughter Sarah married George DeForest, who had an established dry goods business in town. Called one of Oswego's "most popular businessmen,"[129] George became an associate of Charles North & Company, and by 1888, he was listed as a principal of the firm.[130]

In March 1886, Charles ran for mayor again and won, fulfilling the role he had taken on eighteen years earlier. He ran successfully again in 1887.[131] During this time, Charles seemed to shift his focus in terms of his business dealings, as he was not only the proprietor of the tannery but also involved in the sale of leather and findings. The 1888 city directory for Oswego listed him as working both at the tannery and in conjunction with A. F. and W. A. McCarthy, at North, McCarthy & Co.[132]

Charles North, in his later years.[133]

Charles and Harriet's three daughters were married ladies by the time Charles made his will in 1891.[134] The new Mrs. George DeForest and her sister Laura, who had married Walter H. Pulver, lived in Oswego. Sister Louisa married F. C. Osterhout[135] and moved to Glen Ridge, New Jersey.[136]

Charles died a year later on 15 February 1892 at four o'clock in the afternoon at his home on East Seventh Street. He was 72.[137] A funeral was held at his home, and he was buried at Oswego's Riverside Cemetery.[138] Predictably, the town remembered him with fondness. A newspaper obituary referred to Charles as one of Oswego's pioneer citizens, a "staunch businessman," and a charitable soul.[139] "That cheery voice that for so many years was accustomed to greet the smallest urchin and the best known man with the same heartiness and pleasure, is still forever," the obituary continued. "No man was ever more dearly beloved by his neighbors and acquaintances. . . . Nobody ever knew or ever will know the extent of Mr. North's goodness. He never let the left hand know what the right hand gaveth, but for years the poor and needy of the Eighth ward looked to him as a staff to lean on."[140]

Harriet remained at the house on East Seventh Street after her husband's death. At some point, she was joined by her sister, Laura Mitchell White—with whom she had shared a wedding day back in 1844. Laura's husband, William H. White, had died during a visit to Oswego in 1885.[141] Laura eventually relocated and was living with her sister as early as 1892.[142]

Harriet Mitchell North, shortly before her death in 1901.[143]

Harriet Mitchell North died in 1901. According to her obituary: "She was well known in this city and had a host of friends, who are shocked and surprised to learn of the sudden death and who sympathize with the bereaved relatives." She was believed to be the last surviving charter member of the Congregational Church.[144] Harriet lead a life of distinct blessings and sorrows over her seventy-nine years: she gave birth to eight children and buried five of them, and she presumably supported her husband throughout his varied efforts as a business owner as well as a political figure. At the time of Harriet's death, her three surviving daughters were managing households of their own, with four children between them.

One of these daughters had ventured on to new horizons during Harriet's later years. Sarah North DeForest and her husband, George, left Oswego in 1895 and were beginning a new chapter of their lives in the burgeoning city of Utica, New York. There, a new connection with the Maynard family would see their small family into the future.

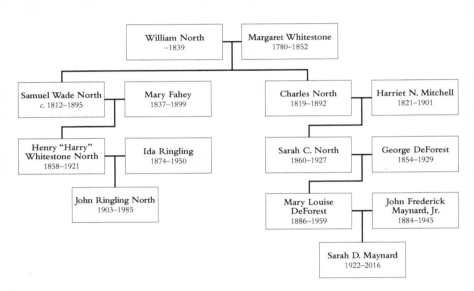

The Circus Connection

ONE OF THE NORTH FAMILY's more notable cousins was John Ringling North, who was the head of the Ringling Brothers and Barnum & Bailey Circus from 1936 to 1967.

John was the grandson of Charles North's brother Samuel Wade North, who came to America sometime in 1849 and settled in Wisconsin.[145] Samuel North's son, Henry "Harry" Whitestone North, an engineer for the Chicago and Northwestern Railroad, married Ida Ringling—who was fifteen years her husband's junior—in 1902 and settled in Baraboo, Wisconsin.[146]

Back in the 1880s, Ida's seven brothers had started the Ringling Brothers Circus at Baraboo, where they housed their large wardrobe department and hundreds of exotic and domestic animals. In 1888, they loaded their circus onto railroad cars and brought it from town to town.

In time, the business grew, in part by absorbing smaller circuses.[147]

Ida and Harry raised their three children, including John Ringling North, alongside this circus. In 1907, however, the Ringling Brothers bought out their biggest rival, the Barnum & Bailey Circus, who called their own attraction "The Greatest Show on Earth." The new combined show adopted the same slogan, as well as the Barnum & Bailey winter headquarters in Bridgeport, Connecticut.[148] The circus left Baraboo in 1918.[149]

John Ringling North (right), animal specialist and circus star Frank Buck, and an elephant.

The following year, the newly merged Ringling Bros. and Barnum & Bailey Circus opened its 1919 season in March with a four-week stint at Madison Square Garden, New York City. The *New York Times* called the new, combined show a "supercircus":

> As is the practice of the circus from time immemorial, the show opens with a pageant . . . [then] the real performance begins. The elephants lead off, five troupes of them, the combined herds of the two old circuses. The giant animals perform all the tricks of elephantine repertoire, with some new ones added, all of them interesting.
>
> After the elephants comes one of the most pleasing acts of the whole show, an act in which seven troupes of aerial performers take part. Among them are three troupes of women aerialists who are hoisted to the top of the Garden, where, suspended by their teeth, and garbed in butterfly raiment, they are whirled at dizzy speeds, the result being, in so far as color is concerned, the most gorgeous picture of the whole performance . . .
>
> The first of the numbers in which the whole Garden is used is the equestrian act of Miss May Wirth, the Australian girl rider. . . . She uses two horses in the act, one of them a frisky spotted animal, upon whose back she executes a series of back somersaults through rings,

ending her performance by a leap from the ground to the back of the fast-going animal, her feet encased in baskets.

Following Miss Wirth are the trained bears that ride bicycles, walk tightropes, and speed around the stage on roller skates, and after the bears comes a display including five troupes of acrobats, contortionists, and balancers.

Hilary Long . . . performs what is perhaps the most dangerous feat of this year's circus. He wears a tin hat with a groove in it. He climbs to a high perch in the western end of the Garden from which a slender solid steel wire is stretched a fourth of the way across the Garden. On this wire he stands on his head and in that position, while the audience gasps, he slides to the ground.

Display No. 9 is the big riding act. . . . The Wild West act comes next, then five troupes of high perch and head balancing performers.

The trained animal act . . . is one of the best things in the circus. Chiquita, the clown dog, and his partner, Toque, who [do] double somersaults from a high perch . . . and a boxing pony are the top-liners among the animal actors.[150]

Back in Baraboo, Henry North met an early death in 1921. Afterward, his son, 17-year-old John Ringling North, sought a career in finance. John attended the University of Wisconsin then transferred to Yale in 1924, before leaving during his junior year to work for a New York stock brokerage house.[151] Later, he joined his family at the circus's new winter quarters in Sarasota, Florida. Working with his uncle John Ringling, he sold real estate during the winters and handled circus finances during the summers.[152]

John's mother, Ida Ringling, relocated to Florida as well. Beginning in 1934, her home was on Sarasota's Bird Key, which her brother had purchased in 1922.[153] She lived in New Edzell Castle, a Georgian-style mansion that had been built in 1914.[154]

Although young John briefly returned to New York as a broker, he retained his ties to his uncle John and the circus. When the elder John died in 1936, the younger John was well poised to succeed him. Shortly thereafter, he became president and director of Ringling Bros. and Barnum & Bailey Combined Shows, Inc.[155]

John ran the circus for the next thirty years, often with the help of his younger brother, Henry.[156] Each summer, John traveled to Europe in search of new acts—visiting fairs, theaters, and nightclubs.

In 1956, he made the controversial decision to abandon the company's massive tents in favor of booking only indoor arenas. With this came the development of a new kind of show, which the *New York Times* later called "razzle-dazzle entertainment."[157] "Some persons regret the decision," the *Times* reported that year. "They regard this as proof that [John Ringling North's] reliance on whim has forced him to close the tent circus. But Mr. North, a man of considerable loquacity as well as pugnacity, is not likely to be perturbed."[158]

John's first two marriages ended in divorce. A man with a "zest for pleasure," the *New York Times* reported that there were "some reports that he is basically a playboy."[159]

At some point, John's European travels brought him back to his ancestral homeland: the Northbrook Estate in Galway, Ireland, where Charles North and John's grandfather, Samuel Wade North, were born more than 150 years earlier. During the early 1960s, John and his brother Henry became Irish citizens and purchased the estate, thereby returning it to the North family.[160]

At around this time, the Ringlings sold off a large number of real estate holdings in Florida, including Bird Key and the mansion that had been Ida Ringling's home.[161] The buyer of many of these holdings, including the mansion, was Arthur Vining Davis's Arvida Corporation.[162] Arthur was related to the North brothers by marriage: he was the uncle of their second cousin once-removed Sarah Maynard Davis's husband, Holbrook R. Davis.[163] Arthur Vining Davis enlarged the island to 300 acres—enough for 511 home sites.[164] The mansion was razed to make room for the Bird Key Yacht Club.[165]

John Ringling North's circus days came to an end in 1967, when he sold the family business to Irvin and Israel Feld and Roy N. Hofheinz. They consummated the sale at the Coliseum in Rome, Italy—the quintessential circus arena. John moved to Geneva, Switzerland, but during a 1985 trip to Brussels, Belgium, he died in his hotel suite.[166]

John's brother Henry authored *The Circus Kings* in 1960, which told the story of the Ringling family and the circus they created.[167] Henry died in Switzerland in 1993.[168]

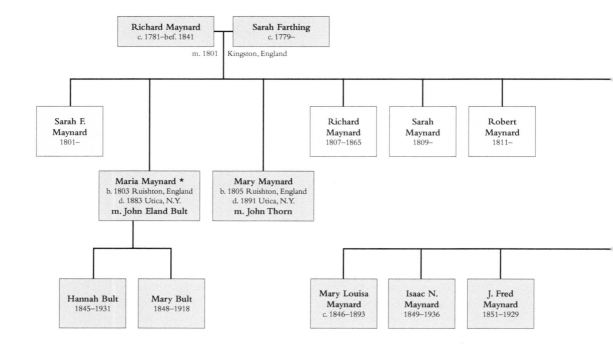

Richard Maynard
c. 1781–bef. 1841

Sarah Farthing
c. 1779–

m. 1801   Kingston, England

Sarah F.
Maynard
1801–

Richard
Maynard
1807–1865

Sarah
Maynard
1809–

Robert
Maynard
1811–

Maria Maynard ★
b. 1803 Ruishton, England
d. 1883 Utica, N.Y.
m. John Eland Bult

Mary Maynard
b. 1805 Ruishton, England
d. 1891 Utica, N.Y.
m. John Thorn

Hannah Bult
1845–1931

Mary Bult
1848–1918

Mary Louisa
Maynard
c. 1846–1893

Isaac N.
Maynard
1849–1936

J. Fred
Maynard
1851–1929

★ *Maria Maynard Bult had three other children who apparently died young.*

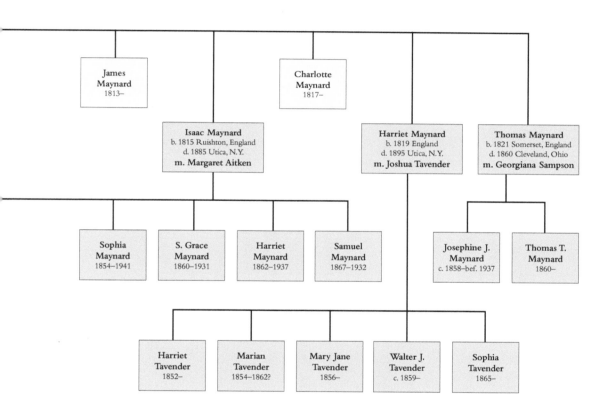

— CHAPTER TWO —

Isaac Maynard

CHARLES AND HARRIET NORTH, as their lives unfolded from Cummington, Massachusetts, to Oswego, New York, may have brushed elbows—or even met—Isaac and Margaret Maynard of Utica.

The two cities of Oswego and Utica—located about 80 miles from each other—had myriad connections for much of the nineteenth century. Utica's political influence was spread out in wide circles across the state, through Roscoe Conkling and his brother-in-law Horatio Seymour, who were key players in the city, the state, and on the national scene. Possibly Charles North's association with Conkling occasionally brought him south to Utica, where for some years Seymour resided just houses away from the Maynards on Whitesboro Street.[169]

If they had even the slightest acquaintance, the two couples—and more significantly the two men—would have found that they had much in common. Charles and Isaac both grew up abroad—Charles in Ireland and Isaac in England. Born less than four years apart, the young men arrived in New York City within three months of each other in 1836: Charles in June, and Isaac later that fall.[170] Uncannily, they were both married within nineteen days of each other in 1844.[171] More importantly, however, with the help of their extended families, each had made an impressive fortune after humble beginnings in small trade shops. While Charles succeeded in the area of leather making, Isaac's experience in the soap and candle trade was the starting point to his varied and lucrative business career.

Little would they have known that their grandchildren would marry each other in 1907.

John Thorn

Isaac Maynard's story is inexorably linked to the story of his lifelong friend and business partner, John Thorn. Isaac and John met as boys in England. John was the son of a shoemaker, but Isaac grew up in the environment of soap and candles, where his father, Richard Maynard, was called a "tallow chandler."[172] John worked in Isaac's father's shop.

Richard Maynard's business was located in a fairly rural setting in the village of Ruishton, about 2 miles from Taunton and 8 miles from Bridgewater, all in County Somerset. The home and shop sat on 16 acres of orchard and meadow surrounded by a ring fence and included a house, two walled gardens, a workshop, a barn, stables, a "gighouse" (carriage house), cellars, and outhouses.[173] The Maynards had eleven children, of which Isaac was the eighth.[174]

Isaac was a teenager when his older friend John came of age and made some ambitious plans. John became engaged to Isaac's 27-year-old sister, Mary, and announced his intention to seek his fortune in America. On July 12, 1832 John left his friend Isaac and his fiancée in Ruishton and boarded a ship for New York City.[175]

New York

It was a rather shaky beginning. After a voyage of seven weeks, John arrived in New York, expecting to find work. Instead, he found a city in the grips of a cholera epidemic. He had come with about £25 in his pocket, and now needed a new plan for a different location.[176]

He found his way to Albany, where he could travel by boat west to Buffalo. As John floated along the Erie Canal, he had plenty of chances to see all the towns that had begun to prosper along its path. He was impressed with Utica, but passed it by in favor of moving on west to Ohio. A steamboat brought him from Buffalo to Cleveland, then a canal boat took him from Cleveland to Zanesville. John was quickly unsatisfied with Zanesville, however. He remembered Utica, and once more boarded a canal boat to reverse his course.[177]

Utica, sometime during the early 1800s.[178]

John arrived in Utica on 1 October 1832. He went to work immediately in his new home city, offering his services to Boyd & Chamberlain, a soap- and candle-making business on Water Street. The owner, Mr. Chamberlain, died shortly thereafter, and John was able to buy the business in partnership with Stephen Thorn.[179]

Stephen, who Utica historian M. M. Bagg described as being of "no relation" to John, was certainly not his brother, but possibly had some family connection, given his identical surname and occupation.[180] Family or not, the two Thorns were united in business in Utica, and their shop was up and running by 1834, at the foot of Division Street.[181] John found a home at 58 Whitesboro Street, near Thomas Alley.[182]

Isaac Makes His Move

Meanwhile, back home in Ruishton, Mary Maynard pined for her fiancé, and arrangements were made for her to join him in America. According to the *Utica Daily Observer,* "their hearts were mated ere he left England, and when he saw his way clear to giving her a home of humble comfort, she met him in New York."[183] The two were married in Utica on 17 September 1833.[184]

Many letters must have traveled back and forth between the Ruishton Maynards and the newly wedded Thorns during the ensuing years. Encouraging news from Utica was just the thing to inspire Isaac, nearly 21, to make plans to join his friend and sister in the United States. He made his sea voyage in 1836, arriving in Utica that fall to join John and Mary in their home at 26 Whitesboro Street.[185]

The following year, John Thorn purchased Stephen Thorn's interest in the soap and candle business. He took his young brother-in-law on as a partner and moved the firm to a new building on the south side of Water Street.[186] Here, Isaac and John began a strong business relationship that would continue—through many and varied endeavors—for the rest of their lives.

Soap and Candles

During America's colonial era, soap had been mostly produced by colonists at home. Using fat retained in fry pans after cooking, housewives were able to combine it with lye to make a soft, jelly-like soap.[187] The immigrants, however, were accustomed to a far more sophisticated product. In London, soap was made from whale oil, olive oil, and tallow, using ashes imported from Denmark for lye. In addition, perfumed soaps were available from Italy.[188]

Because a steady supply of wood ash was needed for the soap-making process, the untouched forests of the New World attracted soap makers just as they did tanners. By about 1800, New England had become the principal center for soap manufacturing in the country.[189]

Compared to tanning, soap making was a fairly short-term process. According to Samuel Colgate, "settled" soaps were poured into wooden frames "until rendered thick from cooling, or were finished by boiling down. The material was ladled by hand from the kettles into the frames, or put into buckets or tubs and carried and emptied into the frames. . . . The waste lye was run off through a pipe reaching through the wooden curb to a point near the bottom the kettle. The kettles were heated by open fire, and the contents were kept from burning by stirring them with a long iron rod flattened at the end."[190]

Like other industries, soap making had been taken up by increasingly larger establishments within small cities and towns. New advances were made by 1841, including the use of steam in the process, as well as new vegetable and animal oils. These changes allowed the American industry to offer fancy soaps, perfumed soaps, and shaving soaps that rivaled European products.[191]

The candle and tallow industry was frequently an offshoot of the soap business, as both processes required the use of animal fats. Candles, the primary source of portable domestic light during this period, were manufactured mostly in the winter, when demand was high and hot wax could set more rapidly. Like tanneries, candle manufacturers usually were located near a river.[192]

Utica

The city of Utica was an excellent location for two businessmen like Isaac and John. Utica had been incorporated in 1832, after seeing marked advancement after the completion of the Erie Canal in 1825.[193] When Isaac joined John in 1836, work was also nearly complete on the Chenango Canal, which would join Utica and the Erie Canal to Binghamton, New York, and Pennsylvania's coalfields. This connection was essential to the industrial growth of the city over the next twenty years.[194]

Like other New York towns, Utica indulged itself in the early 1830s. According to Utica historian T. Wood Clarke, "ready money . . . led to tremendous speculation and lavish spending. Everybody bought; everybody built; real estate skyrocketed." A horrifying financial correction came in 1837, and progress slowed for a time.[195]

Map of Utica, 1838, with Water Street at Division Street highlighted.[196]

During this time, a devastating fire enveloped much of Utica's downtown area and represented a significant blow to the city.[197] On 31 March 1837, flames spread down Genesee Street and John Street, burning buildings on a portion of Whitesboro Street before finally being extinguished at a structure nearly across the street from the home shared by John, Mary, and Isaac. The soap and candle shop on Water Street was situated between the fire and the canal, which likely provided water for those fighting the blaze.[198] Both the home and the business were thankfully spared.

In spite of these temporary setbacks, Utica continued to move forward. Canal travel revolutionized transportation and fed the marketing of new industries across the state, and railroads made small appearances on the transportation and shipping stage. The Utica and Schenectady Railroad was completed in 1837 and was linked later to the Syracuse and Auburn Railroad. Other short-line railways sprang up over the state. At first, travel was awkward, requiring freight and passengers to transfer to different lines at every large city. Later, as railroads merged, smoother connections could be made.[199]

Transportation was popular for recreation as well as industry, and Utica was a frequent stop for those with the means to take a pleasure trip. The *New York Daily Herald* reported in 1840:

> The greater part of fashionable travelling will, this year, pass westward by Oswego and the Great Lakes. Families leaving New York should give preference to those boats for Albany, having deck and state rooms, where, for one dollar extra, they secure privacy as well as much comfort. Night travelling is cooler, and will enable them to proceed with the [railroad] cars to Utica, with less delay than day boats. The cars allow time to snatch a hasty dinner at Bagg's Hotel, Utica. They arrive at Syracuse at six, where comfortable lodgings may be obtained at Syracuse House.[200]

Thorn & Maynard

Meanwhile, the firm of Thorn & Maynard prospered.[201] Isaac presumably took the helm when his sister Mary became ill in 1838 and returned to Ruishton to recover. John made the journey to England with her, and then came back to Utica alone until her health was improved.[202]

Isaac appeared to have gone back to England for a time as well. He was listed on the 1841 census in his widowed mother's household on South Street in Taunton, England, shortly after his father's death.[203] It was likely a tumultuous year for his mother, who placed the house and property in Ruishton—including the soap and candle business— up for auction. According to a notice in the *Taunton Courier*, the business was still operating successfully at the time. Perhaps she took some comfort that her son, Isaac's brother Richard, served as the auctioneer for sale.[204]

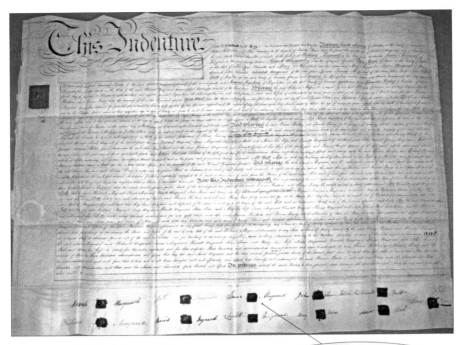

The deed of sale for the house and property once
belonging to Richard Maynard, signed by his heirs—
some in England, some in the United States.

Back in Utica, Thorn & Maynard expanded their partnership in 1840 by purchasing a wool and pelt business.[205] "Tact and energy distinguished their enterprise," the *Utica Morning Herald and Daily Gazette* later recalled.[206]

Isaac and John's working relationship can only be surmised, but their pattern of initiative may be a clue. Throughout their lives John Thorn took the first step, and Isaac Maynard followed. Just as John first journeyed to America, he also married first, and later was first to move his family to a larger home. In the 1860s, John would act as president of the company with Isaac in the supporting role of director.

Possibly, this pattern owed itself to their individual temperaments. Isaac was described as "modest and retiring in his disposition and demeanor" and "of generous and gentle instincts." In contrast, John, despite stating that he was "not a talker," later gave an account of his life to an audience of five hundred at a celebration that he commissioned and proposed.[207] This is not to say that Isaac was ineffective, however. The *New York Times* later lauded him for "his business tact and shrewdness,"[208] and the *Utica Morning Herald and Daily Gazette* praised his habits of industry and close application.[209]

The Family Grows

In 1841, Isaac and John welcomed a new housemate when Isaac and Mary's brother Thomas joined the family at the 26 Whitesboro Street home. Initially, Thomas worked as a tailor, but he later opened a soap and candle establishment on Fulton and Jay Streets with a partner, Joseph Wright.[210]

Two years later, in 1843, a young woman named Margaret Aitken came to Utica from Scotland. Born at Falkirk in 1826, this daughter of Thomas and Mary Aitken was just 18 years old. [211] Although little is known of Margaret's early life or ancestry, she apparently captured Isaac Maynard's heart. The two were married the following year, and they occupied a new home, adjacent to the Thorns, at 22 Whitesboro Street.[212] Their daughter, Mary Maynard, was born in about 1846, and their son, Isaac Newton Maynard, in about 1848.[213]

As young wives in the 1830s and 1840s, Mary Thorn and Margaret Maynard would have devoted themselves to supporting their husbands and children. In 1836, John C. Rudd preached at Utica's Trinity Church on "The Influence of the Female Character," outlining three areas in which the "female character" held the highest importance: domestic life, regulating the affairs of society, and encouraging the Christian faith. "When adorned as every woman should be by the virtues of grace and faith of Gospel, she shines in her brightest lustre," according to Rudd. "Home is the sphere of her best exertions, and while she is not to be immured like the slaves of oriental jealousy, while she is to be qualified for a dignified and interesting appearance in social life, still, it is in the shade of domestic retirement, and in the discharge of domestic duties that she will bring most lasting honor to herself, and the most happiness to those around her."[214]

Margaret Maynard apparently carried out this ideal. Her life "was a happy and beautiful one," as the *Utica Morning Herald and Daily Gazette* described later. "She was devoted to her home and family, and in her life exemplified the highest type of womanhood. She lived for her family and to it she gave all the energies of a warm and generous nature, ever seeking the happiness of her children."[215]

Mary Thorn—perhaps because no children came her way—became noted for her devotion to charitable causes outside her home. During her life, Mary was associated with the Utica Orphan Asylum, which came into being through the work of the Female Society of Industry.[216] She would later offer financial assistance to college students and would also join her husband in supporting the poor back in their hometown of Ruishton.[217]

More women joined Mary and Margaret in Utica when two Maynard siblings arrived from England sometime before 1850. Harriet and her husband, Joshua Tavender, were newlyweds when they made the trip; older sister Maria and her husband, John E. Bult, had been married several years and brought with them their two daughters, Hannah (about 4) and Mary (about 1).[218] Initially, the two newly arrived families shared a home at 3 Seneca Street, with Joshua Tavender immediately beginning work at the Thorn & Maynard chandlery.[219]

By the end of the 1840s, Isaac and four of his siblings lived within a few houses of each other, more than 3,000 miles away from their English birthplace. Sister Mary Thorn and brother Thomas Maynard lived a few doors down, and Harriet Tavender and Maria Bult were around the corner. Isaac also had two of his brothers-in-law, John Thorn and Joshua Tavender, as coworkers. After just a few short years, the Maynards and the Thorns had established themselves firmly in America.

Utica Progresses

Utica moved forward during these years, but with the fits and starts that often characterize the progressions of large communities. Surprisingly, new advances in transportation backfired in the 1840s. Without the need to make numerous transfers during rail travel, fewer people stopped in Utica, which was damaging to profits for hotels, stores, and ultimately the city's entire well-being.[220]

In response, the *Utica Daily Gazette* published a series of articles in 1845 that encouraged the idea of new industry in town. A small committee visited New England, where steam power was being employed in textile mills. Inspired by this example, the people of Utica raised enough money to enable the creation of the Globe Woolen mills, the Utica Steam and Cotton mills, and the Utica Steam Woolen mills, which were all operating within two years. Coal, delivered from Pennsylvania on the Chenango Canal, powered these new companies, and a new stream of German immigrants offered a ready supply of workers.[221] Both Isaac Maynard and John Thorn were directors at the Globe Woolen Company and the Utica Steam Woolen mills.[222] The mills would be important to Utica's future, and to the future of the Maynard family as well.

Utica in 1848.[223]

Utica also produced innovations in the area of communication during this time. The Buffalo, Albany, and New York Telegraph Company—the first of its kind in the world—had its main office on the corner of Genesee and Whitesboro streets in 1845. It completed a line from Albany to Utica in January of 1846, and nine months later, messages could be sent from New York City to Buffalo.

Utica also gained in political importance. Horatio Seymour of Whitesboro Street was elected governor of the state of New York in 1852 and would be reelected twice more, even running for president in 1868 against Ulysses S. Grant. Later moving to an estate in nearby Deerfield, Seymour, called "the Sage of Deerfield," remained influential in the policies of the Democratic Party.[224]

The 1850s

Isaac Maynard branched out to become one of the directors of the newly formed Utica Insurance Company. In September 1850, the company looked for new investors. An advertisement on the front page of the *Oneida Morning Herald* made the case:

> Utica Insurance Company: Capital 100,000!
>
> The directors in soliciting the patronage of the public for this Company, do so, with the fullest confidence that it is based upon the cheapest and best system that experience and well founded calculation could devise. This Company is organized under the provisions of the General Insurance Law of this State, and has been issuing policies for one month with a very favorable result, and the public are assured that no large risks to exceed $5,000 will be taken, and then, only upon the best kind of hazards.[225]

The company insured dwellings, stores, furniture, and merchandise against fire and travel risks.[226]

Around this time, the Maynard family grew with the births of new babies. Isaac and Margaret had son John Frederick Maynard (known as "J. Fred") in 1851,[227] and daughter Sophia Maynard in 1854.[228] The other Maynard siblings welcomed children as well.

Only the Thorns remained childless. Perhaps John and Mary Thorn enjoyed the company of their many nieces and nephews, who likely made the neighborhood around their house loud and lively. Sometime in the early 1850s, John's teenage nephew Edwin Thorn came to live with them, and he later became John Thorn's primary heir.[229]

Isaac and Mary's brother, Thomas Maynard, married and left the Thorns' home to begin a new household with his wife, Georgiana. Thomas made his mark on Utica in the twenty years that he lived there. He worked as a jeweler, at his own soap and candle factory, and later at the Utica Lock Company. He also served as the superintendent of the First Presbyterian Church Sunday School and was well known there for creating a book of hymns. Sadly, he died of "brain fever" in Cleveland, Ohio, in 1860, while living or visiting there "for business considerations."[230]

Railroad Rescue

At the end of the 1850s, John Thorn and Isaac Maynard took a leap and together entered into a fresh initiative. The Black River & Utica Railroad was in trouble and in need of new leadership.[231]

The railroad had first formed in 1853. It opened for service from Utica to Boonville on 13 December 1854 and to Trenton, New York, on 1 January 1855. However, it became clear the following year that the organization had exhausted its capital and had begun operating at a loss.[232]

When a bond issue failed to solve the problem, John Thorn and Isaac Maynard stepped in as trustees. They reorganized the company, renaming it the Utica & Black

River Railroad, with John as president. Twelve new directors were elected, including Isaac. According to M. M. Bagg, "John Thorn and his associates immediately inaugurated a system of economy in management, improvement of the roadbed and rolling stock, and soon changed the whole aspect of the affairs of the company.[233]

John Thorn[234]   *Isaac Maynard*[235]

John accepted only a $250 salary for himself, and other expenses were drastically reduced.[236] The company gradually extended the railroad "by safe and sure steps" to Lowville, Carthage, and Watertown, New York; to Philadelphia, Pennsylvania; and to the St. Lawrence River. It also absorbed rail line branches that gave it a powerful position for controlling trade with Canada.[237] Isaac was elected treasurer of the railroad in 1861.[238]

Both men later received praise for their efficacy in making the struggling railroad a success. According to a later editorial in the *Utica Herald*, "this was the critical point in the history of the road; it required brave men, ready to take risks and make sacrifices, to assume the responsibility of its management and extension."[239] The *Herald* continued: "It is to [Isaac Maynard's] skillful management that the great success of the road is due. . . . Mr. Maynard has managed the finances of the road with prudence and care and has placed it on a sound basis. The success which attended his efforts is the best evidence of their efficiency."[240] "There is not in the state, we doubt if there is in the United States, a more striking illustration of the thrifty, conservative, and successful management of a railroad corporation, than the Black River Road has presented."[241]

John remained president of the railroad almost continuously for the next thirteen years. By the 1870s, the railroad had a fleet of about twenty locomotives—some of them with familiar names: the *John Thorn*, the *Isaac Maynard*, and the *J. F. Maynard*, which was named after Isaac's son, who later became a leader at the company.[242]

Expansion: Before the War

Sometime in 1855 or 1856, John and Mary Thorn, along with their nephew Edwin, made the move to a new home. Leaving the family enclave on Whitesboro and Seneca

Streets, they now opted for a large house at 269 Genesee Street, where many of the city's residents erected sizeable mansions.[243]

Isaac and Margaret Maynard followed suit sometime in 1859 or 1860, moving down the road from the Thorns to a brick home at 283 Genesee Street.[244] In 1860, Isaac employed three servants and a coachman at his new residence. Isaac and Margaret's fifth child, daughter Sarah Grace, was born that same year.[245]

The Thorn home at 269 Genesee Street, about 1890.[246]

The Maynard house at 283 Genesee Street, about 1898 and in 2020 in insert.[247]

The following year, Isaac and John joined forces with West Utica chandler James S. Kirk in opening a satellite soap and candle company in Kirk's hometown of Chicago.[248] In 1861, that city's directory listed the company as James S. Kirk & Company, soap and candle manufacturers, located at 18 and 20 River Street, with all three men listed as principals.[249]

The Civil War

Like Oswego, Utica prided itself on being ready to act when the Civil War broke out. The city held a meeting on 15 April 1861, the very day that President Lincoln called for 75,000 volunteers after the end of the Battle of Fort Sumter. The 14th New York Volunteer Infantry (also called the "1st Oneida"), served at the battles of Gaines Mills, Hanover Courthouse, Malvern Hill, Fredericksburg, and Chancellorsville before mustering out in May of 1863. The 2nd, 3rd, 4th, and 5th Oneida regiments included Utica residents as well.[250]

Isaac Maynard and John Thorn, by then approaching their fifties, did not enlist as soldiers but aided the war effort in other ways. They served on the boards of major cotton mills, which no doubt supplied fabric and clothing for the troops. They also supported railroad transportation, which was vital to the movement of soldiers to the front.

The war created an opportunity outside the home for Mary Thorn. "The union cause found no more ardent supporter at heart than Mrs. Thorn," the *Utica Morning Herald and Daily Gazette* described later. "Her labors in behalf of the northern soldiers were unceasing."[251] In the spring of 1861, she and others sent a box of goods to the 26th New York Regiment (also called the 2nd Oneida), stationed in Elmira, for which they were thanked in a letter from the regiment's commander: "Indeed, it is a gift truly appreciated, for which the volunteers return grateful thanks. For very many kindnesses the citizens of Utica will ever be thankfully remembered by us."[252] In 1863, Mary served on the executive committee planning a "Soldiers' Bazaar," a sale of second-hand goods that was held for the benefit of sick and wounded soldiers.[253]

Mrs. Thorn also became a leader in Utica's Freedman's Relief Association, which sought to send tools, provisions, and clothing to newly freed Southern populations.[254] In 1863, she collected money for the purchase of material from Margaret Maynard and others, then sewed twenty-nine skirts, twenty "sacques," and twenty-seven women's undergarments for donation.[255] That year, Mary was one of the "lady managers" of the Utica association and responsible for tracking donations, which included cash and her own bundle of clothing. The group shipped three boxes of clothing to Memphis, and one box of clothing to "white refugees" in Cairo, Illinois.[256]

During these years, John Thorn made charitable contributions as well. He donated land on Hopper Street in 1864 to their church—the Tabernacle Baptist Church—when the congregation was looking for a new location for its edifice.[257] John had joined the church in 1833 when he first arrived in Utica. He remained a trustee there for fifty years.[258] His brother-in-law Joshua Tavender was a deacon, and Isaac Maynard also belonged to the congregation.[259]

New Horizons

After the war, life expanded for both the Maynards and the Thorns. In 1867, Isaac and Margaret Maynard welcomed a son, Samuel.[260]

John's nephew, Edwin Thorn, established himself in Chicago and worked there in partnership with Nathan Ely Platt.[261] The firm of Platt & Thorn sold wholesale "pig metals," including nails, spikes, and bar and sheet iron manufactured in Pennsylvania.[262] The company also had an interest in the shipping of wheat, flour, corn, and farm products.[263] Isaac and Margaret's son Isaac Newton Maynard later joined this firm.[264]

The Utica soap and candle business also broadened to include other ventures, such as wool pulling, wool dealing, and sheepskin tanning.[265] After forty years of success, however, in about 1875, Isaac and John sold Thorn & Maynard to William Heath and Joshua Tavender.[266]

Isaac took on new responsibilities. His son John Frederick Maynard, called "J. Fred," took over the management of the Utica & Black River Railroad in 1872,[267] freeing up Isaac to become vice-president of the Utica Water Works Company in 1875.[268] Thorn & Maynard had been on the list of original subscribers when the water works firm was incorporated back in 1848.[269] The system provided domestic water and fire protection through a series of pipes and conduits laid throughout Utica. When Isaac took his position, they had just created a new reservoir and put it to use. Construction of another reservoir began in the fall of 1885.[270]

The End of the Era

Isaac and John sold their Chicago interests to James. S. Kirk in 1880,[271] and Isaac became president of Utica's City National Bank,[272] where John Thorn had been a director almost from the time of its organization back in 1848.[273] Isaac and John also served as directors of the Utica, Clinton, and Binghamton Railroad.[274]

Sadly, these were Isaac's final years. In the winter of 1885 a "congestive chill" set in, and he died on 23 February 1885.[275] He left behind, according to the *Utica Herald,* "that most precious of inheritances[:] a spotless reputation and the memory of a useful and influential life."

"[Isaac] was a type of the class of citizens . . . whose names are indissolubly connected with the enterprise and public spirit which have developed the city of Utica," the *Herald* continued. "His success was due to his habits of industry and close application, and to the persistency and consistency with which he applied business principles to the conduct of business. In these respects we recall the name of no citizen of Utica whose career affords a better example and guide for the generation of young men which have grown up around him while he, tho' advanced in years beyond the period when most men are glad to retire, pursued the even tenor of his way, meeting and enjoying the activities of his life quite as much as they."[276]

A less personal obituary appeared in the *New York Times*, praising "his business tact and shrewdness," and estimating his fortune at nearly a million dollars.[277]

Isaac left all of his wealth to his family. He provided money, furniture, and other essentials for his wife Margaret—in lieu of inheriting his estate directly—along with the right to remain at 283 Genesee Street as long as she chose. To each unmarried child he left a sum of money, with the residue to be divided among his seven children. Isaac made a special provision for his daughters, stipulating that whatever they inherited would be theirs outright, "free from the interference and control of their husbands should they marry." John Thorn was one of the estate's executors. The other two were his sons Isaac Newton Maynard and John Frederick Maynard.[278]

Final Years

Margaret and the Thorns did their best to carry on. The Thorns made another visit to their hometown of Ruishton in 1886, and their arrival was afforded a grand celebration. In honor of their emigration to America fifty-four years previously, the village, decorated with welcoming arches, hosted a luncheon for five hundred parishioners.[279]

That same year the Utica & Black River Railroad, the recipient of so much of Isaac and John's energy, was absorbed financially into the Rome, Watertown, and Ogdensburg Railroad Company, in the form of a perpetual lease.[280]

John Thorn's nephew Edwin, who had made a life for himself in Chicago, returned to Utica with his wife, Jennie, and settled in with John and Mary, by then in their mid-70s.[281] Mary's health slowly declined, and she eventually became an invalid. She took a drive each morning, however, and after returning home from one such drive in 1891, she died unexpectedly. She was 85. According to the *Utica Daily Observer*, many friends had seen her that morning. "When, therefore, it was announced that she had passed away in the afternoon, the news was a shock and was received almost with incredulity."[282]

"Probably no person in Utica has done more for the cause of charity than Mrs. Thorn," the *Utica Morning Herald and Daily Gazette* reported after her death, "and her giving has ever been quiet and unostentatious. . . . Her purse has ever been open to the needy, and no cry from the unfortunate was ever allowed to go unheeded."[283]

"Prostrated by his great affliction," on October of 1891, John donated a large sum to the treasury of the Baptist Missionary Convention in his wife's memory.[284] The following year, he took his annual trip to England, this time accompanied by Edwin and Jennie.[285]

John carried on for four years after his wife's death, and then he died suddenly on New Year's Eve in 1894, at the age of 83. His passing was felt acutely, both at home and abroad. The *Utica Morning Herald and Daily Gazette* reported: "Utica is called upon to mourn the death of one of its oldest and most respected citizens. [John Thorn] ended the career of a most loyal, philantropic [*sic*], and useful citizen of Utica. He did much for the city in which he had long dwelt, and his purse was ever open to anything that advanced its interests or helped its institutions.[286]

In England, the sentiment was similar. "Considerable regret will be felt throughout the town and neighborhood at the news of the death of Mr. John Thorn," *The Courier for Taunton and Western Counties* reported. "Unlike the very large proportion who go out to the new world with the idea that it will be to them a veritable El Dorado without effort on their part, he diligently set to work, and by persistent effort succeeded in becoming very wealthy. In his prosperity he did not forget his friends and neighbors in the old country."[287]

Predictably, John's last will and testament was a mark of generosity. He remembered many family members in both England and America, the Tabernacle Baptist Church, and also employees both of the Utica & Black River Railroad and Thorn & Maynard.[288] The church later used his bequest to build a new chapel, called the Thorn Memorial Chapel, which was dedicated on 1 July 1906.[289] The residue of John Thorn's estate went to his nephew Edwin and Jennie, who continued to occupy the house at 269 Genesee Street.[290]

Margaret Aitken Maynard died just a year later in 1896, after a long decline in health. According to one obituary, she "never identified herself with the management of any charitable institutions, but gave generously to their support, and all such movements found in her a warm supporter."[291]

The last of their original foursome, Margaret's death represented the end of the era for the Maynard family. Isaac and Margaret Maynard, along with John and Mary Thorn, had taken the leap to find new success in America, and the two couples had worked together to establish a solid foothold on new soil in less than sixty years' time. Already, the Maynard children were establishing their own families and careers, built on the foundations set by their elders. Before their deaths, Isaac and Margaret Maynard were looking to their son J. Fred to carry on many of Isaac's legacies. As the turn of the century loomed and the nation matured, J. Fred would manage to take these legacies into a new realm.

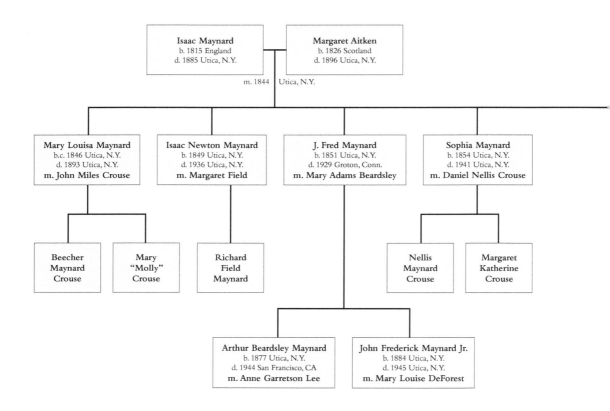

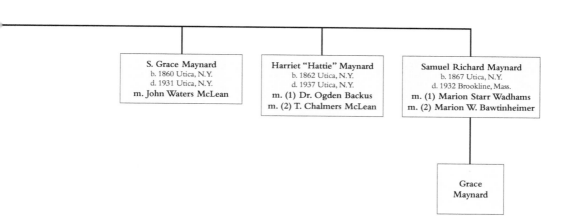

S. Grace Maynard
b. 1860 Utica, N.Y.
d. 1931 Utica, N.Y.
m. John Waters McLean

Harriet "Hattie" Maynard
b. 1862 Utica, N.Y.
d. 1937 Utica, N.Y.
m. (1) Dr. Ogden Backus
m. (2) T. Chalmers McLean

Samuel Richard Maynard
b. 1867 Utica, N.Y.
d. 1932 Brookline, Mass.
m. (1) Marion Starr Wadhams
m. (2) Marion W. Bawtinheimer

Grace
Maynard

Chapter Three

The Textiles Era

I saac Maynard's life had borne many similarities to the life of Charles North. Both men died in their 70s as noted community leaders and successful businessmen who, as immigrants to America, amassed considerable fortunes from challenging beginnings. Through their hard work, their families came to enjoy the comforts of large and sturdy homes, and the two men achieved reputations as notable business and community leaders of enviable character.

Predictably, their deaths did not leave either of their interests in limbo. Charles's and Isaac's successes were rooted in family and would continue to be centered there as their sturdy foundations were inherited by a new generation. The gradual development from home craft to increasingly larger shops—the backdrop of Charles North's and Isaac Maynard's accomplishments—would now move from large workshops to factory settings as the city of Utica became a leader in American textiles production.

Sarah North and George DeForest

George DeForest became a partner at Charles North's Oswego tannery during Charles's final decade.[292] Having lived in Oswego since about 1879, George arrived at the firm as a young businessman, experienced in the retail and wholesale clothing business. With Hubbard & North still recovering from Joseph B. Hubbard's death in 1882,[293] George became the second principal in the firm, then known as Charles North & Company.[294]

In addition to joining Charles in business, George DeForest also joined the North family. In 1885 he married Charles and Harriet North's daughter Sarah C. North in a quiet ceremony in Oswego.[295] Sarah, age 25, was the second of Charles and Harriet North's three surviving daughters.

Born on the eve of the Civil War, Sarah may have had a fairly public existence during her childhood at the house on Seventh Street in Oswego. While she was growing up, her father served in important political positions in the town and the state, including as mayor of Oswego. The Norths led a life of relative comfort, often employing a live-in servant in their home.[296] Sarah presumably had the support and community of the extended family group that centered on her father's tannery, which had had its beginnings in Cummington many years earlier.

George had grown up in comfortable surroundings as well. Born in 1854 at Woodbury, Connecticut, he was the only child of George DeForest Sr. and Mary Ann DeForest, née Linsley.[297] When George was young, his father worked as a shoemaker and then became an insurance agent.[298]

George Sr. provided his son with the start to a good education. He set an example for other members of his community by sending George Jr. to Wesleyan Academy in Wilbraham, Massachusetts, in preparation for college. An 1870 report from Woodbury in the *Waterbury* [Connecticut] *Daily American*, described the new trend:

> Knowledge is power as the youthful mind is trained. As education becomes thorough and spread abroad, so society is improved, and the welfare of the race advanced. There is a growing interest on the subject in this town. The good example lately set by Mr. Cornelius J. Minor and Mr. George DeForest in sending their cherished youth to that excellent institution, the Wilbraham Academy, has thus early produced abundant fruit. Nine additional youths go this morning with these young men to the same institution. It augurs well for this town where such an interest is taken in the advancement and education of its children and youth. When these eleven young men return to their homes with minds well stored with useful knowledge, the town will have 'whereof it may well be proved.'[299]

The Wesleyan Academy offered "equal advantages" to both males and females, with a four-year program that featured "Common and Higher English," mathematics, science, and ancient and modern languages. The school also had offerings in fine arts and music.[300]

Young George's early good fortune ended abruptly in April of 1871 when his father, just 46, died rather suddenly, after a short and "painful" illness. According to the *Waterbury Daily American*, "Mr. George DeForest . . . [died] in the full strength of his manhood, and of his usefulness. For many years, he has moved in his quiet course among us, mingling with us in all the charities and good offices of life—a kind husband and father, a true and sincere friend, and a worthy and consistent christian [*sic*] gentleman."[301] Even two years later, his demise was remembered by the same newspaper as a loss to the community. "Woodbury . . . has been depleted sadly for a few years past," reported the *Daily American* in 1873. "Such men as the late George Drakely, Solomon Minor, and George Deforest, she can hardly afford to lose! To say nothing of the more aged worthies! They were men that the community could rely upon for the support of its *highest* interests.[302]

His college plans scrapped, George and his widowed mother endured the loss, and George set his sights on an early career.[303] At 21, he moved 25 miles southeast to New Haven and found a job as a salesman at Adam & Taylor, selling both wholesale and retail dry goods.[304]

George was in New Haven for only a few years. By 1879, he had made his way to Oswego, taking his skills in dry goods with him.[305] The following year he worked on West First Street in partnership with James Roy at the firm of Roy and DeForest, specializing in "black silks." Calling itself a "one price dry goods house," the establishment sold a variety of ready-made clothing items, such as shawls, dresses, gloves, laces, fringes, woolens, flannels, underwear, shirts, and "neck-ware." A display ad in the Oswego city directory claimed: "The decidedly greatest variety! The latest styles and lowest cash prices."[306]

In 1882, George ran another dry goods establishment, this time with Frederick K. Massey. Massey & DeForest was later remembered as "one of the most successful in their line ever engaged in business in the city."[307]

Sometime over the next three years, George became Charles North's partner and married his daughter Sarah. George and Charles had quite a bit in common. Both had grown up in comfortable circumstances yet had fashioned careers for themselves independent of the direct guidance of their forebears. Like Charles, who had made a major shift as a young man and set out from Ireland for America, the death of George's father had sent him first to New Haven and then to Oswego, in search of making a living on his own.

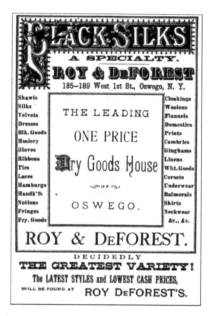

Advertisement for Roy & DeForest, from the 1880 Oswego City Directory.[308]

After their wedding in 1885, George and Sarah DeForest settled in at 163 East Sixth Street. Their daughter, Mary—who would be their only child—was born in 1886. In addition to working alongside him, George joined his father-in-law in the government of Oswego as well. In 1886—the year that Charles reprised his role as mayor of the city—George became Oswego's city chamberlain.[309] He served in that capacity for three years, during which Charles successfully ran for a second term.[310]

Sarah was also involved in the community. She was a member of the Afternoon Whist Club, which met weekly, and she donated money to the Trustees of Oswego

Hospital.[311] George and Sarah attended the 1893 world's fair in Chicago, along with other residents of Oswego.[312]

To Utica

Things were about to change for the DeForest family, however. After Charles North died in 1892, George set a higher goal for himself. For fifteen years he had worked on the retail end of the clothing business. In 1895, he became involved with the manufacture of fabric itself, accepting a position as assistant treasurer of the Utica Steam and Cotton Mills, a textile mill in Utica. George, Sarah, and 11-year-old Mary moved to Utica to begin a new chapter of their lives.[313]

Utica had grown since the arrival of Isaac Maynard and John Thorn back in the mid-1830s. By the time the DeForests arrived, many of the city's roads were paved, electricity lit the streets at night, and a street railway system (run by electricity) connected destinations within the city and beyond. Textiles, shoes, and knitwear were among the city's chief industries.[314]

Genesee Street, Utica, looking Down from City Hall Tower, about 1898.[315]

The economic growth that had begun in the 1840s had continued rapidly up until 1893, when, following an expansion of the city's major mills, a protective tariff bill was repealed on the national level, putting textile profits in jeopardy. An economic panic ensued, and Utica's textile industry, as well as its shoe industry, saw closings and layoffs. Building came to a stop, and hundreds were put out of work.

Things improved after the 1896 election of William McKinley, just as the DeForests were arriving in Utica. With the return of high protective tariffs, factories were enlarged, new businesses started, and the economy moved toward revival.[316]

The city also developed in other ways. A bicycle academy and a golf club were opened, horse racing commenced at Utica Park, and crowds of residents got their first glimpse of an automobile when one traveled through the city *en route* from Cleveland to New York.[317]

As the city flourished, many of Utica's elite had followed Isaac Maynard and John Thorn to occupy Genesee Street mansions, southwest of the center of town.[318] According to historian T. Wood Clarke, "Genesee Street with its double row of stately elms contained only private homes except for one hiatus: the small group of stores at Oneida Square. These fine residences, with their gardens extending through to Union and King Streets on the east and Broadway on the west, housed the descendants of the Utica pioneers, people of wealth and culture.[319] The newly arrived DeForests found their home literally on the edge of this enclave—just off of Oneida Square on Plant Street.[320]

Textiles

George's new role at Utica Steam and Cotton Mills was an important one, and he advanced quickly. Working under president John M. Crouse, George moved from assistant treasurer to treasurer in just six months. He represented the mills as a member of the New England Cotton Manufacturers' Association in 1897.[321] The mills became well known for their production of "Utica Sheets."[322]

An advertisement for Utica Sheets, appearing in the Sunday edition of the Chicago Tribune, *1929.*[323]

Beyond a change in position, George's new role also represented a move away from the world of small shops to the emerging factory scene. Like the tanning and soap and candle industries, textile manufacturing had gone through changes over the previous two hundred years. A home-based industry in colonial times, early American women made their own cloth and clothing for their families; they also made sails, curtains, and other items. Because New York's climate was ill-suited to growing cotton, most of these textiles in the state were made of wool or flax, and they were created from start to finish in the home. It wasn't until the 1770s that carding mills began to offer their services to local families, completing some of the time-consuming process of generating fabric. Even with this advancement, however, material was generally kept by each family for personal use rather than sold or traded for other goods.[324]

England actively discouraged advancement in the textile industry in America, particularly after the Revolutionary War. Because they feared a dwindling of the market for the more sophisticated fabrics that they exported to the colonies, the British discouraged the rise of American manufacturing by prohibiting plans or models of industrial machinery to leave their country. England also discouraged the emigration of skilled workers who might bring machinery designs to the United States.

In opposition to this, during the late 1780s, a number of American businessmen offered rewards to English mill workers for immigrating to America and sharing their knowledge.[325] One of these was Samuel Slater, who committed a British textile operation to memory and created a working replica of it in Pawtucket, Rhode Island, in 1790. "Slater Mills" soon appeared all over New England.[326]

Shortly thereafter, with the invention of the cotton gin in 1793, the southern states and the Caribbean began shipping ginned cotton. This spurred the opening of large-scale mills in the northeast. New York State saw its first cotton mill in 1808 at Whitestown, just a few miles from Utica. In 1817, Whitestown put a power loom into operation.[327]

Beginning in 1825, after the opening of the Erie Canal enabled easy and inexpensive transportation for supplies and products, New Englanders sought out Mohawk Valley locations for their new textile mills.[328] By 1845, New York had more than three hundred woolen mills in operation—twenty-one of them in Oneida, Madison, and Herkimer counties.[329]

The city of Utica jumped on board in a significant way in 1845, when leaders visited New England and brought plans for steam-powered textile mills home. The new factories were operational by 1847,[330] and with this good investment, Utica quickly gained a reputation as a textile center. By the 1870s, the city and environs hosted eleven cotton mills and seven woolen mills. "Utica is naturally proud of her cotton mills," the *New York Times* proclaimed in 1872, "with their thousands of looms, and their thousands upon thousands of spindles, which cluster around her."[331]

The Utica Steam and Cotton Mills, where George would work, were of particular note. In 1872, the company was composed of two adjacent mills—the older one used for making a coarser grade of goods; the newer one for a finer grade. The 900 steam-powered looms and 34,000 spindles produced a daily product of about 17,000 square yards of cloth per day and consumed 5,000 bales of cotton per year. Each mill performed its own picking, cleaning, carding, drawing, spinning, and weaving.[332]

In 1901—six years after he joined the Utica Steam and Cotton Mills—George was instrumental in the company's merger with the nearby Mohawk Valley Cotton Mill, which had begun operation in 1880. After the merger, the capacity of each mill doubled.[333]

J. Fred Maynard and Mary Beardsley

Also involved in textile production at this time was John Frederick Maynard. Unlike George DeForest, "J. Fred" had lived in Utica all of his life. Born in 1851, he was Isaac and Margaret Maynard's third child and second son. [334]

As a young boy, J. Fred lived in his family's brick house in the extended-family compound on Whitesboro Street. This allowed him to be near J. Fred's aunt and uncle Mary and John Thorn and also near two other aunts and uncles: the Tavenders and the Bults, both parents to young girls.[335]

In 1859 or 1860, when J. Fred was about 10, he and his family—which now included two younger sisters, Sophia and Sarah Grace—followed John and Mary Thorn out of the Whitesboro Street neighborhood and into a larger house on Genesee Street.[336] Fred spent the next ten years of his life on this tree-lined boulevard.

Once he was old enough to begin his own career, J. Fred followed in his father's and his uncle's footsteps by clerking at the Utica & Black River Railroad.[337] He became superintendent there in 1872.[338]

Four years later in 1876, J. Fred married his Genesee Street neighbor Mary Adams Beardsley. "A brilliant event," the *Utica Morning Herald and Daily Gazette* called the nuptials, describing Mary as "one of the most charming young ladies of our city." The wedding "was witnessed by a very large number of the elite and many others. The happy couple starts out in life with a wealth of congratulations and good wishes from a widely extended circle of friends."[339]

Mary came from a remarkable family. She was 10 in 1860 when her paternal grandfather, Samuel Beardsley, died. He had served in the U.S. Congress from 1831 to 1836, and again from 1843 to 1844. Samuel had also been the Attorney General for the state of New York and was an associate justice—then chief justice—of New York's Supreme Court.[340]

Samuel Beardsley, grandfather of Mary Adams Beardsley.[341]

During her childhood, Mary's father, Arthur Moore Beardsley, published the *Utica Observer,* but he later worked as an attorney. According to the *Rome Daily Sentinel*: "He ranked with the leaders of the bar of [C]entral New York, and in the earlier days of his practice was a familiar figure in the highest courts in this state."[342]

Arthur was also a man of notable personality. According to the *Rome Daily Sentinel:*

Mr. Beardsley certainly had the complete courage of his convictions, which he never hesitated, when occasion demanded, to express. He hated above all things a coward and a 'quitter,' a wabbling weakling who dared not stand by the principles for which he had at some time declared and who ran to the cover of sham and deception in time of stress. . . . Mr. Beardsley would give utterance to speech which cut like the keen scalpel of the surgeon, and many a man who has come under the sharp blade of his sarcasm has writhed in mental anguish. . . . He was not given to small talk for the mere purpose of appearing amiable, nor did he seek to increase or extend this list of friends by clap-trap methods; he was essentially honest and sincere.[343]

As newlyweds, young J. Fred and the new Mrs. Maynard settled in at 19 Hopper Street, just off of Genesee Street, and within walking distance of both of their parents' homes. J. Fred and Mary had two boys: Arthur B. Maynard in 1877, and John Frederick Maynard Jr. in 1884.[344]

Over the years, J. Fred rose to become vice president and general manager of the Utica & Black River Railroad, which his father and uncle had rescued back in the 1850s. The railroad grew to include 24 locomotives, 26 passenger cars, 14 baggage cars, and 361 freight cars.

A letter to railroad telegraph operators, penned and signed by J. Fred in 1882.[345]

A big change came in 1886, when the Utica & Black River was perpetually leased to the Rome, Watertown, and Ogdensburg Railroad Company.[346] The *Herald* barely hid an air of dismay at this new arrangement, calling the deal "a genuine surprise in business circles. The change is a radical one. . . . The road was largely built by Utica capital, most of its stock is owned here, and it has long been ably managed by Utica men."[347] J. Fred joined his Uncle John Thorn on a trip to New York City to solidify the agreement. It was a long day for the two men: the *Utica Morning Herald and Daily Gazette* reported the next morning that J. Fred and John "returned from New York last evening, but they were too weary to speak of the matter at so late an hour." Although they gave up control of the railroad's administration, J. Fred was appointed as general traffic manager of the entire system.

Changing Lives

J. Fred's success enabled him to enjoy frequent trips abroad with his family. The first one took place in 1888, when Arthur was 10 and John was 4.[348] Eight years later in 1896—the boys now young men—they crossed the ocean again for a nine-month tour of Europe, followed by a summer trip abroad in 1898.[349]

For their son Arthur, the latter two trips were interspersed with his studies at Yale University's Sheffield Scientific School, where he was enrolled as a freshman in 1897–98 and was listed as a member of the (second year) "junior class" in 1898–99.[350] For the Maynard family, Arthur was the first in his direct line to enter college. John would later become a student at Yale as well.

Globe Woolen Company

J. Fred became part of Utica's textiles scene in 1904, when he left his railroad position to become president of Utica's Globe Woolen Company,[351] one of the mills that had been built through community funding back in the 1840s.[352] Both Isaac Maynard and John Thorn had been directors at Globe in their day, but the move represented a leap for J. Fred, who had little experience in the industry. "After I ceased active participation in railroading, I had no other special business," he later noted. "I never [had] been actively engaged in any other manufacturing business of any kind, operated by any kind of power whatever.[353]

Utica had grown and expanded directly following the turn of the century. According to T. Wood Clarke, "taken all in all, this first decade of the twentieth century marks the peak of peacetime prosperity in Utica." The population increased by 29 percent, and "Utica . . . gave promise of becoming the most important industrial city in the State of New York." In particular, the textile industry, the center of Utica's strength, reached its height during these years. Cotton and wool were manufactured in the city, and Utica also became the headquarters of the two largest knit goods corporations in the world by 1910.[354]

From an ad in an 1894 copy of the Philadelphia Inquirer*: "The above is an exact reproduction of the Trade-Mark and ticket of the 'Globe Woolen Co.,' Utica, N. Y. We have in stock and in course of manufacture Two Thousand (2000) Globe Suits and One Thousand (1000) Trousers for Men and Boys, made in our own workshop under our personal supervision."[355]*

Globe Woolen Company products already had a favorable reputation in markets across the state and elsewhere. The company featured a sales location on Broadway in New York City, and ads boasted that there was "no better cloth made in the world":

The Globe Worsteds are made of pure wool worsted yarn; . . . the fabrics made by high-class merchant tailors at $40 to $50 per suit. The ready-to-wear suits are usually sold for $28 and $30, and can only be had in leading retail houses. . . . Our guarantee goes with every garment. This means a suit of Globe Worsted absolutely first-class in all things. The Globe Woolen Company stands at the top as cloth makers. We have carried our best efforts into the makeup, style and character. This combination will give the buyers an A No. 1 suit. [356]

The Globe Company had two mills—a worsted mill and a woolen mill, which manufactured yarn and cloth. Each mill had a separate house for dyeing. In 1903, the mills were mostly operated by steam power, but also using a small amount of electricity.[357]

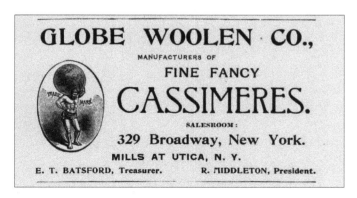

Advertisement in the Bulletin of the National Association of Wool Manufacturers for 1895.*[358]*

Closing Circles

In 1906, two years after J. Fred took his new position at the Globe, George DeForest was promoted from treasurer to president of the Utica Steam and Mohawk Valley Cotton Mills, after the death of mill president John M. Crouse.[359] J. Fred and George were now in counterpart roles, giving their families many reasons to become acquainted and their children to marry each other. In actuality, however, the Maynards and DeForests had had opportunities to meet as soon as the DeForests arrived in Utica in 1895. In addition to living within walking distance of each other, George DeForest's superior, the now-deceased John M. Crouse, was J. Fred Maynard's brother-in-law, married to his sister Mary.[360]

The men also shared an interest in banking. George DeForest was a director of Oneida National Bank and Utica Trust & Deposit Company,[361] and J. Fred Maynard was one of the organizers of City National Bank of Utica and was actively engaged in its management.[362]

George and J. Fred's wives may have also met through their many community endeavors. Mary Maynard was a hostess at the first New York state conference of the Daughters of the American Revolution, which was held in Utica on 4 June 1896.[363] In December 1902, she joined the reception committee for a "bachelor's ball," which was largely attended and featured two orchestras that managed to provide continuous music for the entire evening.[364] That same year, Sarah DeForest was hostess at the lemonade table for a lawn fete given by the nurses of Faxton Hospital for the benefit of a piano fund for the nurses' home. "The piazza and the dancing platform were decorated with American flags and Japanese lanterns, tastefully arranged, and an exceedingly pretty effect was presented," one newspaper reported. The event took place on the hospital lawn, with an orchestra providing music for dancing.[365] Sarah also won a ladies' croquet tournament at a golf match at Yahnundahis Golf Club in 1904.[366]

Wedding

Their children, Mary Louise DeForest and John Frederick Maynard Jr., may have also met, likely through Mary Louise DeForest's association with the Crouse girls—John's first cousins.

John and Mary had definitely met by the summer of 1906, when their interest in each other was clearly public, and one of their dates was described in the newspaper. John's parents hosted a short automobile trip to the town of Richfield—known for its mountain and lake scenery as well as its medicinal springs—about 35 miles southwest of Utica.[367] Mary DeForest joined their party, a fact that was chronicled in the *Brooklyn* [New York] *Life*: "Automobiling through the state usually means a stop for a day or two at Richfield," the newspaper mused on 28 July. "Mr. and Mrs. J. Fred Maynard, Miss de Forest and Mr. F. [*sic*] Maynard, junior, drove from Richfield to Utica, Thursday."[368]

John was 22 and Mary was 21 when they wed on a June afternoon in 1907—an event that commanded significant coverage in the *Utica Observer*.

With a beautiful and impressive service, Miss Mary Louise DeForest and John Frederick Maynard, Jr., were married at 12 o'clock to-day in Christ Church. Guests at the edifice while the ceremony was solemnized were relatives and close friends of those before the altar, including many who are prominent socially in Utica and in other cities. It was a charming function, one of the distinctive and conspicuous nuptial events of late June in Utica.

The bride is a daughter of Mr. and Mrs. George DeForest and the groom is a son of Mr. and Mrs. J. Fred Maynard. Each family is very well known in Utica.

Mary DeForest Maynard, 1907.[369]

The decorations of the church were beautiful in their simplicity. Green and white were the colors, and Florist Baker worked out a happy conception. Roses, long-stemmed and of rich white, studded banks of green that had been artistically placed, and the effect of the whole arrangement was charming. At the residence of Mr. and Mrs. DeForest, the decorations were alike simple and beautiful. This home was visited after the ceremony at the church was concluded, and there a wedding breakfast was partaken of. Chester served, and a programme was rendered by Rath's orchestra.

The gowns worn by the ladies of the bridal party were notable. Each was in white, and the bride had a charming robe of white satin. Other gowns of especial beauty were worn by guests at the church and the home. Many cities of New York and other states were represented in the company that assembled.

Mr. Maynard and his bride have the favor and the sincere congratulations of their many friends in Utica and elsewhere. Mr. Maynard is a young man whose worth is recognized, and his bride's life has been richly blessed with pleasant friendships. For a continuance of the happiness that has been theirs, many good wishes will go out to Mr. and Mrs. Maynard.[370]

And so, John and Mary Maynard began their life together.

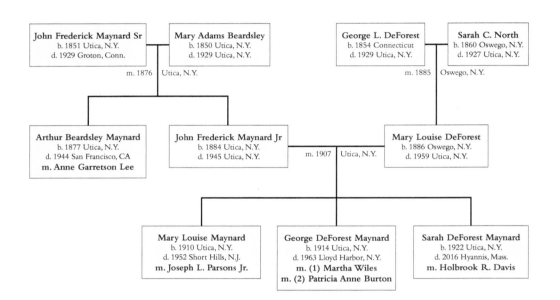

— CHAPTER FOUR —

Into the Future

J OHN F. MAYNARD JR. AND MARY (DEFOREST) MAYNARD faced the future as a married couple seventy years after their grandfathers Charles North and Isaac Maynard set foot on American soil. Well poised for success, both John and Mary had inherited a comfortable situation stemming from the hard work of their ancestors. Their forebears had seen American industry through the stages of home craft to small business to large factory, and their fathers had worked their way to the top of the local industrial structure, serving as presidents of two of the largest mills in one of the nation's most important textile cities.

These realities afforded both John and Mary generous upbringings, with private school educations, European travel, and teenage years filled with parties and balls. Their families reached the top of Utica's social hierarchy, and at times their lives were the talk of the town, with newspaper coverage providing the details of their gatherings and their plans.

Although the future may have seemed nothing but bright on their wedding day in 1907, John and Mary Maynard would face some sobering trials during their next forty years, including a national pandemic, two world wars, and the loss of their four parents. Channeling the community spirit of his forbears, John would emerge as a leader in Utica as an able and available manager in times of crisis.

John Maynard

John F. Maynard Jr., son of J. Fred and Mary, grew up in and around the lower section of Genesee Street, where two previous generations of Maynards had established themselves. His older brother, Arthur Beardsley Maynard, was 7 when John was born in 1884.

Sometimes called "Jack," John was part of a small bevy of Maynard first cousins of similar age, who lived and socialized in Utica during their childhood and teenage years. John and his cousins Nellis, Margaret, and "Mollie" Crouse all were born within two years of each other. The Crouse children were descended from two of John's aunts— Mary Louise (Maynard) Crouse and Sophia (Maynard) Crouse—sisters of J. Fred Maynard's who had married brothers. Beecher Crouse, Mollie's brother, was sixteen years older than the younger four cousins, while John's brother Arthur was seven years older.[371]

John's parents employed servants in their home, and nurse/governess Mary Murphy may have cared for John during his childhood years. When the family traveled to Europe in 1888, Mary traveled with them. Later, when John traveled abroad, he frequently wrote to Mary.[372]

Trips Abroad

John was just 4 years old when he boarded his first ship for Europe. In addition to his family and governess, their party also included a "Miss Maynard," 25, who was the right age to have been his aunt Harriet—his father's younger sister. "Miss Williams," 27, may also have been a member of their group. They arrived home to New York City in October aboard the R.M.S *Aurania*, having boarded the boat in Queenstown, Ireland.[373]

Later, at age 12, John joined his family on a tour of Europe that lasted the better part of a year. "Mr. Collins," presumably a tutor, came along for part of the trip.

John kept a journal that noted the daily events of his journey. Rarely delving into emotion or reflection, the diary reads as one of a quiet boy, interested in his novel surroundings but spending most hours in the company of grown-ups. He occupied much of his time taking pictures.[374]

John's journal began on Saturday, 28 November 1896, the day he departed New York aboard the S.S. *Columbia* of the Hamburg-American line:[375]

> We are off. Left wharf 5 min. behind time. Uncle Sam came down to see us off and Mrs. Collins and Mr. Collin's brother came down to see him off. As soon as we started the band began to play and so did the *Normania*'s so as to say good-by. We went up the harbor at a pretty slow rate, so we could see the things pretty well. At the Brooklyn navy yard we could see the *Columbia*,[376] the *Maine*, the *Massachusetts*, the *Montgomery*, and that was all. They looked very pretty, they were all so white and clean. We saw the statue of Liberty in the harbor and it looked fine. . . . The Cunard liner *Etouria* [*Etruria*] followed us out. She was listed quite a little to port, by her cargo. When we were nearly to Sandy Hook we passed the *St. Paul* of the American line going in.[377]

Page from 12-year-old John F. Maynard Jr.'s diary, 1896.[378]

Transatlantic travel had changed considerably since John's grandfather Isaac first crossed the ocean from England to America in 1836. Ships during Isaac's time were wooden-hulled sailing vessels that relied on prevailing winds for propulsion. Speed and safety were far from guaranteed, with weather often leading to long delays, or worse. The introduction of steam engines and iron hulls had revolutionized the shipping and travel industry, offering speed, safety, and the promise of a regular schedule of arrivals and departures.[379]

Luxury was also a new offering. First-class passengers could now enjoy private rooms that rivaled the finest hotels, and access to public spaces that were as elaborate as they were elegant.[380]

John and his family were among those assigned to Cabin 29, one of a handful of *chambres de luxe* on board. According to a 1900 brochure, the Hamburg-American line offered "the entire absence of all offensive odours or noises, and a complete and first-class service throughout, with the conveniences of barber's shops, baths, toilet-rooms, &c. The ships are lighted throughout with electricity."[381]

Safety was also assured. The *Columbia* was one of the fleet's "twin-screw" steamers that operated with two sets of boilers and engines, "dividing the vessel in two non-communicating halves, each of which is fully equipped to propel the ship. . . . An accident to one side of the ship can in no wise affect the other, the machinery of which will continue to work and propel the ship with perfect ease."[382]

"An Evening in the Grand Saloon," from a travel pamphlet issued by the Hamburg-American Line in 1900.[383]

John enjoyed visiting the workings of this massive boat. "We went down to see the engines this afternoon and it was lots of fun," he wrote during the early days of the voyage. "We also went down in the stoke-hold, where it was awfully hot. When we came up we had to go up the iron stairs which were very hot. I had to pull my sleeves over my hand so as to hold on."[384]

In Naples, Italy, John left the ship to explore the city in the evening. "We went into the arcade and had some chochlate [*sic*] which was as strong as the deuce," he wrote. "The town is an awfully queer place. We took a ride in a crazy old carriage which was drawn by two old plugs made of skin and bone and about the size of a donkey. They had bits which came out about 2 inches on each side of the mouth."[385]

From Genoa, Italy, the family boarded a train for the 200-mile trip to Nice, France. "The train was an awfully long one and did not go at all fast," John wrote. "When ever we would pull out of a station[,] somebody in the station would blow a whistle and then somebody a little farther on would blow a ten cent horn and then the engine would whistle and then we would start."[386]

In Nice, they checked into the Cosmopolitan Hotel for a month-long stay. The first full day there, John's father bought a dictionary "so he could jabber French. It is lots of fun to listen to Papa try to be understood by the people. Some of the words are in English and some in French."[387]

Each day featured study for both John and his brother, Arthur, in the morning, and a walk or drive in the afternoon. John tried to document the sights in his journal and with his camera. Nice did not have much to offer in the way of fun for a 12-year-old, and his brother and Mr. Collins, perhaps similar in age, spent time together without him. "It seems more like the fourth of July than it does Christmas, seeing all the flowers out," he wrote on 19 December. "There is nothing to do in this place except play billiards which Mr. Collins and Art do most of the time. I played billiards for a little while this afternoon with another kid."[388]

Christmas did not disappoint, however. "Merry Christmas. Weather fine. Papa gave me a camera case and a dandy knife. Mama gave me a pair of field-glasses, they are fine. Arthur gave me a Pocket Kodak Picture Album. In the evening, there was a Christmas tree down stairs, it looked very pretty. The hotel gave presents to every one. You drew a number[,] and then there was a number like it on some present. Papa got a smelling bottle, Mama a blotter, Arthur a toy, Mr. Collins a picture ease[l], and I a box of sealing wax. We had a lot of fun." Two days later, another present arrived: "a very nice calendar of dogs," from his cousin Margaret Crouse.[389]

Taking the train back to Genoa, they met John's aunts and uncles—J. Fred's sisters Grace and Hattie, and their husbands, John Waters "Jack" McLean, and Dr. Ogden Backus—who had just arrived on the *Columbia*. The whole group boarded the boat once again, and headed for Alexandria, Egypt. "Uncle Jack, Pop, Art, and I played domino whist in the evening" on board the boat. "I beat. Pile of fun."[390]

They took a train to Cairo, where John "went through the narrow bazars [*sic*] on donkey back . . . Some of them were so narrow we had to get off and walk. It was very, very, dirty." They saw the pyramids on 28 January ("monster heaps!"), then traveled up the Nile to Luxor and back, a trip of two weeks. They returned to Cairo on 18 February. Then they once again boarded the *Columbia*, bound for Italy. They arrived back in Naples on 5 March, and checked into the Grand Hotel of Naples. Young John found little enchantment with this city or its people. "If Rome is a clean city in comparison with Naples, it is pretty dirty. The Italians are the dirtiest and cruelest people I ever laid eyes on."[391]

The aunts and uncles presumably parted with them as John and his family continued on to Rome, where they remained about a month. After seeing the Colosseum, John wrote: "Saw place where they used to keep the wild animals. They used to put people in there and turn the animals in and see the people and animals killed. Just for fun. At one time 5,000 animals were killed in 100 days, 50 a day. For fun."[392]

One positive moment in Rome was the procession that marked the opening of Parliament on 5 April. Impressed, young John took twenty pictures and added another entry to his diary:

> The procession came in two divisions. In the first division came the Queen and some members of the court. They were accompanied by a detachment of the King's guard. The King's guard are a dandy lot of men, I don't believe there is one among them that is under 6 ft. They were mounted on beautiful horses and they wore a breast shield of armor. They had a very pretty uniform. The carriages were drawn by immense horses all dressed up in great big harnesses. The driver and the footman wore wigs and scarlet uniform[s]. . . . The carriages in the first division were drawn by two horses. The carriages were very fine.[393]

Later, on a tour of the palace, the Queen walked by "in a common blue dress," and young John mistook her for a housekeeper.[394]

Once they had passed through Italy, they continued on to Switzerland and Germany, where the boys' school year apparently ended. John's brother, Arthur, passed various academic exams, and John declared: "I am not going to study anymore."[395]

Although John did not admit that he found the trip dull, he cheered when his father booked their passage out of Europe. "Papa has bought rooms on '*Etruria*' on August 28th. Hurrah! 54 days more!" From there, each diary entry included a countdown of days. His excitement shone through particularly on 14 July: "Left Kissengen at 2:25 p.m. Whoop!"[396]

From Hamburg, the group went to The Hague, then to Amsterdam, then London, before making the long voyage home.[397]

Second Trip

A second European tour took place just eight months later, beginning 19 May 1898, when John and his parents boarded the *Auguste-Victoria* of the Hamburg-American Line. After a lengthy stay in Germany, they took a cruise up the Norwegian coast, with passengers alighting to explore various stops along the way. At one point, the captain stopped their boat as "a small whale jumped clear out of the water." In Tromsø, they arrived at a whaling station, where they saw many whales being brought in on boats. They went as far north as Hammerfest, located almost at the northern tip of Norway. "Landed and walked up to the glacier," John wrote on 27 July. Beautiful blue in the ice."[398]

In Sweden, his aunt Sophia and uncle Daniel Crouse and their children—John's cousins Nellis and Margaret—arrived on the S.S. *Wellona* from St. Petersburg. They spent some time with the Maynards, including a game of catch played by John and Nellis. Although Margaret was about John's age, he didn't mention spending time with her in his diary.[399]

A view from the deck of the Auguste-Victoria, *about 1900.*[400]

This second trip seemed to carry less luster for John. His customary remarks about the scenery and the sights, usually neutral and descriptive, were peppered with negative comments. "The dinner was not as good as the one we had going up"[401];"Fireworks . . . in the evening. Not much good";"A very filthy town";"Went to see an old museum in A.M. Very uninteresting. We also went to see an old church. Nothing."[402]

They continued to Russia, then Stockholm and Copenhagen.[403] Apparently weary with the journey, John again was thrilled when his father made arrangements to leave Europe earlier than planned:

> Copenhagen. Thursday. Reduced to 7 days. Hurrah! Papa received telegram this morning offering two rooms on the Auguste Victoria, sailing in a week! He telegraphed for two yesterday, but I didn't know it. We are going to sail on the old Victoria in a week. Whoop. Hip! Hip! Hurrah!

They arrived on American soil on 2 September.[404]

Pomfret

Young John presumably was delighted to be back in Utica. A few years later, however, he left his home city again: this time as a student at the Pomfret School in Pomfret, Connecticut. The school, established just a few years earlier in 1894, enrolled about 130 boys, mostly from eastern cities.[405]

John attended Pomfret during the 1900–1 and 1901–2 school years, during which he completed his junior and senior years of high school. His studies consisted of Latin, Latin composition, algebra, trigonometry, literature, English composition, German, history, writing, sacred study, and botany. With the exception of botany, for which he earned all As, his other grades were modest, consisting of mostly Bs and Cs. His deportment grades were exemplary, however: he earned consistent As in punctuality, neatness, and behavior.[406]

Life at Pomfret wasn't all academics. John had the opportunity for some good fun with his peer group there. The school was still developing its sports program, but tennis, football, hockey, and baseball teams had been formed. The entire school sometimes joined in a large field hockey game on the football field across from the school.[407]

Skating and sledding were frequent activities in the wintertime, and warmer weather allowed for other pursuits as well. "We caught and tamed innumerable squirrels, both red and gray," remembered student William B. Boulton, who was a student there from 1895 to 1900. "[We] capsized canoes on the Quinebaug River, always too early in spring to enjoy the water; built huts in the woods; trapped anything that would be trapped; got poison ivy collecting birds' eggs; swam in leech-infested Paradise Pond, and loved it all."[408]

John spent his school breaks back in Utica, but far from a chance to relax, the weeks comprised an ambitious social schedule involving the families—many related— in the Genesee Street area. Dancing lessons, receptions, debuts, and balls with live music always abounded during the week between Christmas and New Year's Day.

Both John and Arthur almost certainly attended the large dancing party in Oneida Hall that their parents hosted shortly after Christmas in 1901. According to the *Utica Sunday Journal*, "Upwards of 200 were present, and the affair was one of the most brilliant and successful of the season."[409]

John F. Maynard Jr.[410]

The Maynards, Crouses, and Beardsleys all welcomed Yale's Glee, Banjo, and Mandolin Club when they came to Utica to perform a concert that same December. John's parents hosted an afternoon reception at their home, and John's aunts, including Mary Louise Crouse and Sophia Crouse, were on the receiving line. The Oneida Dancing Academy gave a ball afterward, with many of the same women as patronesses.[411]

Following New Year's Day in 1902, John's mother was a patroness at a "fancy dress ball" that was attended by about 200 young people, and that December, John's parents gave their annual after-Christmas dancing party, this time in honor of John and Arthur. The occasion gathered between 200 and 300 guests at "one of the most enjoyable of the society events of the holiday season."[412]

John would have been well schooled in a young man's behavior at such affairs. At the very least, he would have known how to dance. "A gentleman should know how to box, fence, ride, drive, shoot, swim, and dance," one etiquette book of the time period suggested. "He should practice every 'accomplishment' that will give him strength and grace." Manners held importance to the young men in John's sphere. "High moral character, a polished education, a perfect command of temper, delicate feeling, good habits and a good bearing are the indispensable requisites of good society," according to the same authority. "These constitute good breeding and produce good manners."[413]

Balls such as these typically began at ten o'clock in the evening and lasted until two or three o'clock in the morning. Introductions and dancing were followed by dinner at midnight and a "cotillion," or "German,"—a series of dances that were overseen by a leader and involved multiple partners, preprinted cards, and party favors.[414]

Utica's holiday social schedule was tightly packed. The same week as the 1902 holiday ball, John's mother served on the reception committee at a "bachelors' ball," which John likely attended. He may also have been among the twenty "young people" who enjoyed a sleigh ride followed by a supper given by his aunt Sophia Crouse at her home that likely included his cousins Nellis and Margaret. One December, J. Fred and Mary hosted a Japanese costume party during Christmas week.[415]

By this time, John and his cousin Nellis were students at Yale's Sheffield Scientific School, John's brother Arthur's *alma mater*.[416] John belonged to the class of 1905, studying in the field of mechanical engineering. He was a member of the Cloister Club, the Book and Snake, and the Kopper Kettle Club.[417]

Mary Louise DeForest

In the midst of this vibrant atmosphere, John had myriad opportunities to become acquainted with his future wife, Mary Louise DeForest, who had been part of his social realm since her arrival in Utica as an 11-year-old.

Born in 1886, Mary spent her earliest years in with her parents, George and Sarah North DeForest, at their home on East Sixth Street in Oswego. Her grandfather Charles North was mayor of Oswego the year she was born, and he died when she was 5. An only child, Mary's world changed considerably when her father accepted a new position with Utica Steam and Cotton Mills, and she and her parents moved to Utica.[418]

Young Mary's new house was located in a row of connected brick residences just off of Oneida Square, on the edge of the fashionable end of Genesee Street and within a short walking distance of John.[419] She quickly became a member of the social circle in this part of town. Two of the girls her own age—daughters of her father's boss—were young John Maynard's first cousins, Margaret and "Mollie" Crouse.

In December 1898, Mary DeForest was one of the "sixteen little misses" who, for the benefit of charity, sponsored a "fancy sale" at Mollie Crouse's Genesee Street home. Margaret Crouse attended that sale, and a similar sale in 1899, which included a puppet show put on by the girls. Her neighbor Anne Gibson later remembered Mary DeForest as "beautiful," and noted that her special "pal" was her next-door neighbor Priscilla Chamberlain, who was also a member of this group of young girls.[420]

Mary displayed a penchant for public speaking and acting. She—along with Margaret, Mollie, and Priscilla—participated in an elocution recital in 1899.[421] In May 1900, she performed in a "farce" called the "The Heartsville Shakespeare Club," and she was in a play for the benefit of playgrounds for children that summer. In September that year, she gave two recitations at a meeting of the New Century Club.[422]

During this turn-of-the-century era, opportunities for young women were increasing. "It is difficult to picture a happier life or one of greater freedom than that enjoyed by the girls of the present day," wrote manners author Mrs. Burton Kingsland in 1901. "Sports and pleasures formerly the monopoly of young men are allowed to be her privilege to enjoy as well. Life is replete with varied interests."[423]

In April 1903, Mary turned 17, old enough for her social debut. "The time for a young lady's first appearance in society is usually from seventeen to twenty," according to Mrs. Sara B. Maxwell, the author of a manners guide published in 1890. "The mother decides when her daughter shall make the transition from girlhood to young ladyhood and invites friends to her house that she may present this daughter to them as a member of their circle." According to Maxwell, young ladies did not attend parties until they had "come out," unless it was for a wedding, funeral, or birthday.[424] Mary probably made her debut before January 1905, when she was on the receiving line, along with Mollie Crouse, at a tea given in honor of Margaret Crouse.[425]

Like John, Mary received her high school education away from Utica. From 1904 to 1906, she studied at Miss Baldwin's School in Bryn Mawr, Pennsylvania, where she was a member of Glee Club.[426]

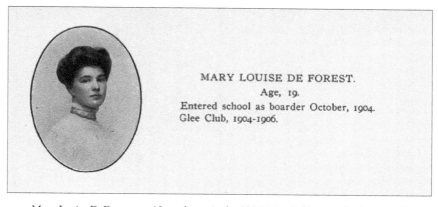

MARY LOUISE DE FOREST.
Age, 19.
Entered school as boarder October, 1904.
Glee Club, 1904-1906.

Mary Louise DeForest, age 19, as shown in the 1906 Miss Baldwin's School annual.[427]

The girls' school, founded in 1888 by Florence Baldwin, was intended for preparation for entrance into Bryn Mawr College—or to Vassar, Smith, or Wellesley.[428] Mary did not opt for higher education, although many of her fellow students probably did. When Miss Baldwin, the original proprietor of the school, took Mary and some of her classmates to spend a few days at the Gladstone Hotel in Atlantic City, New Jersey, one newspaper called the group an "attractive company of accomplished maids."[429]

Courting

Although John and Mary likely were well acquainted, they may not have acknowledged it openly if they passed each other on Genesee Street. According to manners authority Sara Maxwell:

[A lady] does not stop to gaze in at shop windows, nor talk to acquaintances. She is always unobtrusive. She never talks loudly or laughs boisterously, or does anything to attract the attention of passers-by. She simply goes about her business in her own quiet lady-like way, and by her preoccupation is secure from all the annoyance to which a person of less perfect breeding might be subjected.[430]

Mary Louise DeForest[431]

Similarly, Maxwell offered this advice to young men:

Carefully avoid all semblance of staring at ladies passing in the street, alighting from a carriage, etc., and make no comment, even of a complimentary nature, in a voice that can possibly reach their ears.[432]

Socializing and courting in these days happened in home parlors and on spacious dance floors. A complex system of conventions governed home visits, involving carefully kept lists of acquaintances and preprinted calling cards. Cards were left on the table in the entrance hall at each residence, and callers made visits of fifteen to twenty minutes on days that their friends and acquaintances were "at home."[433] According to Kingsland:

By three o'clock the hostess, dressed in becoming afternoon toilet, should be in her drawing-room ready to receive her friends on the afternoon of her weekly day at home. Visiting hours are sensibly restricted to between three and six o'clock. . . . In making an afternoon call[,] a man usually leaves his overcoat, stick or umbrella, hat and gloves in the hall before entering the drawing room. . . . He puts his card on the hall table or on the tray tendered him by the servant who holds open the door or portière and announces him if the hostess is in the drawing-room. . . . If a lady is behind her tea-table, she need not rise to greet a man caller, but bow, give her hand, if convenient, and gracefully include him in the conversation, introducing him or not, as she pleases, to those near her. She also bows her adieux. A lady never goes into the vestibule to meet a man, . . . [and] neither should she ever accompany a man to the hall, but take leave of him in the drawing-room. Under no circumstances does a lady help a man on with his overcoat, struggle as he may.[434]

John would have had to wait for an invitation from Mary's mother before calling on Mary at her home. Presumably the invitation was offered, and the guest was well received. John and Mary's engagement was announced in the *Utica Herald-Dispatch* during the December 1906 holiday season.[435]

Marriage

The *Herald-Dispatch* described John and Mary's wedding as "one the most important of the June weddings in local society circles," which took place "in the presence of a large and fashionable assemblage."[436] A breakfast and reception followed, and the new Mr. and Mrs. Maynard left for their bridal trip. Upon their return, they made their home on Clinton Place, near the Genesee Street neighborhood where they had both grown up.[437]

John established himself quickly as a cotton merchant, first working in partnership with Leslie W. Brennan, then joining Cromwell Woodward in 1911.[438] In 1918, Maynard & Woodward's offerings included American, Egyptian, Sea Island, and Peruvian cotton.[439]

John also remained close to his family's other interests. He followed his brother's lead to become a member of the board of directors of the Globe Woolen Company in 1909.[440] That same year, he and Mary served as best man and bridesmaid at Arthur's wedding to Anne Garretson Lee. The new couple settled in on nearby Plant Street.[441]

Like her own mother, Mary's focus would have been the support of her husband and her home. "It is a duty to all concerned for the wife and mother to take her stand with quiet dignity, at the head of her household," author Sara Maxwell advised in 1901. "If she be firm, gentle, self-reliant, allowing no coarseness . . . she can educate her family up to her standard. She can diffuse through the home an atmosphere of sympathy, kindness and love, in which the tender buds of humanity which may be given to her care, can grow and expand into noble manhood and womanhood."[442]

Mary and John's "tender buds of humanity" arrived in due course. Daughter Mary Louise Maynard was born 9 June 1910, and son George DeForest Maynard arrived in 1914.[443]

Sarah (North) DeForest and her oldest grandchild, Mary Louise Maynard, about 1913.[444]

Getting Around

Transportation advances were coming to the nation, including to Utica. By the 1910s, automobiles began to be a regular sight in the city. John was part of the trend with his own Peerless 30.[445]

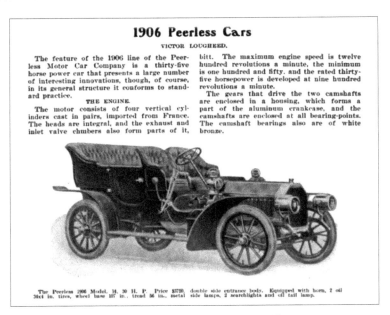

The 1906 version of the Peerless 30.[446]

In 1911, John and Mary may have watched when an airplane flew over the city "to the intense excitement of the citizens" on its way from St. Louis to New York. Just a few weeks later, another airplane provided a flight demonstration for twenty-five thousand people as part of "Utica Day," which also featured a parade, an automobile tour, and fireworks in the evening.[447]

George DeForest and his grandchildren: George DeForest Maynard and Mary Louise Maynard, about 1919.[448]

War and Disease

Aside from being a novel spectacle, these transportation advancements were integral to the defense of the nation when the United States entered World War I in 1917. The efficacy of Utica's textile industry was a boon to the effort as well. The city's textile mills were "working around the clock," during the war, in order to produce supplies for the allied armies and the government.[449]

John and his family members represented a complex web of key figures in the industry during this time: John as a cotton merchant and supplier at Maynard & Woodward; his father, J. Fred, as president of Globe Woolen Company; his father-in-law, George DeForest, as president of the Utica Steam and Mohawk Valley Cotton Mills; and his cousin Beecher Crouse, as president of the American Knit-Goods Association.[450]

Perhaps John's most memorable contribution during this time period, however, came in the form of community volunteer work. Taking a leap away from his business interests, John served as the head of the Red Cross Auxiliary when the 1918 flu ravaged Utica in October of that year, taking 177 lives in the first twenty days. The *Herald-Dispatch* reported on October 21: ". . . this figure exceeds the total number of deaths for a given time of any disease ever recorded by the health department." Thousands of others fell ill and recovered.[451]

"It was very scary as it came along slowly, but surely, from the East," Utica resident Anne Gibson Moffett remembered later. "It swept across the country leaving death in its path. Corpses piled up at the cemetery."[452] Utica's mayor, James D. Smith, later reported that the flu "took a heavy toll in death. Its spread throughout the city was very rapid, and in numberless cases whole families were incapacitated at the same time."[453]

On 3 October of that year, the American Red Cross issued its plan for combatting the "ever-increasing epidemic," which included supplying nursing personnel, hospital supplies, doctors, and the organization of local chapters. They also started an education program, with informational pamphlets that were distributed through schools, local businesses, and the Boy Scouts.[454]

In Utica, many of the city's trained nurses were unavailable—some, already committed to war service; others, victims of the epidemic themselves.[455] As temporary head of the local Red Cross chapter, John took charge of accepting donations and getting nurses to the hospitals where they were needed. He also led the chapter in the dispatching of medical aid, supplies, and food to the homes of the ill, and in repurposing city saloons to serve as soup kitchens for those who needed food.[456]

"I wish to express my gratitude to the Emergency Committee of the Utica Chapter of the American Red Cross," the mayor offered in December. "These splendid Uticans came to my aid in a manner which left nothing to be desired. This body speedily effected a splendid organization, through which medical and nursing attention was provided in the homes of the needy, as well as foodstuffs and other necessities furnished those in poor circumstances."[457]

Tragedies

Although none of the Maynards died as a result of the war or of influenza, during this time several tragic deaths occurred in John's extended family.

The first of these was 17-year-old Caroline Crouse, daughter of John's cousin Beecher. While home for a holiday break from boarding school in January of 1913, Caroline succumbed to meningitis and died after just forty-eight hours of illness. The death, according to the *Utica Observer*, "was most unexpected and comes as a crushing sorrow to her parents, who idolized her." The obituary described her as being "of the sweetest and gentlest of dispositions."[458]

Seven years later in 1920, another of John's cousins, Nellis Crouse, lost two sons (aged 11 and 20 months) and his mother-in-law in a catastrophic train wreck in Schenectady. The crash also injured Nellis and his 7-year-old daughter, Catherine. The family's nurse, Olwen Jones, and the family's cook, Annie Sullivan, also died.[459] The *Utica Herald-Dispatch* reported that another train rammed into theirs when Nellis and his family were asleep in a Pullman sleeper car on a train that was stopped for repairs. Eleven others were killed and twenty were injured in the accident.[460] The family originally kept the news of the tragedy from Nellis's wife, who, pregnant with her fourth child, had remained at home.[461]

The 1920s

In spite of these unfortunate losses, a national mood of progress prevailed in the early 1920s, and Utica saw some optimistic growth. The city became home to new buildings, it annexed land to its southern border, and it built new roads. The town gained two radio stations, and also an airport, located in nearby Marcy.[462]

In addition, John and Mary's family also grew. In 1922, they welcomed their third child, Sarah DeForest Maynard.[463] They called her "Sally."

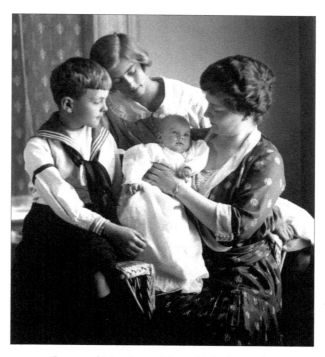

George and Mary Louise Maynard help their mother,
Mary Louise DeForest Maynard, welcome their new sister, Sally.[464]

As heartening as this progress may have been however, a national economic depression hit Utica hard in 1922. Cotton mills closed, and the demand for knit goods waned. In 1928, John F. Maynard Jr. lamented: "During the past five years . . . many of the cotton manufacturing mills in Utica and its vicinity have been closed, and several have moved to a location in the South where conditions for manufacturing were more favorable. Other mills in Utica and its vicinity have decreased their production because of unfavorable manufacturing conditions."[465]

In truth, textile manufacturing had been moving south for decades. The entire Southern region became ripe for industrialization after the Civil War, and textile production represented an attractive opportunity for an impoverished workforce that was unskilled but trainable.[466] In the South, laws discouraged the formation of unions and encouraged a liberal tax and regulatory environment. In addition, the Southern mills were closer to the source of growing cotton, making transportation costs for cotton mills minimal.[467]

By the 1920s, the South equaled the North in terms of textile production and had surpassed it by the 1950s.[468] Perhaps anticipating this, John's father, J. Fred Maynard, sold the Globe Woolen mills in 1916 to then become part of the American Woolen Company.[469] Ten years later, Mary's father, George DeForest, resigned from the Utica Steam and Mohawk Valley Cotton Mills.[470]

The Parents Continue On

Both George and J. Fred remained engaged in other business pursuits, however. George continued as chairman of the board of the cotton mills even after his retirement, and he was a director of the Utica Chamber of Commerce, a director of the Avalon Knitwear Company, and a member of the board of trustees of the YMCA.[471]

Likewise, J. Fred kept his ties to the New York Telephone Company, retaining a position on its board of directors. In 1929, he was considered the oldest surviving member of the board. He also was also an active director of the Utica Gas & Electric Company. Throughout, he was "frequently sought in adjusting business entanglements."[472]

Mary Louise DeForest Maynard.[475]

Their wives remained active as well. In December 1916, Mary attended the first convention of the National Association Opposed to Woman Suffrage, held in Washington, D.C.[473] "Antisuffragists believed that women and men were suited for very different tasks and had very different sensibilities," according to author Steven M. Beuchler. "Antisuffragists believed that the ballot would be a burdensome, destructive influence that would corrupt women and drag them into the unwholesome arena of partisan political struggle. Perhaps most important, antisuffragists believed that the ballot would undermine true womanhood, the sanctity of marriage, and the stability of the family."[474]

Mary held a card party in her home on behalf of the antisuffragists in January 1917. Guests, including many from surrounding towns, made up thirty-eight tables of whist. "Generous contributions [were] made toward the work of the local association" at the party.[476]

In 1927, Sarah DeForest served on the Board of Trustees of Faxton Hospital.

Leisure

The Maynards and the DeForests also found time for leisure away from home. J. Fred and Mary Maynard, who had taken their young children to Europe back in the 1890s, traveled there again in 1922.[477] On their passport, J. Fred was described as being 70 years old, five-feet six-inches tall, with a medium-large mouth, medium forehead, round chin, brown but partly gray hair, gray eyes, a medium light complexion, a straight nose, and a full face. He had a mustache and wore glasses. In addition, he had no little finger on his left hand, a fact that may confirm a family story that, during his railroad career, his hand was injured by getting caught between two heavy train cars.[478]

J. Fred Maynard.[480]

Mary Louise Deforest Maynard.[479]

J. Fred and Mary Maynard, as pictured on their passport in 1922.[481]

George and Sarah DeForest traveled closer to home. They regularly stayed at the Hotel Ormond in Ormond Beach, Florida, and George came close to winning a golf tournament there in 1919. The resort offered a beach, tennis, and horseback riding during the day, and in the evening, activities included bridge, concerts, and dancing. They also visited the Biltmore Hotel in North Carolina in 1924.[482]

Over his lifetime, George joined the Fort Schuyler Club, the Oneida County Historical Society, and the Dutch Reformed Church, and he was a member of the Yahnundasis Golf Course. His sometimes-acerbic personality came across in a 1925 letter in which he gave his opinion concerning some changes at the course. He quipped:

> I am pleased that you propose to inaugurate a new policy in reference to the . . . course and bring about a condition which will make it possible for the ordinary player to go over the course without breaking several of the Ten Commandments.
>
> The policy which has been pursued, of making the course so difficult that only professionals can get any pleasure out of it, and leaving the "rough" so that a man is liable to lose a box of golf balls in making the rounds, and also leaving the "rough" and sand traps so that they are practically unplayable if you do find a golf ball, has tended to drive a great many of the men who are supposed to play golf simply for exercise and pleasure out of the game.
>
> In following this program, you will, I think, have the earnest cooperation of that section of the members of the golf club who want to get a little pleasure and recreation out of their golf experiences.[483]

In December 1923, George purchased a new car for his wife just in time for Christmas. The vehicle was a Packard Single-6, a 7-passenger limo sedan, with wheels lettered with Sarah's initials: "SNDF."[484] Being a limousine in both name and size, the car was presumably driven by a chauffeur, rather than by Sarah herself.

1922–1923 Packard, first series single-six, 6-cylinder, 54-horsepower, 133-inch wheelbase, 7-person sedan-limousine, body type #229.[485]

Both the Maynards and the DeForests spent summers on Eastern Point in Groton, Connecticut. Located along the banks of the Thames River where it meets Long Island Sound, Eastern Point was a popular summer resort community beginning at the turn of the twentieth century.[486]

A Time of Endings

Sad times approached, however. Sarah (North) DeForest became ill during the fall of 1927 and did not recover, dying on 20 November at her home on Clinton Place. She was remembered for her work for the hospital, and her obituary in Oswego's *Palladium-Times* mentioned the many friends still remaining in that city, as well as her father Charles North's illustrious career as a community leader. She was 67.[487]

Sarah's death was first in a series of unfortunate losses for the Maynard family. After a short reprieve in 1928, John and Mary endured several blows to their family in 1929—the year that also marked the halt of the national economy and the advent of the Great Depression.

The first loss of the year came in June, when John's mother, Mary Adams Beardsley Maynard, died.[488] John's father, J. Fred, only lived a few months afterward. According to his obituary in the *Utica Observer-Dispatch*, "it was said by those close to him . . . [that he] had failed greatly following the death of his wife."[489] He had headed to their summer home in Groton in July, then died suddenly on 4 September—a "distinct shock to friends and relatives" in Utica. The *Observer-Dispatch* described him as a "prominent figure in the commercial and industrial life of this community."[490]

Just a month after J. Fred's death, George DeForest succumbed to a heart attack and died 6 October. His obituary in the *Utica Daily Press* called him a "sterling citizen and businessman. . . . By his death, the city suffers a severe loss. . . . He was known all over the country as a man of executive ability and of careful and conservative management."[491]

In just two years, all four of John and Mary's parents had died. Their children, 18-year-old Mary Louise, 14-year-old George, and 6-year-old Sarah, had lost of all four of their grandparents.[492]

Surprisingly, John's strength was especially evident that dismal autumn. In November, he again took the helm in terms of volunteer work for the community when he chaired a committee to raise funds for a new maternity unit and nurses' home at Faxton Hospital. This committee garnered substantial support, even in the face of the devastating economic crisis.[493]

That same month, John's skills as a manager and organizer—which had been so vital in response to the pandemic of 1918—were a distinct advantage when a crisis concerned a member of his extended family. On 14 November, Beecher Crouse's wife wandered away from their home on Genesee Street in the middle of the night and remained missing two days later. Authorities began a search that included the questioning of streetcar conductors and taxi drivers and aid from the Boy Scouts. According to the *Observer-Dispatch*, Louise Crouse had "suffered a breakdown about a year ago" [but] had greatly improved since then.[494] Two local experts suspected that Mrs. Crouse had amnesia.[495]

John F. Maynard was part of the inner circle of those concerned with her disappearance. The *Observer-Dispatch* reported that a small conference was held at the Crouse home and that "all present were of the opinion Mrs. Crouse was alive and was probably in a secluded spot."[496]

As days turned to weeks, the story received national attention, and rumors that Mrs. Crouse had been spotted as far away as West Virginia spiked at the end of November. Along with Beirne Gordon Jr. (Mollie Crouse's husband), John headed up a makeshift office in the Crouse home, with two floors of investigators and a bevy of telephone lines. "Probably no more systematic search has ever been conducted for a missing person," the *Utica Herald-Dispatch* reported. "Aerial maps of Utica and the surrounding country are being studied. Barns and old buildings within a radius of many miles have been thoroughly inspected and even wells, cisterns, and other out of the way places."[497] They offered a $5,000 reward for her discovery, and thousands helped in the search. Airplanes, radio, telegraph, and newspapers spread the word of her disappearance nationwide.[498]

Heartbreak came in March of the following year, when Louise Crouse's body emerged from melting ice in the barge canal, within a short walking distance from her home. Her death was considered a suicide.[499]

Final Years

After this blow, John focused on the business world again. Clearly an able and adept manager, he explored other spheres of work. He and his father had become involved with the Xardell Corporation back in 1923, which later changed its name to Utica Products, Inc.[500] The company manufactured and sold household appliances, including garage heaters.[501]

John began working there on weekends in 1924 and also in the afternoons during the week, arriving at 3:30 p.m. after spending the bulk of his day at Maynard & Woodward. He became president of the Utica Products the following year.[502]

Taking a page from his deceased father's book, John also made railroading a new focus. He became president of the Utica, Clinton and Binghamton Railroad in 1932, a position that he maintained until 1940.[503]

A versatile leader and businessman, he made contributions across a varied spectrum, serving as a chairman of the board of directors for the Utica and Mohawk Cotton Mills, as well as serving on the boards of the Utica and Willowvale Bleaching Company, Duofold Incorporated, and the New York Telephone Company. He also served as a trustee of the Savings Bank of Utica.[504]

Meanwhile, the children matured into adulthood. John and Mary's oldest, Mary Louise, attended the Finch School in New York City, graduating in 1930.[505] She married Joseph Lester Parsons Jr. in 1935, with her siblings, Sally and George, as members of the large wedding party. The Utica wedding held "unusually wide interest."[506]

George attended Cornell University and married Martha Wiles in about 1937.[507] He stayed in Utica during the 1930s, working with his father at Utica Products.[508]

Sally, a decade younger than her siblings, graduated from the Masters School in Dobbs Ferry, New York, in 1941, before moving on to Vassar College, from which she graduated in 1944.[509] She married Holbrook Reineman Davis in Utica in 1946.[510]

Sarah "Sally" Maynard's wedding to Holbrook Reineman Davis, Utica, 1946.[511]

Sadly, John did not live to see the wedding of Sally, his youngest daughter. Just a few weeks after her engagement, John died at age 61 on 22 November 1945.[512]

The *New York Times* headlined John's importance as "Utica Industrialist and Banker, Ex-Head of Railroad," and the *Utica Daily Press* described him as "prominently identified with the industrial life of Utica and vicinity."[513] Both obituaries—however laudatory in their nature—merely hinted at the flexibility and command that John exhibited during his lifetime. His ability to take new leaps in myriad directions characterized his business career as well as his contributions to his community. Neither tribute mentioned John's management of the Red Cross during the 1918 epidemic or his leadership in the search for Louise Crouse—efforts that may have presented the best examples of the ability and generosity with which he shared his talents.

Into the Future

By the time John died, Utica's heyday was admittedly behind it. As the textile industry moved south, Utica's prominence as a center of industry waned. The city's former role in the American economy remained immeasurable, however, and the contributions from the Maynards and the DeForests were invaluable to that success. More than one hundred years earlier, when Isaac Maynard made the first trepid steps toward making Utica his home, little could he have imagined that his grandson would exhibit the kind of influence on Utica that John Frederick Maynard Jr. enjoyed and nourished during his final years.

Predictably, new changes appeared on the horizon in 1945 for the cities of upstate New York and for the country. Mary (DeForest) Maynard, who lived until 1959,[514] witnessed the beginning of these: a move toward more globalized economy and the dawn of the electronic age. She and John's descendants—Mary Louise, George, and Sally—going forth with the strength and experience of their forebears, would make their own marks on this new society.

Lee De Forest Opens the Electronic Era

J UST AS AMERICA'S INDUSTRIAL REVOLUTION played out in the lives and work of the Norths, the Maynards, and the DeForests, so did progress continue in the hands of one of the DeForest cousins: Lee De Forest. Lee, who became widely known for his patents and inventions in the field of radio, television, motion pictures, and telegraph, was purportedly George DeForest's fifth cousin—both men likely being seventh-generation descendants of David DeForest, whose father, Isaac, came to America in about 1636.[515]

Lee was born in Council Bluffs, Iowa, 26 August 1873,[516] son of Henry Swift and Anna Margaret (Robbins) De Forest.[517] His father was an 1857 graduate of Yale University, where he had stayed on to earn a divinity degree.[518] Henry De Forest worked at first as a minister, and then brought his family to Talladega, Alabama, to take a position as president of Talladega College.[519]

Young Lee, a lonely boy in Talladega, occupied himself by building and "inventing" things.[520] Eschewing his father's wishes for a career in the ministry, he enrolled at Mount Hermon School for Boys in Massachusetts because he wanted to study electricity. Tuition there was free in exchange for work on the school's farm. He graduated in 1893.[521]

From there, Lee enrolled at Yale's Sheffield Scientific School, taking advantage of the David C. De Forest Scholarship Fund established in 1823 by Lee's distant cousin, David Curtis De Forest.[522] The scholarship gave priority to descendants of David's mother and to "others of the name DeForest, giving preference to the next of kin of the donor."[523] Lee took a course in electricity—the first to be offered at any American college.[524]

He was an unusual young man. According to a 1942 article in the *Saturday Evening Post*, "Some of his Yale fellows who are still alive recall De Forest as brash and loud. . . . He was named 'homeliest' and 'nerviest' in the class; received one vote as 'brightest'; sixteen for 'thinks he is.'"[525] He graduated in 1896 (three years after Beecher Crouse earned his degree there), and then stayed on an additional three years for his doctorate.[526] He was perhaps on the New Haven campus contemporaneously with John F. Maynard Jr.'s brother, Arthur B. Maynard, who earned his undergraduate degree in 1900.[527]

Lee De Forest "lived at a feverish pitch," according to the *New York Times*. He took inspiration from the work of Italian inventor Guglielmo Marconi,[528] who was developing radio transmitters out of London beginning in 1896, just as Lee was completing his undergraduate studies. In 1902, Marconi was using radio signals to send messages across the Atlantic.[529] Lee went to Chicago after earning his PhD. Sixty years after Utica opened the first commercial telegraph office in the world,[530] Lee and a friend spent nights developing "an electrolytic detector" that enabled wireless messages to be heard on headphones. It was Lee's first patent, and it put him on par with Marconi. Subsequent patents reinforced his position.[531]

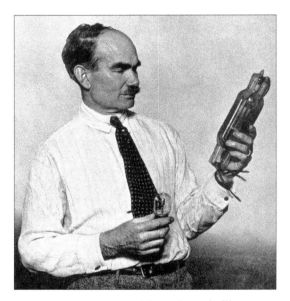

Lee De Forest and the audion tube.[532]

Lee created what turned out to be his most important invention early on in his career: the audion tube, which he developed in 1906. Similar to the two-element "Fleming valve" that had been invented previously by Dr. J. A. Fleming, Lee's three-part tube later made radio broadcasting, talking pictures, and television possible. According to the *New York Times*, "the three-element vacuum tube ushered in the modern era of electricity and is regarded by many as the greatest single invention of this or any other age."[533]

Lee first put the audion tube to the test in 1909, when he persuaded the Metropolitan Opera House to erect a radio-telephone transmitter to broadcast the opening night of an opera featuring Enrico Caruso. With public receivers set up in New York, New York; Jersey City, New Jersey; and Bridgeport, Connecticut; it was the first broadcast address to the general public in history. It had a limited public effect. "Although only a few amateurs and hip operators had heard the opera," Lee later commented, "we knew that it had been a success." Later, he broadcast a Yale-Harvard football game in 1916.[534]

In 1919, Lee patented "Phonofilm," a sound-on-film process. Most previous attempts at infusing silent films with sound involved playing recordings of dialogue and music that matched action on the screen. Lee's invention embedded the soundtrack into the film, paving the way for the motion picture industry that would later flourish. In 1924, he was responsible for the first "talking" newsreel.[535]

Lee also took an active part in the development of radar, long-distance telephones, cosmic ray measurements, electric phonographs, and diathermy machines. At his death in 1961, he was credited with more than three hundred patents in the United States and abroad.[536]

In spite of his many achievements, however, Lee often struggled financially. His intense focus on his work often left money matters in the background. In addition, he drained his funds through fighting over ownership of many of his inventions, beginning with the audion tube in 1906, which was the subject of a major court battle.[537]

He also worried that his inventions would be used for less-than-noble pursuits. "[He] struggled to keep radio and television as instruments of education and culture," according to the *New York Times*. He disdained "crass commercialism."[538]

Lee married four times. He proposed to his first wife, Lucille Sheardown, using a wireless apparatus that he installed in her house. She accepted the same way. The 1906 marriage was annulled the following year. In 1908, he married Nora Stanton Blatch, daughter of suffragist Harriet Stanton Blatch, and they had a daughter, Harriet. They were divorced in 1911. The following year, he married concert singer Mary Mayo, and they had two daughters, Eleanor and Marilyn, before divorcing. Finally, after a six-week courtship in 1930, he married motion picture actress Marie Mosquini. They were married for 31 years, until his death.[539]

Even into his later years, Lee remained an active inventor. He worked in a "cloistered" laboratory in Los Angeles when he invented a terrain altimeter (patented in 1946) and "a television device for the transmission of colors" (patented in 1948). In 1957, at the age of 84, he patented an automatic dialing device for telephones.[540]

In his time, he was well known. He was featured in a lengthy three-part biographical sketch of his life and career in the *Saturday Evening Post* in 1942, and he published his autobiography, *Father of Radio,* in 1950. He was also the subject of an episode of the biographical television show, "This is Your Life," in 1957.[541]

During his later years, his money troubles apparently behind him, he lived in a comfortable fifteen-room house in the Hollywood Hills, California.[542] He and Marie loved the outdoors and made "trips into the desert and mountains on horseback, by car, often roughing it."[543]

When Lee De Forest died in 1961, the *New York Times* called him "a genius in the field of communications . . . a great dreamer, a poet and an enthusiastic advocate of radio and television for uplifting the masses." He was survived by Marie and his three daughters.[544]

His legacy more than outlived him, even if it was not necessarily attached to his name. When he died, the audion tube had already opened the door to the myriad electronic and communication advances that characterize the modern world, bringing progress well beyond the advances of the early 1900s. According the *New York Times:*

> [The audion tube's] immediate achievement was to make possible radio broadcasting and the long-distance telephone. Later it led to the talking motion picture and later still to television. . . . But these were only the early manifestations of an age that is just now beginning to unfold. . . . [The invention] has opened up the age of automation, more revolutionary in its social implications than the industrial revolution. And finally, it has made possible the age of satellites and interplanetary travel, which has opened for man the road to the stars.[545]

— CHAPTER FIVE —

Genealogy

The North Family

1. **WILLIAM**[A] **NORTH** (Joseph[B]), oldest son of Joseph North of Northbrook, County Galway, Ireland,[546] died on or before 21 October 1839.[547] He married, perhaps in Northbrook, on or after 19 October 1804, **MARGARET ANNE WHITESTONE**,[548] born 17 September 1780,[549] and died at Kingstown, County Dublin, Ireland, 16 September 1852,[550] daughter of Henry and Ann Elizabeth (_____) Whitestone.[551]

William and Margaret's son, Samuel Wade North, claimed that his mother was born in Spain, and Samuel's descendants claimed that she was named Letizia and was of Spanish descent.[552] These claims are precluded, however, by William and Margaret's 1804 marriage agreement, which precedes Samuel's birth (and likely the births of all of the children listed here) and Margaret's 1852 death.[553]

Tradition also claims that William was an officer in the English army and was a commander during the Napoleonic Wars.[554] His participation in this regard has not been confirmed. William was not referred to by military title in his wife's 1852 death notice.[555]

According to their son Charles's 1892 obituary, William and Margaret had twelve sons, most of whom immigrated to the United States.[556] Eight children have been confirmed, many of whom did eventually relocate to America.

Known children of William and Margaret Anne (Whitestone) North:

  i. JOSEPH NORTH,[557] probably the Joseph North, gentleman, b. about 1812; d. Tobergrellane, Ballinasloe, County Galway, Ireland, 3 December 1886.[558] Joseph was probably b. Northbrook, County Galway, and certainly did m. (1) about 1835, LETITIA LAMBERT, daughter of Henry Lambert of Aggard, Galway,[559] who was probably the Letitia Sophie North who d. 13 February 1856 "near Ballinasloe."[560] He was probably the Joseph North listed as a tenant at Tobergrellane, Ballinsloe, in 1855,[561] and who was of "St. Grellan's" (the same place as Tobergrellane), when he m. (2) at Dublin, County Dublin, Ireland, 7 August 1857, ARABELLA SELINA NAGHTON of Dorset Street, daughter of Edward Naghton.[562]

ii. HENRY W.[1] NORTH, b. Northbrook, County Galway, about 1811;[563] d. at the home of his daughter in Adams, Jefferson County, New York, 1 May 1894.[564] He m. at Lickerrig Parish, Loughrea, County Galway, 8 December 1845, MARY BOULGER, b. Cape of Good Hope, South Africa, 15 June 1815, daughter of Persse O'Keefe Boulger.[565] Her father was a major in the 93rd Regiment, Sutherland Highlanders.[566]

Henry's 1845 marriage registration listed him as a "gentleman," the son of William North, "gentleman."[567]

A naturalization document shows that Henry entered the United States through the port of New York in July 1865.[568] Possibly, he was in the company of his daughter, Anna, who was listed on the 1900 census as immigrating that same year.[569] His wife and son, William, arrived in 1866.[570] The family settled briefly in New York before moving to La Crosse County, Wisconsin, where they joined Henry's brother, Samuel Wade North, in Onalaska.[571] Henry was naturalized in La Crosse County on 2 November 1867.[572]

Children of Henry W. and Mary (Boulger) North:

a. *Anna B.*[2] *North,* b. Ireland 1847 or March 1850;[573] bur. Adams, Jefferson County, New York, 1922.[574] She m. (1) *Dr. W. C. Tracy* of Brooklyn, Kings County, New York, and m. (2) at Brooklyn, 21 May 1889, *Rufus P. White* of Adams.[575]

b. *William N. North,* b. Ireland about 1854.[576] He m. *Henrietta* _____ about 1880.[577]

iii. ANNE/ANNA E. NORTH, m. 1838, HENRY PILKINGTON.[578]

iv. SAMUEL WADE[1] NORTH, probably b. at Northbrook, County Galway,[579] about 1820, 1812, or August 1810;[580] d. 3 July 1895; bur. Onalaska, La Crosse County, Wisconsin.[581] He m. in the Shopiere section of Turtle, Rock County, Wisconsin, 6 December 1852, MARY FAHEY.[582] She was b. either Montreal, Quebec, Canada; Quebec, Canada; New York; or Ireland,[583] 3 September 1837;[584] d. 3 April 1899, bur. Onalaska Cemetery, Onalaska.[585]

Children of Samuel Wade and Mary (Fahey) North:

a. *Joseph E.*[2] *North,* b. Wisconsin[586] about 1855;[587] m. *Addie J.* _____, b. Wisconsin about 1857. In 1895, Joseph was the secretary and treasurer of the C. H. Nichols Lumber Company. He was living in New Orleans in 1921.[588] Their son, *Raymond North,* was b. Wisconsin, 1879.[589]

b. *Henry "Harry" Whitestone North,* b. 1858.[590]

c. *Frances ("Fanny") M. North,* b. Onalaska, Wisconsin, about 1862.[591]

d. *Mary North,* b. Onalaska about 1864.[592]

e. *Rachael North* (perhaps also called "Gertrude"), b. Wisconsin about 1869.[593] In 1895, she was living in Baraboo, Wisconsin.[594]

f. *Samuel P. North* (perhaps also called "Charles"), b. Onalaska about March 1870;[595] d. 1922. He was living in Onalaska in 1895[596] and in Raceland, Louisiana, in 1921.[597]

g. *Florence E. North,* b. Onalaska about 1875.[598]

v. ALICIA MARGARETTA ("LISSIE") NORTH,[599] d. Saint Servan, France, 11 November 1903.[600] She m. in 1853, CHARLES PRESTON.[601]

vi. RICHARD A.[1] NORTH, b. probably Northbrook, County Galway, 1819;[602] d. probably Hagaman, Montgomery County, New York, 26 April 1858.[603] He m., probably between 1850 and 1853 (birth of first child), ELLEN A. PALMATEER, probably the daughter of Joseph Palmateer.[604] She was b. Fulton County, New York, between 1827 and 1829;[605] d., probably Hagaman, 29 March 1858.[606]

Richard and his brother Charles were in New York State by 29 March 1840,[607] and in West Cummington, Massachusetts, by October of 1841.[608] Richard was 25 and a resident of Mohawk, Montgomery County, New York, when he was naturalized on 11 September 1844.[609] The 1850 census shows Richard, 25, living in St. Johnsville, Montgomery County, working as a teacher.[610]

On 8 August 1854, Richard and his wife, Ellen, "of St. Johnsville," purchased land in the same town from Stephen B. and Emily Nellis for $620. They sold the same land to Aaron Smith for $700 just a few weeks later on 21 August.[611]

In 1855, Richard was living with his wife and daughter in Amsterdam, Montgomery County. The census, taken 8 June, showed the family had been living there for two months.[612]

Richard's wife, Ellen, died 29 March 1858, and Richard himself died less than a month later on 26 April. A probate document was issued the following day naming his apparent father-in-law, Joseph Palmateer, as the administrator of Richard's intestate estate.[613] Their daughter, Anna, orphaned at age 4, was living with her apparent grandfather and several aunts and uncles in the adjacent town of Perth, Fulton County, in 1860.[614] She died in 1863 at the age of 8.[615]

Child of Richard and Ellen A. (Palmateer) North:

a. *Anna Alicia[2] North,* b. Montgomery County, New York, 10 October 1854; d., probably Perth, Fulton County, New York, 26 June 1863.[616]

2 vii. CHARLES[1] NORTH, b. about 1819; d. 14 February 1892. He m. 8 September 1844, HARRIET NEWELL MITCHELL.

viii. GEORGE A. F.[1] NORTH, b. Northbrook, County Galway, about April 1825;[617] d. East New York, Brooklyn, Kings County, New York, 4 November 1910.[618] He m. about 1849, SARAH A. _____. She was b. Montgomery County, New York, January 1832.[619]

George was employed for a short time in Dublin from 1841 to 1842, then immigrated to the United States in 1842. He began his teaching career in Fonda, Montgomery County. In 1850, he was living in Turtle, Rock County, Wisconsin, with his wife, son, and his brother Samuel. George and his family moved to Fulton County, New York, sometime before 1853, then to New Lots, Brooklyn, Kings County, New York, before 1855. He taught in the public schools from 1853 to 1889 and served in the Civil War with the 2nd New York Cavalry.[620]

Children of George A. F. and Sarah (_____) North:

   a.   *William W. North*, b. Montgomery County, New York, about 1849.[621]

   b.   *Charles North*, b. Fulton County, New York, about 1853.[622]

   c.   *George A. F. North Jr.*, b. New York, January 1860.[623]

   d.   *Arthur W. North*, b. Kings County, New York, about 1863.[624]

   e.   *Stephen North*, alive in 1910.[625]

   f.   *Henry L. North*, b. New York, May 1874.[626]

 ix.   LONGWORTH NORTH, d. Ireland, about 1842.[627]

2. **CHARLES**[1] **NORTH** (*William*[A]*, Joseph*[B]) was born in probably Northbrook, County Galway, Ireland,[628] in 1819,[629] and died in Oswego, Oswego County, New York, 14 February 1892.[630] He married at Cummington, Hampshire County, Massachusetts, 8 September 1844, **HARRIET NEWELL MITCHELL**,[631] daughter of Capt. Chester and Venila Mitchell.[632] She was born in Cummington, 27 December 1821,[633] and died in Oswego, 27 January 1901.[634]

Children of Charles and Harriet (Mitchell) North, probably all born in Oswego:

   i.   WILLIAM LORENZO[2] NORTH, b. 26 September 1845; d. of a heart ailment, Oswego, 23 October 1865.[635]

  ii.   ALICIA M. NORTH, b. 23 June 1849;[636] d. of scarlet fever, Oswego, 9 May 1855.[637]

 iii.   VENELIA M. NORTH, b. 11 August 1851; d. Oswego, 13 or 16 August 1853.[638]

  iv.   LAURA W. NORTH, b. January 1855;[639] d. Oswego, 21 October 1938.[640] She m. about 1878, WALTER H. PULVER, b. New York, September 1851;[641] d. 19 April 1928,[642] son of William W. Pulver.[643]

Children of Laura W. North and Walter H. Pulver:

   a.   *Harriet N.*[3] *Pulver*, b. June 1881.

   b.   *Helen C. Pulver*, b. October 1883.

   c.   *Harold N. Pulver*, b. August 1890.

   d.   _____ *Pulver*, d. before 1900.[644]

v. CHESTER M. NORTH, b. 19 October 1857; d. of consumption in Oswego, 27 April 1859.[645]

vi. SARAH C. NORTH, b. 25 March 1860; d. Utica, 20 November 1927.[646] She m. 8 April 1885, GEORGE L. DEFOREST.[647]

vii. HATTIE N. NORTH, b. 1863; d. Oswego, 12 July 1868.[648]

viii. LOUISA NORTH, b. 5 September 1865;[649] d. Utica, 1960.[650] She m. about 1890, FREDERICK C. OSTERHOUT. He was b. September 1851; d. New York City, 5 October 1930.[651] The couple resided in Glen Ridge, Essex County, New Jersey, in 1900.

According to her obituary, Louisa resided in Utica following the death of her husband in 1930. She was living at Clinton Place in that city at the time of her death in 1960.[652] They had no children.[653]

The DeForest Family

1. **GEORGE[7] DEFOREST** (*Marcus[6], Philo[5], John[4], Edward[3], David[2], Isaac[1]*)[654] was born in Connecticut[655] on 15 January 1825, and died 2 April 1871,[656] son of Marcus and Laura Colton (Perkins) DeForest.[657] He married, probably in Connecticut, 3 October 1849,[658] **MARY ANN LINSLEY**, born 18 October 1823, and died 10 September 1883,[659] daughter of Harvey and Mary (____) Linsley.[660]

Child of George and Mary Ann (Linsley) DeForest:[661]

2   i. GEORGE L.[8] DEFOREST, b. 15 July 1854; d. 6 October 1929. He m. 1885, SARAH C. NORTH.

2. **GEORGE L.[8] DEFOREST** (*George[7], Marcus[6], Philo[5], John[4], Edward[3], David[2], Isaac[1]*) was born in Connecticut on 15 July 1854,[662] and died in Utica, 6 October 1929.[663] He married at Oswego, 8 April 1885, **SARAH C. NORTH**. She was born in Oswego, 25 March 1860, daughter of Charles and Harriet (Mitchell) North.[664] She died in Utica, 20 November 1927.[665] (See North Family Genealogy.)

Child of George and Sarah (North) DeForest:

i. MARY LOUISE[9] DEFOREST, b. Oswego, 22 April 1886; d. in Utica, 5 July 1959.[666] She m. 1907, JOHN FREDERICK MAYNARD JR.

The Maynard Family

1. **RICHARD[A] MAYNARD** (*Richard[B]*) was born perhaps in Ruishton, Somerset, England,[667] about March 1781, son of Richard and Sarah (Lyssant) Maynard.[668] He was baptized in Taunton, Somerset, between 4 and 9 April 1781,[669] and died probably before 1841.[670] He married on 5 February 1801 at Kingston St. Mary, Somerset, **SARAH FARTHING**, daughter of Robert Farthing.[671] She was born about 1779 in Kingston, Somerset, England.[672] She was called "Sally."[673]

Children of Richard and Sarah (Farthing) Maynard: [674]

   i. Sᴀʀᴀʜ Fᴀʀᴛʜɪɴɢ Mᴀʏɴᴀʀᴅ, b. Ruishton, Somerset, England, 2 December 1801; bp. at Paul Street Church, Taunton, Somerset, 31 December 1801.[675] She likely died young, as another child was later named Sarah.[676]

  ii. Mᴀʀɪᴀ[1] Mᴀʏɴᴀʀᴅ, b. Ruishton 29 June 1803;[677] d. Utica, Oneida County, New York, 15 or 16 November 1883.[678] She m. at Ruishton with banns dated 24 April 1831, Jᴏʜɴ Eʟᴀɴᴅ Bᴜʟᴛ.[679] He was b. England, 1802; d. Utica, 5 November 1874.[680]

Maria was described in her death notice as a "well-known and estimable lady"; John was a deacon at the Tabernacle Baptist Church in Utica.[681]

Children of Maria Maynard and John Eland Bult:

   a. *Hannah M.[2] Bult*, b. England about 1845; d. Utica, 14 February 1931.[682]

   b. *Mary E. Bult*, b. England about 1848; d. Utica, 14 April 1918. She m. *Newell Johnson*.[683]

   c. *Three other children*, who presumably died young.[684]

 iii. Mᴀʀʏ[1] Mᴀʏɴᴀʀᴅ, b. Ruishton, 28 July 1805;[685] d. Utica, 23 April 1891.[686] She m. New York, 17 September 1833, Jᴏʜɴ Tʜᴏʀɴ.[687] He was b. England, 6 December 1811; d. 31 December 1894,[688] son of Robert and Betty (Palmer) Thorn.[689] They did not have children.

 iv. Rɪᴄʜᴀʀᴅ Mᴀʏɴᴀʀᴅ, b. Ruishton, 20 August 1807;[690] d. Taunton, 22 January 1865.[691] He m. (1) before 1829, Hᴀʀʀɪᴇᴛ Gᴏᴏᴅʟᴀɴᴅ Jᴇɴɴɪɴɢs, daughter of Robert and Harriet (_____) Jennings of Cannington.[692] He m. (2) at Taunton, 4 August 1858, Eꜱᴛʜᴇʀ Cᴀʀᴏʟɪɴᴇ Hᴏʀꜱᴇʏ of Upper Crescent, Taunton.[693] He was an auctioneer.[694]

Children of Richard and Harriet Goodland (Jennings) Maynard:

   a. *Richard Maynard*, b. Ruishton, 24 September 1829.[695]

   b. *Alfred Maynard*, b. Ruishton, 12 February 1831;[696] d. Taunton, 30 July 1900, age 69.[697] He lived in Taunton, Somerset, England,[698] at Henley Lodge, Wellington Road, and was head of the firm of Messers. A. & H. Maynard, auctioneers and real estate agents. He was also a deacon at Silver Street church, Taunton. Alfred was the father of Howard Maynard, b. Taunton, about 1860; d. West Lea, Wellington Road, Taunton, 29 August 1936, who succeeded his father as principal of the auctioneering firm.[699]

   c. *Harriet Maynard*, b. Ruishton, 8 April 1833.[700]

   d. *Walter Maynard*, b. 4 November 1834.[701]

  v. Sᴀʀᴀʜ Mᴀʏɴᴀʀᴅ (again), b. 15 May 1809.[702]

vi. ROBERT MAYNARD, b. 26 June 1811.[703]

vii. JAMES MAYNARD, b. 17 June 1813.[704]

2 viii ISAAC[1] MAYNARD, b. 10 June 1815; d. 23 February 1885. He m. 20 August 1844, MARGARET AITKEN.

ix. CHARLOTTE MAYNARD, b. Ruishton, 10 August 1817.[705] She m. at Taunton, 11 March 1858, as his second wife, JOHN DAVID WOOLEN, son of John Woolen.[706] She came to Utica in 1839 but moved back to England by 1851 and lived with her mother in Taunton.[707]

x. HARRIET[1] MAYNARD, b. in England, 15 July 1819;[708] d. Utica, 1 January 1895. She m. in England, 1849, JOSHUA TAVENDER. He was b. Somerset, England, 6 January 1822; d. October 1895.[709]

Harriet was listed as a milliner on the 1841 English census for Taunton.[710]

Children of Harriet Maynard and Joshua Tavender, probably all born in Utica, based on their parents' residential history:

a. *Harriet[2] Tavender,* b. Oneida County, New York, about 1852.[711]

b. *Marian A. Tavender,* b. New York about 1854,[712] probably the Mary Emma Tavender who was b. Utica, 11 January 1854 and d. Utica, 8 April 1862 of heart disease, with no parents listed on burial record.[713]

c. *Mary Jane Tavender,* b. Oneida County about 1856.[714]

d. *Walter J. Tavender,* b. New York about 1859.[715]

e. *Sophia Tavender,* b. New York about 1865.[716]

xi. THOMAS[1] MAYNARD, b. Somerset, England, 26 July 1821;[717] d. of brain fever, Cleveland, Ohio, 31 January 1860.[718] He m. before 1855, GEORGIANA SAMPSON.[719] She was b. "Hindastan" (India) about 1833 and d. Jamaica, Queens County, New York, 13 December 1916.[720]

Thomas came to Utica in 1841. He was the superintendent of the First Presbyterian Church Sunday School there. According to M. M. Bagg, Thomas was "diligent in mission Sunday schools in the remote parts of the city and in Deerfield Corners, [and he] delighted to address a juvenile audience, and his hearty good nature, his direct appeals to the feelings of his little parishioners, made his voice clear and eloquent. He collected and had printed hymns for his own and their use, calculated to encourage young heart and ear. His collection reached its fourth edition and numbered nearly 200 pages."[721]

He died in Cleveland, Ohio, in 1860, while visiting there.[722]

After Thomas's death, Georgiana continued to live in Utica for a time.[723] Georgiana and her family were enumerated adjacent to John and Mary Thorn on the 1865 census of New York.[724]

Children of Thomas and Georgiana (Sampson) Maynard:

a.   *Josephine Julia[2] Maynard,* b. Oneida County, New York, about 1858;[725] d. Los Angeles County, Calif., before 21 December 1937.[726] She m. at Utica, 23 April 1884, *William M. Griffith.*[727]

b.   *Thomas T. Maynard,* b. Oneida County about 1860, d. perhaps shortly after 1880, when he was listed on the census as having consumption. He was not mentioned as a beneficiary in probate documents for his mother's estate in October of 1917.[728]

2. Isaac[1] Maynard (*Richard[A]*) was born in Ruishton, 10 June 1815,[729] and died in Utica, New York, 23 February 1885.[730] He married at Utica, 20 August 1844, **Margaret Aitken**.[731] She was born in Falkirk, Stirlingshire, Scotland, 27 March 1826, probably the daughter of James and Mary (Henderson) Aitken.[732] Margaret died in Utica, 2 December 1896.[733]

Children of Isaac and Margaret (Aitken) Maynard, all living in 1885:

i.   **Mary Louisa[2] Maynard,** b. Utica, New York, about 1846;[734] d. Utica, 29 June 1893.[735] She m. say 1869 (first-known child),[736] **John Miles Crouse,**[737] son of Daniel and Catherine Jane (Beecher) Crouse and brother of Daniel N. Crouse, who married Mary's sister Sophia.[738] He was b. Canastota, New York, 12 December 1847, and d. Salisbury, England, 9 July 1906.[739] He m. (2) at Hartford, Hartford County, Connecticut, 18 March 1896, **May Hamilton Conklin**.[740] She was b. Hartford, 8 June 1862,[741] daughter of H. W. Conklin.[742]

Mary was ill for six weeks before her death. According to her obituary, "her circle of relatives by blood and marriage is unusually large, but vastly larger is the circle of friends. Happily married some twenty years ago, gifted with a kindly and generous spirit which found expression in deeds of kindness as well as in charms of face and manner, she has lived a life of singular domestic and social felicity. To her husband and her son, and to her mother and brothers and sister, this bereavement is one of the heaviest than can fall on human hearts."[743]

John Crouse inherited the grocery business started by his uncle and his father, Daniel, which Daniel brought from Canastota, New York, to Utica in 1827. John's son Beecher joined him in the business in 1894, renaming it John M. Crouse & Son. "The firm did an extensive wholesale grocery trade and was one of the most prosperous of the kind in central New York," according to his obituary. John sold the business about 1899 in order to "devote his attention exclusively to his large interest in the cotton manufacturing industry." He was president of the Utica Steam and Cotton Mills and vice president of the Roberts-Wicks Company. He was also a director of the Rome, Watertown & Ogdensburg Railroad Company.[744]

Children of Mary Louisa (Maynard) and John M. Crouse:

a. *Beecher Maynard³ Crouse,* b. Utica, New York, 22 August 1870; d. Utica, 1 October 1934.[745] He m. at Guilford, New Haven County, Connecticut, 5 September 1894, (1) *Louise Shultas Knous.*[746] She was b. Hartford, Connecticut, 10 August 1871;[747] d. Utica, 15 November 1929,[748] daughter of Jacob and Caroline (____) Knous of Hartford.[749] He m. (2) New York City, *Mabel Wheeler,* b. Utica, 27 September 1880; d. Utica, 10 December, 1964, daughter of Frank E. and Louisa V. (Ames) Wheeler.[750] Beecher graduated from Yale University in 1893.[751] He retired from his father's grocery business in 1898 and founded the Avalon Knitwear Company. He was also a director of the Utica Steam and Mohawk Valley Cotton Mills and the New York Telephone Company.[752]

b. *Mary Louise "Mollie" Crouse,* b. Utica, 14 February 1886; d. New Hartford, Oneida County, 27 November 1971.[753] She m. at Utica, 6 September 1911, *Beirne Gordon Jr.*[754]

ii. ISAAC NEWTON MAYNARD, b. Utica, 6 May 1849; d. Utica, 11 February 1936. He m. St. Louis, Missouri, 7 March 1873, MARGARET FIELD, b. Bound Brook, Somerset County, New Jersey, 27 May 1849; d. Utica, 7 August 1929.[755] She was the daughter of Jeremiah and Margaret (____) Field.[756]

Isaac, who was called "Ike," moved to Chicago, and was a partner in the firm of Platt, Thorn & Maynard, along with Edwin Thorn, the nephew of his father's associate, John Thorn.[757] According to his 1936 obituary, he was engaged in the grain and flour business in Chicago.[758]

He eventually returned to Utica, where he served on the boards of directors for the Utica Steam and Mohawk Valley Cotton Mills; the Utica City National Bank; the Rome, Watertown & Ogdensburg Railroad; the Mohawk Valley Cap Factory; the Roberts-Wicks Company; and the Utica, Clinton & Binghamton Railroad. He was also a member, and for some time the president, of the board of trustees of the Utica Cemetery Association.[759]

Child of Isaac Newton and Margaret (Field) Maynard:

a. *Richard Field Maynard,* b. Chicago, Illinois, 23 April 1875;[760] d. Greenwich, Fairfield County, Connecticut, 2 March 1964.[761] He m. at New York City, New York, 4 January 1917, *Lorraine Huling.*[762] She d. Old Greenwich, Connecticut, 27 November 1971.[763] Richard graduated from Harvard University in 1898, where he was editor of the Harvard *Lampoon.* He was a portrait painter, with his works shown in major American galleries, and his writing appearing in national magazines.[764] He lived in Utica and New York City before moving to Greenwich in 1939. Lorraine was an actress, making her Broadway debut in 1913, and appearing afterward in silent films. She also wrote a number of short stories and four books.[765]

3   iii. JOHN FREDERICK MAYNARD ("J. FRED"), b. 15 August 1851; d. 4 September
          1929. He m. 6 September 1876, MARY ADAMS BEARDSLEY.

    iv. SOPHIA MAYNARD, b. Utica, 10 June 1854; d. Utica, 30 April 1941.[766] She m. 5
         January 1881, as his second wife,[767] DANIEL NELLIS CROUSE,[768] son of Daniel
         and Catherine Jane (Beecher) Crouse and brother of John Miles Crouse, who
         married Sophia's sister Mary.[769] He was b. Canastota, Madison County, New
         York, 4 April 1855;[770] d. Utica, 19 February 1919. Daniel was "engaged in
         various enterprises" in Utica and was a director of the Rome and Clinton
         Railroad Company. He was an avid traveler, crossing the Atlantic at least thirty
         times during his life.[771]

         Children of Sophia (Maynard) and Daniel N. Crouse:

         a.   *Nellis Maynard*[3] *Crouse,* b. Utica, 5 January 1884; d. Irvington, Lancaster
              County, Virginia, 12 May 1957.[772] He m. at Utica, 28 April 1909, *Rebecca
              Leggett Bowne,* daughter of Watson H. and Catharine (Doherty) Bowne.[773]
              Nellis was the author of many books, including *Search for the Northwest
              Passage, In Quest for the Western Ocean,* and *French Pioneers in the West Indies.*[774]

         b.   *Margaret Katherine Crouse,* b. 14 December 1885; d. New York City, New
              York, 16 June 1961.[775] She m. on or after 17 November 1909, *Hon. Merwin
              K. Hart.*[776] She was called Margaret.

    v.   SARAH GRACE MAYNARD, b. New York, April 1860; d. Utica, 9 November
         1931.[777] She m. at Utica, 4 April 1888, JOHN WATERS MCLEAN,[778] son of Charles
         and Anne (Waters) McLean and brother of Thomas Chalmers McLean, who
         married Sarah Grace's sister Harriet.[779] John was b. New York, January 1853;[780]
         d. 7 December 1945.[781]

         Sarah Grace was called "Grace."[782] She was known for her devotion to charity.
         She served on the executive boards of the Associated Charities, the Utica
         Visiting Nurse and Child Health Association, and the Old Ladies Home.[783]
         The couple had no children.[784]

    vi. HARRIET "HATTIE" MAYNARD, b. Utica, 10 July 1862;[785] d. Utica, 23 August
         1937.[786] She m., as his second wife, DR. OGDEN BACKUS, son of Azel and Mary
         (Ogden) Backus.[787] He was b. 15 April 1858;[788] d. Rochester, New York, 10
         February 1906,[789] son of Dr. Azel Backus.[790] The couple had no children. She
         m. (2) at Utica, 23 September 1909, as his second wife,[791] THOMAS CHALMERS
         MCLEAN, son of Charles and Anne (Waters) McLean and brother of John
         Waters McLean, who married Harriet's sister Sarah Grace.[792] Thomas was b.
         New Hartford, Oneida County, 25 October 1847; d. 19 August 1919. He was
         buried at Arlington National Cemetery.[793] The couple had no children.

         Hattie was educated in Utica and New York City. She lived in Rochester, then,
         after the death of her first husband, returned to Utica. She was a member of
         Christ Reformed Church there and a member of the board of directors of the
         Old Ladies' Home and Associated Charities for many years.[794]

Ogden Backus was a physician in Rochester;[795] Thomas Chalmers McLean was a rear admiral in the U.S. Navy who served a lengthy and illustrious career, visiting almost every country in the world. His most notable service was in connection with the building of the Panama Canal.[796] He was called "Chalmers."

vii. SAMUEL RICHARD MAYNARD, b. Utica, 17 or 12 September 1867;[797] d. Brookline, Norfolk County, Massachusetts, 6 February 1932.[798] He m. (1) at Utica, 25 September 1894,[799] MARION STARR WADHAMS, daughter of Moses Wadhams.[800] She was b. Plymouth, Luzerne County, Pennsylvania, 5 September 1866;[801] d. Colorado Springs, Colorado, 18 October 1907.[802] He m. (2) at New York City, 22 September 1915,[803] MARION WALLACE BAWTINHEIMER, daughter of Chrysler and Sarah Jane (Mitchell) Bawtinheimer. She was b. Canada, 3 May 1883; d. Utica, 5 July 1959.[804]

Samuel attended schools in Utica[805] and Phillips Academy in Andover, Massachusetts.[806] According to his 1932 obituary, he graduated from Yale, but he was listed as a non-graduate in a 1926 alumni directory.[807]

He listed himself as "retired" at age 30 on an 1897 passport application,[808] and as having no occupation on the 1930 census.[809] His 1915 marriage certificate, however, listed him as a farmer.[810]

Child of Samuel Richard and Marion (Bawtinheimer) Maynard:

a. *Grace Maynard*, b. Boston, Suffolk, Mass., 16 July 1923; d. Greenwich, Fairfield County, Connecticut, 30 April 2003,[811] She m. at New York City, New York, 18 December 1941, *Edward Vernon Nunes*.[812]

3. JOHN FREDERICK ("J. FRED")[2] MAYNARD SR. (*Isaac[1], Richard[A]*) was born in Utica, 15 August 1851,[813] and died in Groton, New London County, Connecticut, 4 September 1929.[814] He married at Utica, 6 September 1876,[815] MARY ADAMS BEARDSLEY, daughter of Arthur Moore and Louisa Howland (Adams) Beardsley. She was born in Utica, 21 April 1850 and died there, 30 June 1929.[816]

Children of John F. and Mary Adams (Beardsley) Maynard:

i. ARTHUR BEARDSLEY[3] MAYNARD, b. Utica, 28 August 1877;[817] d. San Francisco, San Francisco County, California, 21 April 1944.[818] He m. at Columbiana County, Ohio, 28 August 1909, ANNE GARRETSON LEE, daughter of Joseph Garretson and Elizabeth (Knowles) Lee.[819]

4   ii. JOHN FREDERICK MAYNARD JR., b. 14 September 1884; d. 22 November 1945. He m. on 20 June 1907, MARY LOUISE DEFOREST.

4. JOHN FREDERICK[3] MAYNARD JR. (*John Frederick Sr.[2], Isaac[1], Richard[A]*) was born in Utica, 14 September 1884, and died there, 22 November 1945.[820] He married at Utica, 20 June 1907, MARY LOUISE[9] DEFOREST (*George[8], George[7], Marcus[6], Philo[5], John[4], Edward[3],*

David², Isaac¹), daughter of George and Sarah (North) DeForest.[821] (See DeForest Family.) She was born in Oswego, Oswego County, New York, 22 April 1886,[822] and died in Utica, 5 July 1959.

Children of John Frederick and Mary Louise (DeForest) Maynard:

    i. MARY LOUISE⁴ MAYNARD, b. New York, 9 June 1910;[823] d. Short Hills, Millburn, Essex County, New Jersey, 18 December 1952.[824] She m. at Utica, 27 April 1935, JOSEPH LESTER PARSONS JR., son of Joseph Lester Parsons of Llewellyn Park, West Orange, Essex County, New Jersey.[825] She attended Simmons College, Boston, Massachusetts; and Finch Junior College, New York City.[826]

    ii. GEORGE DEFOREST MAYNARD, b. Utica, 9 May 1914;[827] d. Lloyd Harbor, Suffolk County, New York, 14 November 1963.[828] He m. (1) at Kansas City, Jackson County, Missouri, on or after 3 September 1937, MARTHA WILES.[829] They were divorced in August 1957.[830] He m. (2) PATRICIA ANNE BURTON.[831] She was b. New York City, 10 July 1930;[832] d. High Point, Guilford (and other) counties, North Carolina, 14 September 2011.[833]

    iii. SARAH DEFOREST MAYNARD, b. Utica, 4 April 1922; d. Hyannis, Massachusetts, 31 March 2016.[834] She m. at Utica, 25 March 1946, HOLBROOK REINEMAN DAVIS.[835]

Endnotes

1   From the collection of Holbrook Davis.

2   David J. LaVigne, "Immigrants," *Industrial Revolution: People and Perspectives,* Jennifer L. Goloboy, ed., part of *Perspectives in American Social History,* Peter C. Mancall, series ed. (Santa Barbara, California: ABC-CLIO, Inc., 2008), 140.

3   In the nation's infancy, this move had not been without its detractors. Thomas Jefferson was in favor of farming as the national occupation and thought a factory system would lead the way to the unequal class system that dominated England. Alexander Hamilton disagreed, asserting that a dependence on Europe for manufactured goods weakened the economy, and thereby the new nation's world status: Hamilton was a proponent of replacing the home crafts system of production with machine-driven factories. Slowly, Hamilton's ideas dominated. Farmers who had taken trades into their homes during the winter expanded on those industries, and Americans gradually found ways to compete against British products (Sonia G. Benson, *Development of the Industrial U.S. Almanac* [Detroit: Thomson Gale, 2006], 7–10. Timothy R. Mahoney, "Industrialization and the Market," *Encyclopedia of the United States in the Nineteenth Century,* vol. 2, Paul Finkelman, ed. [New York: Charles Scribner's Sons, 2001], 107).

4   Passenger manifest for the brig *Pratincole,* arriving 1 June 1836, p. 1, Richard North and Charles North, lines 62 and 63, viewed on Ancestry.com: "Passenger and Crew Lists of Vessels Arriving at New York, New York, 1820–1897," National Archives and Records Administration (NARA), Washington, DC, Record Group 36, microfilm publication M237, 675 rolls, roll 030. The ship was captained by Benjamin Rogers Jr.

5   "For the City of New-York, the Fine Fast-Sailing Ship *Pratincole,*" advertisement, *The Galway Patriot,* 19 March 1836, p. 3. "The Flourishing City of New York, the Fine New Fast-Sailing Brig *Pratincole,*" advertisement, *The Telegraph, or Connaught Ranger* (Castelbar, County Mayo), 6 April 1836, p. 1.

6   "For the Flourishing City of New York," *The Galway Patriot,* 29 June 1836.

7   Newspaper image © The British Library Board. All rights reserved. With thanks to The British Newspaper Archive (www.britishnewspaperarchive.co.uk).

8   LaVigne, "Immigrants," *Industrial Revolution: People and Perspectives,* 140; Edward P. Keleher, with John Alan Ross, "Great Irish Famine," *Great Events from History: The 19th Century, 1801–1900,* vol. 2, 1835–1854, John Powell, ed. (Pasadena, California, and Hackensack, New Jersey: Salem Press, 2007), 699.

9   LaVigne, "Immigrants," *Industrial Revolution: People and Perspectives,* 141.

10   Passenger manifest for the Brig *Pratincole,* 1 June 1836, Richard North and Charles North. Landed estates were generally large inherited pieces of land that were held in freehold or outright ownership, then parceled out and leased to tenants ("Background to Landed Estates," Ask about Ireland, online at www.askaboutireland.ie, accessed 21 November 2020).

11   Henry Ringling North and Arlen Hatch, *The Circus Kings: Our Ringling Family Story* (Gainesville, Florida: University of Florida Press, 2008), 155.

12   "In the Court of Commissioners for the Sale of Incumbered [*sic*] Estates in Ireland," *The Galway Mercury*, 15 January 1853, p. 3.

13   Major L. Wilson with Judith Boyce DeMark, "American Era of 'Old' Immigration," *Great Events from History: The 19th Century: 1801–1900,* vol. 2, 1835–1864 (Pasadena, California: Salem Press, 2007), 632. S. J. Connolly, ed., *The Oxford Companion to Irish History*, 2nd ed. (Oxford: Oxford University Press, 2011), "Encumbered Estates Court" entry, 180–181.

14   Keleher and Ross, "Great Irish Famine," 697–698.

15   Envelope accompanying the letter from Alicia M. North to Richard [and Charles] North, dated 29 March [18]40, "Eight letters of Mrs. Anne Pilkington, Kingstown, Co. Dublin, to her brother Charles North, Oswego, N.Y., on family affairs, 1840–1853," National Library of Ireland, Ms. 13,093, photostat copy of original letters (contrary to the manuscript title listing at NLI, not all of the letters in this collection were written by Anne). The envelope—which is barely legible—is addressed to Richard, but the enclosed letter's salutation includes both Richard and Charles.

16   Robt. H. Foerderer, "Hides and Leather," *The Encyclopedia Americana* (New York and Chicago: The Americana Company, 1904), 684. Col. William Edwards, William W. Edwards, and William Henry Edwards, *Memoirs of Col. William Edwards* (n.l., Press of W. F. Roberts, 1897), 50.

17   Helen H. Foster & William W. Streeter, *Only One Cummington*, 2 vols. (Cummington, Massachusetts: Cummington Historical Commission, 1974), 1:51.

18   Foster & Streeter, *Only One Cummington*, 1:51.

19   Foster & Streeter, *Only One Cummington*, 1:52–53. "A successful farmer was usually the possessor of one horse, a yoke of oxen, four or five cows, one or two dogs, a flock of sheep, some chickens with a rooster or two, and probably a few geese."

20   Envelope to Letter from Mrs. H. Pilkington to Charles North, dated 24 September 1841 (postmarked Kingstown 13 October 1841), "Eight letters of Mrs. Anne Pilkington," NLI: Ms. 13,093. Massachusetts Historical Commission, *MHC Reconnaissance Survey Town Report: Cummington* (Boston: The Commission, 1982)*,* 6. Foster & Streeter, *Only One Cummington*, 1:222. Hampden (Hampshire) County, Massachusetts Deeds, book A13, p. 201; book 7, p. 555; and book 8, p. 492, viewed on FamilySearch.org 13 December 2019, *Massachusetts Land Records, 1620–1986,* (early Hampshire County deeds are filed in Hampden County and are not downloadable or printable).

21   *MHC Report: Cummington*, 6.

22   Letter from Alicia M. North to Richard and Charles North, dated 11 March [18]42, "Eight letters of Mrs. Anne Pilkington," NLI: Ms. 13,093. Alicia's March letter mentions that George was planning to join his brothers in the United States, as his "situation" in Dublin was not working out. According to George's obituary, he arrived sometime that year ("Obituary: George A. F. North," *The Brooklyn Daily Eagle*, 5 November 1910, p. 16, viewed on Newspapers.com 29 October 2019).

23   Foster & Streeter, *Only One Cummington*, 1:12, 1:47, 1:49.

24   1840 U.S. Census, Cummington, Hampshire County, Massachusetts, p. 210, showing totals for males (1239), females (606), and free colored persons (8), viewed on Ancestry.com. The Norths do not appear on this enumeration.

25   *MHC Report: Cummington*, 6, 52, and 180, showing four tanneries during the town's peak years of 1840 to 1860.

26   Foster & Streeter, *Only One Cummington*, 1:51. Cummington, Massachusetts, Town Records, book 1, p. 44, 56, 64, 68, 80, et al., viewed on FamilySearch.org, *Town Records, 1762–1860,* FHL film. no. 234,538. Only leather that had been inspected and sealed by an officially appointed inspector could be sold "to any person, for any purpose." Each inspector was to "impress [the leather] thereon [with] his name, and the name of the place for which he is inspector, at full length, and also the weight thereof" (Theron Metcalf, Esq., *The General Laws of Massachusetts, from June 1822, to June 1827,* 3 vols. [Boston: Wells and Lilly, 1827], Chapter 99, sections 1 and 2, 3:348–349).

27   Photograph by the author.

28   Cummington, Massachusetts, 1845 marriages, p. 160, items 12 and 13, Charles North–Harriet N. Mitchell, and William H. White–Laura Mitchell; viewed on AmericanAncestors.org 19 July 2019, *Massachusetts: Vital Records, 1841–1910.*

29   Hampden (Hampshire) County, Massachusetts Deeds, book 16, p. 124. The land was described as being in Township No. 5, Lot 22 of the third division, abbreviated on Cummington land maps as 22–3.

30   Author's visit to the house, 21 November 2019. Foster & Streeter, *Only One Cummington,* 1:265; using their own numbering system for their research, Foster & Streeter designated this house as No.110.

31   Photograph taken by the author, 2021.

32   Hampden (Hampshire) County Deeds, book 16, p. 124. Edward was described as a tanner in a 1740 land sale; he was listed as owning a "tan house" on a 1771 valuation list (Ann Smith Lainhart and Robert S. Wakefield, FASG, *Mayflower Families through Five Generations,* vol. 22: *Family of William Bradford* [Plymouth, Massachusetts: General Society of Mayflower Descendants, 2004], 148–49); and on 17 February 1787, he sold to his son Bela Mitchell of Charlestown, tanner, half of his tan yard, half of his bark house and half of his currying shop (Plymouth County, Massachusetts Deeds, book 67, p. 52). A bark house was often located on the site of a tannery to hold tree bark that was used in the tanning process.

33   Seth Bryant, *Shoe and Leather Trade of the Last Hundred Years* (Boston: the author, 1891), 35–36. Bryant's account, which is of a direct father-to-son inheritance over 170 years, is problematic, however. He credits William's great-grandfather Experience Mitchell with starting the Joppa tannery in 1650, but Experience was a resident of "Duxborrow" (Duxbury) between 1647 and 1670 and left no evidence in his will of any equipment specific to tanning (Ralph Wood Jr., *Mayflower Families through Five Generations,* vol. 12: "Francis Cooke of the Mayflower: The First Five Generations" [Camden, Maine: Picton Press, (1999)], 29, 34). In addition, Col. Edward Mitchell, who Bryant credits as inheriting his father Ensign Edward's tanning business, was an infant at the time of his father's death (Ann Smith Lainhart and Robert S. Wakefield, FASG, *Mayflower Families through Five Generations,* vol. 22: Family of William Bradford [General Society of Mayflower Descendants: 2004], 38, 148). It is possible that small-scale tanning began on the Mitchell property in 1650 and was carried out and enlarged into a business by various Mitchell family members—not necessarily fathers and sons—over the 170-year period, authenticating the spirit of the story.

34   Soon after his arrival in Cummington, William married Elizabeth Ward, daughter of William Ward, and in 1777, their first child, Chester Mitchell, was born (Cummington, Massachusetts, Proprietors' Records, p. 100, viewed on Ancestry.com, "Massachusetts, Town and Vital Records, 1620–1988," Cummington Proprietors' Records with Births, Marriages, and Deaths; Cummington Deaths, entry no. 2, Chester Mitchell). After the Revolutionary War broke out, Mitchell left to serve in the war on two separate occasions, coming home from New London, Connecticut, in the summer of 1779 with the rank of lieutenant (Massachusetts Office of the Secretary of State, *Massachusetts Soldiers and Sailors of the Revolutionary War,* [Boston: Wright & Potter, 1902], 855).

35   Cummington Town Records, book 1, p. 44, 56, 64, 68, 80, et al.

36   Author's visit to the ruins of "Shaw Tannery" location, 21 November 2019. Foster & Streeter, *Only One Cummington,* 1:262 and "Map A" folded pull-out between pp. 168 and 169. Foster & Streeter designated this location as No. 104 (Foster & Streeter's description of ownership involves both William Mitchell and his son William Mitchell Jr., without distinction). Stage Road was called "The County Road" on early maps.

37   Hampden (Hampshire) County Deeds, book 28, p. 182, dated 8 March 1805 and book 39, p. 31, dated 13 February 1812, viewed on FamilySearch.org 13 December 2019. Chester was described as a "yeoman" on both deeds.

38   Cummington, Massachusetts, 1845 marriages, p. 160, item 12, Charles North and Harriet N. Mitchell, viewed on AmericanAncestors.org 19 July 2019, "Massachusetts: Vital Records, 1841–1910"; the marriage took place in 1844, despite the page header.

39   Foster & Streeter, *Only One Cummington*, 64. Charles's brothers Richard and George North also went west. (See Note 22 for information on George's arrival in the United States). Richard was a resident of Montgomery County, New York, by September of 1844 (Richard A. North, Naturalization Record, filed 11 September 1844, viewed on FamilySearch.org 2 December 2019, *New York, County Naturalization Records, 1791–1980,* Montgomery [County] Petition evidence 1820–1882 L–P), and George was teaching in Fonda, New York, in 1843 ("George A. F. North, Oldtime Kings County School Teacher, Dead," *New-York* [New York] *Tribune,* 5 November 1910, p. 7). George later moved on farther west to Wisconsin, where he was joined by brother Samuel Wade North by 1850 (1850 U.S. Census, District. No. 21, Turtle, Rock, Wisconsin, dwelling 753, family 830, John Hopkins household; viewed on Ancestry.com).

40   Barbara McMartin, *Hides, Hemlocks, and Adirondack History: How the Tanning Industry Influenced the Region's Growth* (Utica, New York: North Country Books, 1992), 31–32.

41   C. W. Holbrook, *Record of the Descendants of Silence Holbrook of Weymouth, Mass.* (Worcester, Massachusetts: Henry J. Howland, [1851]), 9. "Obituary: Charles North," *The Oswego Daily Palladium,* 15 February 1892, p. 5. Oswego County Deeds, Oswego, Book 43, p. 79.

42   1850 U.S. Census, Oswego, p. 490 (penciled), dwelling nos. 466 and 467, family nos. 517 and 518, William O. Hubbard and Chas. North households; viewed on Ancestry.com.

43   Shirley Louise Purtell Bickel, *Descendants of Richard Coman of Salem, Massachusetts and Providence, Rhode Island* (Boston: Newbury Street Press, 2006), 422. 1860 U.S. Census, Oswego, p. 74, dwelling 564, family 572, Rollin Coman household, viewed on Ancestry.com. Cummington, Hampshire, Massachusetts, Intentions of Marriage (1834), p. 51, Samuel Porter Hubbard and Venila Mitchell; viewed on Ancestry.com, *Massachusetts, Town and Vital Records, 1620–1988.* 1855 New York State Census, Oswego, dwelling 339, family 449, Sam'l P. Hubbard household, viewed on Ancestry.com.

44   "Obituary: Charles North," *The Oswego Daily Palladium,* 15 February 1892.

45   *1880 City Atlas of Oswego, New York: from Official Records, Private Plans and Actual Surveys* (Philadelphia: G. M. Hopkins, 1880), viewed at Library of Congress, www.loc.gov/maps.

46   Lithograph attributed to W. H. Rease. Courtesy of the Oswego County Historical Society.

47   Oswego County Deeds, book 43, p. 79.

48   Peter Eisenstadt, *The Encyclopedia of New York State* (Syracuse, New York: Syracuse University Press, 2005), 1527.

49   Eisenstadt, *The Encyclopedia of New York State,* 1527.

50   McMartin, *Hides, Hemlocks, and Adirondack History,* 11.

51   McMartin, *Hides, Hemlocks, and Adirondack History,* 11, 18, 31–32.

52   McMartin, *Hides, Hemlocks, and Adirondack History,* 13–16.

53   McMartin, *Hides, Hemlocks, and Adirondack History,* 57, 62.

54   *1880 City Atlas of Oswego, New York: from Official Records, Private Plans and Actual Surveys* (Philadelphia: G. M. Hopkins, 1880), Library of Congress, www.loc.gov/maps, 23 October 2020.

55   *1880 City Atlas of Oswego.*

56   Peter C. Welsh, "A Craft That Resisted Change: American Tanning Practices to 1850," *Technology and Culture,* vol. 4, no. 3 (Summer 1963):299.

57   Lucius F. Ellsworth, *Craft to National Industry in the Nineteenth Century: A Case Study of the Transformation of the New York State Tanning Industry* (New York: Arno Press, 1975), Preface, [ii].

58   McMartin, *Hides, Hemlocks, and Adirondack History,* 24–25.

59   McMartin, *Hides, Hemlocks, and Adirondack History,* 14, 16.

60   Ellsworth, *Craft to National Industry,* 30.

61   Crisfield Johnson, *History of Oswego County, New York, with Illustrations and Sketches of Some of its Prominent Men and Pioneers* (Philadelphia: L. H. Everts & co., 1877), 74.

62   David William Moody and Lewis Bradley, "Oswego, N.Y.," lithograph, (New York: Smith Brothers & Co., [1855]), Library of Congress, www.loc.gov.

63 Johnson, *History of Oswego County*, 74.

64 Johnson, *History of Oswego County*, 74. George R. Taylor, *The Transportation Revolution, 1815–60* (London and New York: Routledge, Taylor & Francis, 1951), 30.

65 Johnson, *History of Oswego County*, 75.

66 Riverside Cemetery Office, "Interment Record B," "Charles North & Hubbard," p. 692. Riverside Cemetery Office, Oswego, Oswego County, New York, "Internments [*sic*], Riverside Cemetery, 1855–1910," William Lorenzo North, Alicia M. North, 146. Riverside Cemetery, William L. North and Alicia M. North gravestones, photographs taken by the author, 2019.

67 Courtesy of the Oswego County Historical Society.

68 Keleher and Ross, "Great Irish Famine," 696–99.

69 Letter from Anne E. Pilkington to Charles North, dated 3 March 1847, "Eight letters of Mrs. Anne Pilkington," NLI: Ms. 13,093. Minor additions in punctuation have been added for clarity.

70 Keleher and Ross, "Great Irish Famine," 699. Letter from Anne E. Pilkington to Charles North, dated 1 May 1850, "Eight letters of Mrs. Anne Pilkington," NLI: Ms. 13,093. Minor additions in punctuation have been added for clarity.

71 Letter from Alicia "Lissie" North to Charles North, dated December 1851 (postmarked Liverpool 18 December 1851), from "Eight letters of Mrs. Anne Pilkington . . . ," National Library of Ireland, Ms. 13,093, courtesy of the National Library of Ireland.

72 Letter from Alicia "Lissie" North to Charles North, dated December 1851 (postmarked Liverpool 18 December 1851), "Eight letters of Mrs. Anne Pilkington," NLI: Ms. 13,093.

73 "County of Galway: In re the Estate of Joseph North," *The Dublin Evening Post*, 3 February 1853, p. 4.

74 "Obituary: Joseph B. Hubbard," *Oswego Morning Express*, 18 September 1882, p. 4. 1855 New York State Census, Third Ward, City of Oswego, Oswego County, New York, dwelling 111, J. B. Hubbard household, viewed on Ancestry.com, showing Joseph's birthplace erroneously as Massachusetts. 1850 U.S. Census, Brunswick, Rensselaer County, New York, p. 66 (stamped), p. 131 (penned), dwelling 2, family 2, Daniel Hubbard household, viewed on Ancestry.com. 1855 New York State Census, Brunswick, p. 4, dwelling 95, family 109, Daniel Hubbard household, viewed on Ancestry.com. In 1850, Daniel was listed as a currier and tanner, and in 1855 as a shoemaker, born Hampshire County, Massachusetts.

Daniel and Asenath's brief residence in Worthington was marked by the death and burial of a 3-year-old son, Francis Edward Hubbard (photograph of gravestone at FindAGrave.com, memorial #61398946, which includes his parents' names).

Daniel was born in 1776 and died in Brunswick in 1856 (Photograph of gravestone at FindAGrave.com, memorial #70295377, giving his death date as 11 August 1856 and his age at death as 80). The above-mentioned 1855 New York State Census shows a Francis Edward Hubbard—likely a second child who was given the same name—age 40 (born c. 1815), living in the same dwelling as Daniel and Asenath, and a discharge of a lease recorded in Brunswick, Rensselaer County on 8 March 1852, lists both Francis E. Hubbard and Joseph B. Hubbard as the heirs and assigns of Daniel (New York, Rensselaer County Deeds, book 81, p. 362, discharge given by Gilbert Cropsey of Brunswick, viewed on FamilySearch.org 26 July 2020).

According to Hubbard historian Edward Warren Day, Daniel was the brother of William Hubbard Sr., who was the father William O. Hubbard as mentioned previously. Both Daniel and William Sr. were sons of Edmund (1734–1791) and Ruth (Lyman) Hubbard (Edward Warren Day, *One Thousand Years of Hubbard History, 866 to 1895: From Hubba, the Norse Sea King to the Enlightened Present* (New York: Harlan Page Hubbard, 1895), 232–33.

75 Riverside Cemetery Office, "Internments [*sic*], Riverside Cemetery, 1855–1910: Records of 4th & 5th Ward Cemeteries," Venelia M. North, p. 146, which reads 16 August 1851. Riverside Cemetery, Venelia North gravestone, (which includes only the year of death), photograph taken by the author, 2019. Riverside Cemetery Office, "Interment Record B," Interment record for Section T, Lot 10, "Charles North & Hubbard," Venelia North, p. 692 (which reads 13 August 1851). Venilia's grave,

along with many others, was moved from the East Cemetery and was reinterred 16 June 1859 (Interment Book B record reads 1856 in error for her particular grave).

76   Riverside Cemetery Office, "Interment Record B," "Charles North & Hubbard," Venelia North, p. 692, cause of death left blank.

77   Photograph of gravestone at FindAGrave.com, memorial #141752082, Alicia M. North, buried at Riverside Cemetery. Riverside Cemetery Office, "Internments [*sic*], Riverside Cemetery, 1855–1910: Records of 4th & 5th Ward Cemeteries," Alicia North, p. 146. Her grave was moved from the East Cemetery and was reinterred 16 June 1859. 1900 U.S. Census, First District, Sixth Ward, Oswego, enumeration district 130, Sheet 135A, 156 (crossed out) 165, 181 (crossed out) 176, Walter H. Pulver household; viewed on Ancestry.com, giving the month and year of Laura's birth. Photograph of gravestone at FindAGrave.com, memorial #159122011, Laura W. North Pulver, Riverside Cemetery. "Deaths in the County," *Fulton* [New York] *Patriot*, 27 October 1938, p. 17.

78   "Historical Pictorial Journey of Oswego, New York," Michael J. Colasurdo, administrator, www .oswego-history.com/historic-oswego-pictures.

79   1855 New York State Census, 4th Ward, City of Oswego, dwelling nos. 195 and 196, family nos. 228 and 229, W. O. Hubbard and Chas. North households, viewed on Ancestry.com, showing the two families enumerated consecutively. *The Oswego Business and Residence Directory, and Compendium of Useful Information, for 1852 & '53* (Oswego: Knorr & Hancock, 1852), 228, 244. *Oswego City Residence & Advertising Directory for 1856 & '57* (Oswego, New York: William Hancock, 1856), 52, 102, showing both men living on Syracuse Street.

80   1855 New York State Census, 4th Ward, City of Oswego, Oswego County, New York, dwelling nos. 195 and 196, family nos. 228 and 229, W. O. Hubbard and Chas. North households, viewed on Ancestry.com, showing the North house valued at $1,000 and the Hubbard house at $5,000. Both homes were listed as being frame houses.

81   *The Oswego Business and Residence Directory, and Compendium of Useful Information, for 1852 & '53* (Oswego: Knorr & Hancock, 1852), 51.

82   *Oswego Business Directory 1852 & '53*, 228, which lists Samuel as "P. Hubbard."

83   1850 U.S. Census, Fourth Ward, City [of] Oswego, Oswego County, New York, p. 238 [stamped], 475 [penciled], dwelling 353, family 402, Joseph P. [*sic*] Hubbard household, viewed on Ancestry.com.

84   Johnson, *History of Oswego County*, 75.

85   *The Oswego City Residence & Business Directory, for 1854 & '55* (Oswego, New York: William Hancock, 1854), 24.

86   *Oswego, Oswego County, New York* (New York: Sanborn-Perris Map Co., August 1890), map, 31 pages, p. 18, viewed online at Library of Congress, www.loc.gov., "Sanborn Fire Insurance Map from Oswego, Oswego County, New York."

87   McMartin, *Hides, Hemlocks, and Adirondack History*, 59.

88   *The American Heritage Dictionary of the English Language*, 4th ed., (Boston and New York: Houghton Mifflin Company, 2000), "tailrace," p. 1762. Tom Murphy, "The Clark Tannery in 19th Century Amesbury," Amesbury Carriage Museum, 2019, online at https://amesburycarriagemuseum.org /news/2019/3/22/the-clark-tannery-in-19th-century-amesbury-6d8sp-gf946, accessed 24 October 2020. *Oswego, Oswego County, New York* (New York: Sanborn-Perris Map Co., August 1890), map, 31 pages, p. 18, viewed online at Library of Congress, www.loc.gov., "Sanborn Fire Insurance Map from Oswego, Oswego County, New York."

89   *Oswego City Directory, 1854 & '55*, 75, 97. Charles North is listed on p. 97 as a "farmer," but there is no evidence that he would have had the property or the inclination to take that title; also he was listed consistently as a tanner in city directories before and after this one. Likely, the incorrect listing was a mistyping of the handwritten word "tanner," which could have featured even slight irregularities in the "T" and two "N's" to be mistaken as "farmer."

90   Ellsworth, *Craft to National Industry*, 49–52.

91   Courtesy of Oswego Public Library.

92   *Twenty-Fifth Anniversary of the First Congregational Church, Oswego, N.Y.: An Account of Its Celebration, July 16th and 20th, 1882* (Oswego, New York: R. J. Oliphant, 1882), 9. "Obituary: Mrs. Harriet Mitchell North," *The* [Oswego] *Daily Palladium*, 26 January 1901, p. 5, reporting that she was believed to be the last charter member of the Congregational Church to die.

93   Riverside Cemetery Office, "Internments [*sic*], 1855–1910," Chester North, 146. Riverside Cemetery, Chester North gravestone, photograph taken by the author, 2019.

94   1865 New York State Census, southern 4th Ward, City of Oswego, Oswego County, New York, p. 45, dwelling 270, family 296, Charles North household, viewed on Ancestry.com. Sarah's middle initial is given here as "L." This census, conducted on 21 June 1865, gives Hattie's age as 2 years, 8 months, which would place her birth at about October 1862. Riverside Cemetery Office, "Internments [*sic*], Riverside Cemetery, 1855–1910," Hattie N. North, 146, listing Hattie's birth year only; also Riverside Cemetery, Hattie N. North gravestone, photograph taken by the author, 2019, which shows only the years of birth and death.

95   *History of Oswego County, New York, with Illustrations and Biographical Sketches of Some of Its Prominent Men and Pioneers* (Philadelphia: L. H. Everts, 1877), 75–78.

96   Dorothy Denneen Volo and James M. Volo, *Daily Life in Civil War America*, 2nd ed. (Santa Barbara, California: Greenwood Press, 2009), 167.

97   *Directory of the City of Oswego, for 1864 and 1865, with a Synopsis of Incidents and Events Transpiring in the War for the Union* (Oswego, New York: John Fitzgerald, 1864), 223.

98   Riverside Cemetery Office, "Internments [*sic*], Riverside Cemetery, 1855–1910," William Lorenzo North, 146. Riverside Cemetery, William L. North gravestone, photograph taken by the author, 2019.

99   Eisenstadt, *The Encyclopedia of New York State*, 1164.

100   *Directory of the City of Oswego for 1868–9* (Oswego, New York: John Fitzgerald, 1868), 10–14.

101   *The Oswego Residence & Advertising Directory, for 1861* (Oswego, New York: John Fitzgerald, 1861), 113.

102   Photo of drawer pull, courtesy of Eugene Ossa and Helen Hester-Ossa.

103   1900 U.S. Census, Glen Ridge, Essex, New Jersey, enumeration district 213, sheet 14B, Frederick C. Osterhout household. Photograph of gravestone at FindaGrave.com, memorial #179563012, Louise N. Osterhout, viewed 6 September 2020. "Obituary: Mrs. Frederick C. Osterhout," *The* [Oswego] *Palladium-Times*, 28 May 1960, p. 5.

104   Photograph courtesy of Eugene Ossa and Helen Hester-Ossa.

105   Photograph, taken by the author, with permission from Eugene Ossa and Helen Hester-Ossa.

106   Photograph, taken by the author, with permission from the Oswego County Historical Society.

107   1870 U.S. Census, First Ward, Grand Rapids, Kent County, Michigan, p. 84, dwelling 673, family 626, William Hubbard household, viewed on Ancestry.com. J. A. French & M. T. Ryan, comps., *Grand Rapids City Directory and Business Mirror 1865–'66* (Grand Rapids, Michigan: Daily Eagle, 1865), 34.

108   1870 U.S. Census, Grand Rapids, William Hubbard household.

109   "Oswego Times," *Oswego Palladium-Times*, 20 September 1945, p. 10.

110   *Oswego Directory, 1868–9*, 9.

111   "Obituary: Charles North," *The Oswego Daily Palladium*, 15 February 1892.

112   Courtesy of the Oswego County Historical Society.

113   "Oswego Times," *Oswego Palladium-Times*, 20 September 1945. Arthur M. Schlesinger Jr., *The Almanac of American History* (New York: Barnes & Noble Books, 2004), 323.

114   "Obituary: Charles North," *The Oswego Daily Palladium,* 15 February 1892. T. Wood Clarke, *Utica: For a Century and a Half* (Utica, New York: Widtman, 1952), 51.

115   Photograph by Mary Kay Stone.

116 "The Hon. Charles North," *The* [Oswego] *Palladium,* 16 May 1878, p. 2. "Oswego Officials: Mayors of Oswego," *Oswego Palladium,* 1 April 1891, p. 6.

117 "Oswego Officials," *Oswego Palladium,* 1 April 1891.

118 *Oswego City and County Directory and Gazetteer for 1869–70* (Oswego, New York: R. J. Oliphant, [1869]), 36–37.

119 Riverside Cemetery Office, "Internments [*sic*], Riverside Cemetery, 1855–1910," Hattie N. North, 146. Riverside Cemetery, Hattie N. North gravestone, photograph taken by the author, 2019.

120 Florence Hartley, *The Ladies' Book of Etiquette, and Manual of Politeness . . .* (Boston: J. S. Lock, 1876), 109, 113.

121 *Twenty-Fifth Anniversary of the First Congregational Church, Oswego,* 25–26.

122 "Oswego Times," *Oswego Palladium-Times,* 20 September 1945.

123 "Obituary: Charles North," *The Oswego Daily Palladium,* 15 February 1892. "Oswego Times," *Oswego Palladium-Times,* 20 September 1945.

124 "The Hon. Charles North," *The* [Oswego] *Palladium,* 16 May 1878.

125 "Oswego Times," *Oswego Palladium-Times,* 20 September 1945.

126 *Twenty-Fifth Anniversary of the First Congregational Church, Oswego,* 10, 35.

127 Riverside Cemetery Office, "Internments [*sic*], Riverside Cemetery, 1855–1910, Joseph B. Hubbard, 107.

128 "Obituary: Charles North," *Oswego Daily Palladium,* 15 February 1892.

129 "Oswego," marriage notice for George DeForest and Sara C. North, *The Syracuse* [New York] *Standard,* 10 April 1885, p. 6. For variations in the spelling of George's surname, see Note 292.

130 "Death Removes George De Forest," *Utica Daily Press,* 7 October 1929, p. 3. Although the headline for this obituary reads "De Forest," the subsequent article spells the surname "DeForest." *Oswego City Directory . . . 1888* (Oswego, New York: Oliphant & Boyd, 1888), 258, listing for "Charles North & Co., tanners and leather dealers."

131 "Oswego Officials," *Oswego Palladium,* 1 April 1891.

132 "Death Removes George De Forest," *Utica Daily Press,* 7 October 1929, p. 3. *Oswego City Directory . . . 1888* (Oswego, New York: Oliphant & Boyd, 1888), 258, listing for "Charles North & Co., tanners and leather dealers." Findings are tools and materials used for making and mending shoes (*Oxford English Dictionary* (online), "finding, n." definition 4.c.(a). [in plural], entry updated for the OED Third Edition, December 2016, accessed 20 November 2020).

133 From the collection of Maynard Kirk Davis.

134 1891 Will of Charles North, Oswego County Wills, vol. S, p. 602, viewed on FamilySearch.org 15 August 2019, *New York, Wills and Probate Records, 1659–1999, Oswego Records of Wills.*

135 "Obituary: Charles North," *The Oswego Daily Palladium,* 15 February 1892.

136 1891 Will of Charles North.

137 Charles North death notice, *New York Times,* 16 February 1892, p. 2.

138 "Obituary: Charles North," *Oswego Daily Palladium,* 15 February 1892. Riverside Cemetery Office, "Internments [*sic*], Riverside Cemetery, 1855–1910," Charles North, 146. Riverside Cemetery Office "Interment Record B," Interment record for Section T, Lot 10, "Charles North & Hubbard," 692.

139 "Obituary: Charles North," *Oswego Daily Palladium,* 15 February 1892.

140 "Obituary: Charles North," *Oswego Daily Palladium,* 15 February 1892.

141 Deaths Registered in the Town of Cummington, 1885, p. 54, no. 10, William H. White, viewed on Ancestry.com. William was listed as having died in Oswego but was a resident of Cummington and was also buried there. Photograph of gravestone at FindaGrave.com, memorial #103751784, William H. White, Dawes Cemetery, Cummington, Massachusetts. Laura, who died in 1910, shares the stone with her husband.

142   1892 New York State Census, Oswego, 8th Ward, 2nd Election District, p. 12, Harriet North and
      Laura T. White listed consecutively, viewed on Ancestry.com. R. J. Oliphant, *Oliphant's Oswego
      Directory, 1899* (Oswego: the author, 1899), 363, describing Laura as boarding at 212 E. Seventh
      Street. 1900 U.S. Census, Oswego, enumeration district no. 134, sheet no. 3B, dwelling 55 (crossed
      out) 56, family 56 (crossed out) 57, Hanna [*sic*] North household, 212 [East] Seventh Street, viewed
      on Ancestry.com.

143   From the collection of Maynard Kirk Davis.

144   "Obituary: Mrs. Harriet Mitchell North," [Oswego] *Daily Palladium*, 26 January 1901. See the North
      Family section of Chapter Five.

145   Obituary of Samuel Wade North, *La Crosse County Record*, 11 July 1895, p. 3, courtesy of the La
      Crosse Public Library, La Crosse, Wisconsin. He married Mary Fahey in 1852 (Registration of
      Marriage for Samuel W. North and Mary Fahey, uncertified copy provided by the Wisconsin State
      Vital Records Office, issued 17 January 2020, author's files). Henry Ringling North erroneously
      implies that the marriage took place in Montreal (North, *Circus Kings*, 155), and Samuel Wade
      North's obituary erroneously claims that the couple was married in Albany, New York (Obituary of
      Samuel Wade North, *La Crosse County Record*, 11 July 1895). They lived in Janesville, then settled in
      Onalaska by 1860 (Obituary of Samuel Wade North, *La Crosse County Record*, 11 July 1895. 1860
      U.S. Census, Onalaska, La Crosse County, Wisconsin, p. 236, dwelling 2008, family 1717, Samuel
      North household, viewed on Ancestry.com). See the North Family section of Chapter Five.

146   Chicago and North Western Railroad, Pensioner's Record, no. 1077 (stamped), no. 1262, (typed),
      Harry W. North, viewed on Ancestry.com, *U.S. Chicago and North Western Railroad Employment
      Records, 1935–1970,* Pensioners Records and History, Miller–Ozga. The two-sided card is typed,
      with Harry's address listed as 821 Oak Street, Baraboo, corresponding with his address on the 1920
      U.S. Census. His date of death was added later in red ink. He began his career in 1878 as a "water
      boy" at the Onalaska gravel pit, and he was promoted from there. 1900 U.S. Census, Baraboo,
      Sauk County, Wisconsin, enumeration district 125, sheet 2A, dwelling 27, family 29, Harry North
      household, viewed on Ancestry.com. Henry W. North and Ida Lorana Wilelmina Ringling marriage,
      Cook County, Illinois, Marriage Index, 1871–1920, Ancestry.com, citing Family History Library, Salt
      Lake City, Utah, film no. 1,030,341. North, *Circus Kings,* 157.

      Harry had had a previous marriage that ended in divorce (North, *Circus Kings,* 156), but produced a
      daughter, Lila North, who was born in Wisconsin in April 1886 (1900 U.S. Census, Baraboo, Harry
      North household). Lila married Walter Wilcox, and they were living in Pontiac, Michigan, in January
      1920 with their newborn son, Robert Wilcox (1920 U.S. Census, Pontiac Township, Oakland
      County, Michigan, enumeration district 182, sheet 19A, dwelling 338, family 360, Henry Simpson
      household [Walter, Lila, and Robert Wilcox], viewed on Ancestry.com). The family apparently
      moved to Chicago, where Lila became seriously ill later that year ("Saturday," *Baraboo* [Wisconsin]
      Weekly News, 24 June 1920, p. 8) and was visited by Harry and Ida North before her (Lila's) death
      sometime before 7 July, when her funeral was held in Baraboo ("Saturday," *Baraboo Weekly News,* 24
      June 1920; "Obituary: Mrs. Walter Wilcox," *Baraboo Weekly News,* 7 July 1920, p. 7).

      Lila's son Robert later came to live with Walter's father, Robert H. Wilcox, in Baraboo, and in 1933,
      at age 14, he accidentally drowned in the Baraboo River, near the old Ringling Circus quarters
      ("Girl, 11, Fails in Attempt to Save Boy from River," [Madison] *Wisconsin State Journal,* 7 July 1933,
      p. 1).

147   Sauk County Historical Society, *Images of America: Baraboo* (Charleston, South Carolina; Chicago,
      Illinois; Portsmouth, New Hampshire; and San Francisco, California: Arcadia Publishing Company,
      2004). "Ringlings Buy Out Barnum & Bailey," *The New York Times,* 23 October 1907.

148   "Ringlings Buy Out Barnum & Bailey," *The New York Times,* 23 October 1907.

149   North, *Circus Kings,* 160.

150   "Supercircus Draws Crowds to Garden," *The New York Times,* 30 March 1919, p. 25.

151   Chicago and North Western Railroad, Pensioner's Record, Harry W. North. "John Ringling North,
      of Circus, Dies," *The New York Times,* 6 June 1985, p. 46.

152   "John Ringling North, of Circus, Dies," *The New York Times*, 6 June 1985. The circus began using Sarasota as a winter quarters in 1927 ("Circus Shifts to Florida," *The New York Times*, 24 March 1927, p. 25).

153   John Ringling was endeavoring to create a winter White House for President Warren G. Harding, but Harding died before the plan could be carried out ("Bird Key began as the Isle of Enchantment," [Sarasota, Florida] *Herald-Tribune*, online article posted 4 February 2013, www.heraldtribune.com /article/LK/20130204/News/605192630/SH, retrieved 7 January 2020).

154   "Bird Key began as the Isle of Enchantment," *Herald-Tribune*, 4 February 2013.

155   "John Ringling North, of Circus, Dies," *New York Times*, 6 June 1985.

156   "John Ringling North, of Circus, Dies," *New York Times*, 6 June 1985. "Henry Ringling North, Former Owner of Circus," *Miami* [Florida] *Herald*, 4 October 1993, p.18.

157   "John Ringling North, of Circus, Dies," *New York Times*, 6 June 1985.

158   "Impressario by Instinct," *New York Times*, 17 July 1956, p. 24.

159   "Impressario by Instinct," *New York Times*, 17 July 1956.

160   North, *Circus Kings*, 155. "John Ringling North, of Circus, Dies," *New York Times*, 6 June 1985.

161   Ida died in 1950. (Photograph of gravestone at FindaGrave.com, memorial #21496457, Ida Lorana Ringling North, buried at John and Mable Ringling Museum Grounds, Sarasota, Sarasota County, Florida, viewed 1 December 2019).

162   Bird Key Homeowners Association, "Bird Key Circa 1960 to Current," online at www.bkha.org /historical-marker-2, viewed 13 May 2020. In his later years, Arthur Vining Davis became an avid investor of real estate in Florida.

163   Holbrook often joked that John Ringling North offered him and Sarah an elephant as a wedding present. Although he may have understood the family connection at the time of the purchase, family members don't believe that the relationship represented a motivating factor. Jenifer Kahn Bakkala, *An American Family: Four Centuries of Labor, Love, and Reward: A Story of the Davis Family* (Boston: Newbury Street Press, 2018), 103. Holbrook Davis, personal interview with the author, 5 August 2020.

164   Bird Key Homeowners Association, "Bird Key Circa 1960 to Current."

165   "Bird Key began as the Isle of Enchantment," *Herald-Tribune*, 4 February 2013.

166   "John Ringling North, of Circus, Dies," *New York Times*, 6 June 1985.

167   North, *Circus Kings*.

168   "Henry Ringling North, Former Owner of Circus," *The Miami* [Florida] *Herald*, 4 October 1993, p. 18.

169   The 1849 Utica city directory shows Isaac Maynard living at 22 Whitesboro Street and Horatio Seymour at 36 Whitesboro Street (Bildad Merrell, Jr., comp., *Utica City Directory for 1849–50* [Utica: D. Bennett, 1849], 94, 122).

170   Isaac Maynard in 1815 (Forest Hill Cemetery Office, "Record of Interments, 1849 to 1901," Isaac Maynard, 239). See the Maynard Family section of Chapter Five (2. Isaac Maynard) for the resolution of a conflict in dates regarding Isaac's birth year. Passenger manifest for the brig *Pratincole*, arriving 1 June 1836, p. 1, Charles North, line 63, viewed on Ancestry.com., citing "Passenger and Crew Lists of Vessels Arriving at New York, New York, 1820–1897," NARA RG 36, microfilm publication M237, 675 rolls, roll 030. "Death of Isaac Maynard," *Utica* [New York] *Morning Herald and Daily Gazette*, 24 February 1885, p. 5. M. M. Bagg, M.D., *Memorial History of Utica, N.Y., from Its Settlement to the Present Time* (Syracuse, New York: D. Mason, 1892), 239.

171   Charles and Harriet were married on 8 September (Cummington, Massachusetts, 1845 marriages, p. 160, item 12, Charles North and Harriet N. Mitchell; viewed on AmericanAncestors.org 19 July 2019, "Massachusetts: Vital Records, 1841–1910" [the marriage took place in 1844, despite being grouped with others from 1845]). Isaac and Margaret were married on 20 August ("Married," *Utica Daily Gazette*, 26 August 1844. Isaac's obituary gives their year of marriage incorrectly as 1846 [Death of Isaac Maynard," *Utica Morning Herald and Daily Gazette*, 24 February 1885]).

172   John Thorn attended primary school until the age of 9. He worked on a farm for six years and learned the soap and candle business. He attended school again for about eight weeks when he was 15, then returned to the soap and candle business until 1832. Bagg, *Memorial History of Utica,* 30 (biographical section). "Death of John Thorn: A Well Known and Highly Respected Citizen Passes Away," *Utica Morning Herald and Daily Gazette,* 1 January 1895, p. 6. A tallow chandler is one who makes or sells tallow candles (*Oxford English Dictionary,* online version, "tallow-chandler, n." first published in 1910).

173   "Ruishton, Somerset, Eligible Investment," classified advertisement, *The Taunton* [Somerset, England] *Courier,* 10 March 1841, p. 2. "Gigs on two wheels swarmed mornings and evenings on the suburban roads round London . . . [and] where the establishment was small, and the gig the only carriage kept, the gig-house, built at the side of the residence, was indispensable. . . . " (G. N. Hooper, "Modern Carriages," *Papers Read before the Institute of British Carriage Manufacturers, 1883–1901* [Aspley Guise: The Powage Press, Ltd., 1902], 228).

174   Silver Street (Baptist) Church register, births of Sarah, Maria, Mary, Richard, Sarah (again), Robert, James, and Isaac Maynard, viewed on Ancestry.com, "England & Wales, Non-Conformist and Non-Parochial Registers, 1567–1970," RG4: Registers of Births, Marriages and Deaths, Somerset Baptist Piece 3219: Taunton, Silver Street (Baptist), 1782–1837. Eight children of Richard and Sarah Maynard had births recorded into this register on 4 July 1820 by Rev. Richard Horsey. Below these entries reads: "All of the above was entered at the particular request of the parties concerned and according to their information of the time of the births of each—all of which being before the Establishment of this Interest." Each registration lists the parents as "Richard Maynard and Sarah his Wife of the Parish of Ruishton in the County of Somerset." The birthdates of both Isaac and Mary match the birthdates recorded at their deaths at Forest Hill Cemetery in Utica.

175   "Village Treat at Ruishton," *The Taunton Courier,* 28 July 1886, p. 6. "The Late Mr. John Thorn," *The Courier for Taunton and Western Counties,* 16 January 1895, p. 4.

176   "Village Treat at Ruishton," *The Taunton Courier,* 28 July 1886. "Death of John Thorn," *Utica Morning Herald,* 1 January 1895.

177   "Death of John Thorn," *Utica Morning Herald and Daily Gazette,* 1 January 1895.

178   W. H. Bartlett and Robert Brandard, "Utica," Emmet Collection of Manuscripts Etc. Relating to American History, New York Publc Library, digital collections, Miriam and Ira D. Wallach Division of Art, Prints and Photographs: Print Collection.

179   Bagg, *Memorial History of Utica,* 31 (biographical section).

180   Bagg, *Memorial History of Utica,* 31 (biographical section). Stephen Thorn was the son of James and Elizabeth (Springate) Thorn and was born in Kent, England, about 200 miles away from Ruishton. (Baptism of Stephen Thorn; Pembury, Kent, England, Christenings, 1802, viewed on FamilySearch. org, "England, Kent, Bishop's Transcripts 1560–1911," Pembury Births, Marriages and Burials 1716–1812." Marriage of James Thorn of Brenchley and Elizabeth Springate of Pembury, Pembury, Kent, England, Marriages, 1786, viewed on FamilySearch.org, "England, Kent, Bishop's Transcripts 1560–1911," Pembury Births, Marriages and Burials 1716–1812. Stephen's mother is erroneously listed as Hannah in Forest Hill Cemetery Office, "Record of Interments, 1849 to 1901," Stephen Thorn, 419. "Death of John Thorn," *Utica Morning Herald and Daily Gazette,* 1 January 1895. Ruishton, Somerset, England, marriage registers, marriage of Robert Thorn and Betty Palmer, dated 22 April 1806, viewed on Ancestry.com, "Somerset, England, Marriage Registers, Bonds and Allegations, 1754–1914.")

       According to *History of Oneida County,* Stephen came to the U.S. with his mother and siblings in 1818 and lived in Albany (*History of Oneida County, New York, with Illustrations and Biographical Sketches of Some of Its Prominent Men and Pioneers* [Philadelphia: Everts & Fariss, 1878], 360). Stephen was recorded in Utica as early as 1829, when his son James E. B. Thorn was born there (Forest Hill Cemetery Office, "Record of Interments, 1849 to 1901," James E. B. Thorn, 372, giving date and location of birth). He was enumerated on both the 1830 and 1840 U.S. censuses for Utica (1830 U.S. Census, Utica, Oneida County, New York, p. 11, viewed on Ancestry.com; 1840 U.S. Census, Utica,

Oneida County, New York, p. 26, viewed on Ancestry.com). Although he was briefly in the soap and candle business, Stephen made his living at a variety of trades over his lifetime. The 1832 Utica city directory listed him as a saddler (Elisha Harrington, *The Utica Directory, 1832* [Utica: E. A. Maynard, 1832], 102); in 1855, he was a brewer (1855 New York State Census, Utica, Oneida County, New York, p. 68 (penciled), dwelling 459, family 517, Stephen Thorn household, viewed on Ancestry.com); and in 1870, a farmer (1870 U.S. Census, Utica, p. 35, dwelling 247, family 305, Stephen Thorn household, viewed on Ancestry.com).

181   Elisha Harrington, *The Utica Directory, No. 5, 1834* (Utica: E. A. Maynard, 1834), 170. Stephen lived at 32 Jay Street, next door to Samuel S. Thorn. Samuel worked at Thorn & Curtiss, "forwarders," who had a warehouse located at 25 Jay Street, fronting the canal below John Street.

182   Harrington, *The Utica Directory, No. 5, 1834,* 170.

183   "Death of Mrs. John Thorn," *Utica Daily Observer,* 24 April 1891, p. 5.

184   Bagg, *Memorial History of Utica,* 31 (biographical section). "Mrs. John Thorn," *Utica Morning Herald and Daily Gazette,* 25 April 1891.

185   "Death of Isaac Maynard," *Utica Morning Herald and Daily Gazette,* 24 February 1885. Bagg, *Memorial History of Utica,* 239. *The Utica City Directory for 1837–8* ([Utica]: G. Tracy: 1837), 110, 85, erroneously showing Isaac as boarding with John "Thomas." William Richards, *The Utica Directory: 1840–'41* (Utica: John P. Bush, 1840), 95.

186   Bagg, *Memorial History of Utica,* 597. Stephen Thorn remained in Utica and took on other occupations. (See Note 180.)

187   Samuel Colgate, "American Soap Factories," *One Hundred Years of American Commerce,* Chauncey M. Depew, LL.D, ed. (New York: D. O. Haynes, 1845), 422. Alice Morse Earle, *Home Life in Colonial Days* (New York and London: Macmillan Company, 1899), 253–5. Lye was made by pouring water over wood ashes. It took about six bushels of lye and twenty-four pounds of grease to make one barrel of soft soap, which bore no traces of grease in its end product.

188   F. W. Gibbs, "The History of the Manufacture of Soap," *Annals of Science* (1939), 4:174–175.

189   Colgate, "American Soap Factories," 422–433.

190   Colgate, "American Soap Factories," 423.

191   Colgate, "American Soap Factories," 422, 426.

192   Michael Ball and David Sunderland, *An Economic History of London, 1800–1914* (London and New York: Routledge, 2001), 131–132.

193   Bagg, *Memorial History of Utica,* 199. Noble E. Whitford, *History of the Canal System of the State of New York Together with Brief Histories of the Canals of the United States and Canada,* 2 vols. (Albany, New York: Brandow, 1905), 1:131.

194   T. Wood Clarke, *Utica: For a Century and a Half* (Utica, New York: Widtman, 1952), 39. Whitford, *History of the Canal System,* 1:683.

195   Clarke, *Utica: For a Century and a Half,* 40.

196   David H. Burr, "Utica," Atlas of New York (New York, 1938), New York Public Library, digital collections, Lionel Pincus and Princess Fryal Map Division.

197   Bagg, *Memorial History of Utica,* 230.

198   "Great Fire," *The Utica Observer,* 4 April 1837, p. 2. See *The Utica City Directory, for 1843–'44* (Utica: Roberts & Curtiss, 1843), 105, showing Thorn & Maynard's Water Street location as being near Division Street. A. P. Yates, *The Utica Directory and City Advertiser, Arranged in Five Parts, for 1839–40* (Utica: R. Northway Jr., 1839), 71, 88, showing Isaac Maynard boarding at J. Thorn's at 26 Whitesboro Street. Also refer to the map as shown. At this time, the length of Genesee Street extended up to the canal.

199   Clarke, *Utica: For a Century and a Half,* 43.

200   "Travelling," *New York* [New York] *Daily Herald,* 25 May 1840, p. 2.

201   "Death of Isaac Maynard," *Utica Morning Herald and Daily Gazette,* 24 February 1885.

202   "The Late Mr. John Thorn," *The Courier for Taunton and Western Counties*, 16 January 1895.

203   1841 Census of England, St. Mary Magdalen, Taunton, Somerset, England, p. 18/35, Sarah Maynard household, viewed on Ancestry.com.

204   "Ruishton, Somerset, Eligible Investment," *The Taunton Courier*, 10 March 1841.

205   "Death of John Thorn," *Utica Morning Herald and Daily Gazette*, 1 January 1895. This business also involved the tanning of sheep skins ("Death of Isaac Maynard," *Utica Morning Herald and Daily Gazette*, 24 February 1885).

206   "Isaac Maynard," editorial, *Utica Morning Herald and Daily Gazette*, 24 February 1885, p. 4.

207   "Isaac Maynard," editorial, *Utica Morning Herald and Daily Gazette*, 24 February 1885. "Village Treat at Ruishton," *The Taunton Courier*, 28 July 1886.

208   "Isaac Maynard," *The New York Times*, 24 February 1885, p. 2.

209   "Isaac Maynard," editorial, *Utica Morning Herald and Daily Gazette*, 24 February 1885.

210   Bagg, *Memorial History of Utica*, 279. William Richards, *The Utica City Directory for 1843–'44* (Utica, New York: Roberts & Curtiss, 1843), 71. Bildad Merrell Jr., *The Utica City Directory for 1846–'47* (Utica: H. H. Curtiss, 1846), 89, 148.

211   See the Maynard Family section of Chapter Five for a discussion of her birth date and parentage.

212   "Death of Mrs. Isaac Maynard," *Utica Morning Herald and Daily Gazette*, 3 December 1896. "Married," *Utica Daily Gazette*, 26 August 1844. Merrell Jr., *The Utica City Directory for 1846–'47*, 89.

213   See the Maynard Family section of Chapter Five for a discussion of differing sources regarding Mary's birth. For Isaac's birthdate, see Forest Hill Cemetery Office, "Record of Interments, 1849 to 1901," Isaac Maynard, 81.

214   John C. Rudd, D.D., *The Influence of the Female Character: A Sermon Preached in Trinity Church, Utica, on Sunday March 13, 1836* (Utica, New York: Eli Maynard, 1836), 6.

215   "Death of Mrs. Isaac Maynard," *Utica Morning Herald and Daily Gazette*, 3 December 1896.

216   Henry J. Cookingham, *History of Oneida County, New York: from 1700 to the Present Time* (Chicago: S. J. Clarke Publishing Company, 1912), 2 vols., 1:428. Mary's 1891 obituary claimed that she was the founder of the asylum, but Mary was not yet in the United States when it was founded in 1830 ("Mrs. John Thorn," *Utica Morning Herald and Daily Gazette*, 25 April 1891).

217   "Mrs. John Thorn," *Utica Morning Herald and Daily Gazette*, 25 April 1891. "Village Treat at Ruishton," *The Taunton Courier*, 21 July 1886.

218   "Joshua Tavender, an Old and Respected Utican," *The Utica Morning Herald and Daily Gazette*, 11 October 1895. 1855 New York State Census, City of Utica, Oneida County, New York, p. 14, dwelling 79, family 121, John E. Bult household, viewed on Ancestry.com, showing the family as having been residents of the city for six years.

219   Bildad Merrell Jr., *The Utica City Directory for 1850–51* (Utica, New York: D. Bennett, 1850), 23, 136.

220   Clarke, *Utica: For a Century and a Half*, 50, 43.

221   Clarke, *Utica: For a Century and a Half*, 43–47.

222   Bagg, *Memorial History of Utica*, 239, 32 (biographical section). "Death of Isaac Maynard," *Utica Morning Herald and Daily Gazette*, 24 February 1885.

223   Bradley Lewis, "Utica, N.Y.," (New York: Smith Brothers & Co., 1848), I. N. Stokes Collection of American Historical Prints, New York Public Library, digital collections, Miriam and Ira D. Wallach Division of Art, Prints and Photographs: Print Collection.

224   Clarke, *Utica: For a Century and a Half*, 49–51. Arthur Schlesinger Jr., *The Almanac of American History*, revised and updated edition (New York: Barnes & Noble, 2004), 311.

225   "Utica Insurance Company," *Oneida Morning Herald*, 7 September 1850, p.1, quoting a statement dated 10 June 1850.

226   "Utica Insurance Company," *Oneida Morning Herald*, 16 September 1850, p. 1.

227 Forest Hill Cemetery Office, "Record of Interments, 1927 to 1961," John F. Maynard, p. 239. Passport application for John F. Maynard, 6 April 1922, issued 11 April 1922 (stamped) no. 143397 (penned), viewed on Ancestry.com, "Passport Applications, 1795–1905," NARA RG 59, microfilm publication M1372, 694 rolls, roll 295.

228 Photograph of gravestone at FindAGrave.com, memorial #156314775, Sophia Margaret Maynard Crouse, Forest Hill Cemetery. Passport application of Sophia M. Crouse, issued 28 February 1916 (stamped), viewed on Ancestry.com, citing "Passport Applications, January 2, 1906–March 31, 1925," NARA RG 59, microfilm publication M1490, 2740 rolls, roll 0295.

229 1855 New York State Census, First Ward, City of Utica, Oneida County, New York, p. 14, dwelling 77, family 119, John Thorn household, viewed on Ancestry.com, showing Edwin, age 16.

230 1855 New York State Census, First Ward, City of Utica, Oneida County, New York, p. 8, dwelling 58, family 74, Thomas Maynard household; viewed on Ancestry.com. 1860 U.S. Census, 7th Ward, Utica, Oneida County, New York, mortality schedule, p. 687 (stamped), line 13, Thomas Maynard, viewed on Ancestry.com. "Death of Mr. Thomas Maynard," *Utica Morning Herald and Daily Gazette*, 1 February 1860, p. 4. *The Utica City Directory for 1854–'55* (Utica, New York: S. A. & W. E. Richards, 1854), 96. Bildad Merrell Jr., *The Utica City Directory for 1849–50* (Utica, New York: D. Bennett, 1849), 94. Bagg, *Memorial History of Utica*, 279–280.

231 Bagg, *Memorial History of Utica*, 389.

232 Bagg, *Memorial History of Utica*, 389.

233 Bagg, *Memorial History of Utica*, 390.

234 *History of Oneida County*, 461.

235 *History of Oneida County*, 461.

236 Bagg, *Memorial History of Utica*, 31 (biographical section).

237 "Isaac Maynard," editorial, *Utica Morning Herald and Daily Gazette*, 24 February 1885, p. 4.

238 Bagg, *Memorial History of Utica*, 239.

239 "Isaac Maynard," editorial, *Utica Morning Herald and Daily Gazette*, 24 February 1885.

240 "Death of Isaac Maynard, *Utica Morning Herald and Daily Gazette*, 24 February 1885, p. 5.

241 "Isaac Maynard," editorial, *Utica Morning Herald and Daily Gazette*, 24 February 1885.

242 Bagg, *Memorial History of Utica*, 31 (biographical section). Edward Hungerford, *The Story of the Rome, Watertown and Ogdensburgh Railroad* (New York: Robert M. McBride, 1922), 163.

243 *The Utica City Directory for 1856–7* (Utica: W. W. Richards, 1856), 166.

244 *The Utica City Directory for 1859–60* (Utica: Joseph Arnott, 1859), 134, Isaac Maynard at 22 Whitesboro Street. *The Utica City Directory for 1860–1* (Utica: Joseph Arnott, 1860), 122, listing Isaac Maynard at 283 Genesee Street; also see 1860 U.S. Census, 7th Ward, City of Utica, Oneida County, New York, p. 85, family 681, dwelling 681, Isaac Maynard household, viewed on Ancestry.com. The house was brick (1865 New York State Census, 7th Ward, Utica, Oneida, New York, p. 1, dwelling 1, family 1, Isaac Maynard household, viewed on Ancestry.com).

245 1860 U.S. Census, Oneida County, New York, Isaac Maynard household. 1900 U.S. Census, Utica Town, Ward 7, Oneida, New York, enumeration district 60, sheet no. 1B, dwelling 11, family 11, John W. MacLean household, viewed on Ancestry.com. Will of Isaac Maynard, Oneida County.

246 From *Utica Illustrated* ([n.p.]: H. R. Page & Co., 1890), 9 vols., vol. 6.

247 From *Picturesque Utica* (Utica, New York: W. A. Semple, 1898), [7]; modern photo taken by the author, 2020.

248 Bagg, *Memorial History of Utica*, 597–598.

249 T. M. Halpin, *Halpin & Bailey's Chicago City Directory, for the Year 1861–2* (Chicago: Halpin & Bailey, 1861), 200. Isaac Maynard and John Thorn were listed in the same directory with a home address of "Utica, N.Y." (Isaac on p. 240; John on p. 345); James Kirk was listed as living at 285 Illinois Avenue in Chicago (p. 200).

250   Clarke, *Utica: For a Century and a Half,* 53–54.

251   "Mrs. John Thorn," *Utica Morning Herald and Daily Gazette,* 25 April 1891.

252   "Note from Col. Christian," *Utica Daily Observer,* 21 May 1861, p. 2. Clarke, *Utica: For a Century and a Half,* 54.

253   "Soldiers' Bazaar," *Oneida Weekly Herald,* 18 November 1862, p. 3.

254   "The National Freedman's Relief Association," *New York Times,* 14 May 1865, p. 3.

255   "Utica Freedman's Relief Association . . . " *Oneida Weekly Herald,* 3 February 1863, p. 3. A sacque is a short loose-fitting garment for women and children (*American Heritage Dictionary of the English Language,* 4th ed. [Boston and New York: Houghton Mifflin, 2000], 1529–30).

256   "The Freedm[a]n," *Utica Morning Herald and Daily Gazette,* 25 December 1863, p. 2.

257   Clarke, *Utica: for a Century and a Half,* 238.

258   Bagg, *Memorial History of Utica,* 32 (biographical section).

259   "Joshua Tavender, an Old and Respected Utican," *Utica Morning Herald and Daily Gazette,* 11 October 1895. Bagg, *Memorial History of Utica,* 239.

260   Passport application of Samuel R. Maynard, no. 22993, issued 29 October 1888, viewed on Ancestry.com, citing "Passport Applications, 1795–1905," NARA RG 59, microfilm publication M1372, 694 rolls, roll 315. Passport application of Richard Maynard, issued 17 May 1897 (stamped), viewed on Ancestry.com, citing "Passport Applications, 1795–1905," NARA RG 59, microfilm publication M1372, 694 rolls, roll 315. Forest Hill Cemetery Office, "Record of Interments, 1849 to 1901," Samuel Maynard, 239.

261   "Obituary: Nathan Ely Platt," *Chicago Tribune,* 7 January 1916, p. 17. Nathan's obituary implies that his partnership with Edwin began in 1861, but an article describing the firm's flour and wheat shipping interests claims that the firm was established in 1864 ("Commission House of Platt & Thorn," *Western Home Journal* [Lawrence, Kansas], 30 June 1877, p. 3). Edwin appears in the city directory for Chicago in 1865 (*Halpin's Eighth Annual Edition Chicago City Directory 1865–6* [Chicago: T. M. Halpin, 1865], 623).

262   *Bailey & Edwards' Chicago Directory 1868* (Chicago: Edwards, 1868), advertisement, 718.

263   "Commission House of Platt & Thorn," *Western Home Journal,* 30 June 1877. "Platt, Thorn & Maynard," classified advertisement, *Chicago Tribune,* 17 October 1871, p. 4 ("Platt, Thorn & Maynard, Dealers in Pig Iron, Nails, Flour, and Grain, 9 and 11 North Canal-st, Nails at $4.25 rates").

264   *Edwards' Sixteenth Annual Directory of the . . . City of Chicago for 1873* (Chicago: Richard Edwards, 1873), 768, listing for Platt, Thorn & Maynard: "(Nathan Platt, Edwin Thorn and Isaac M.[sic] Maynard), pig iron, 9 and 11 N. Canal." Edwin was listed on p. 933 of the same directory, residing at 144 Park Avenue, and Isaac on p. 660 with no address. In 1875, the partnership was dissolved, with Edwin continuing to focus on the pig iron and nail business, and Isaac working in the grain and provision commission business ("Dissolution," *Chicago Tribune,* 28 January 1875, p. 1).

265   "Death of Isaac Maynard," *Utica Morning Herald and Daily Gazette,* 24 February 1885.

266   Bagg, *Memorial History of Utica,* 597. Heath & Tavender was located on the north side of Whitesboro Street above the junction of Fayette Street, and near Wiley Street. Joshua later purchased Mr. Heath's interest and went into a partnership with his son Walter. The firm moved to North Genesee Street ("Joshua Tavender, an Old and Respected Utican," *Utica Morning Herald and Daily Gazette,* 11 October 1895).

267   Hungerford, *The Story of the Rome, Watertown and Ogdensburgh Railroad,* 162.

268   "Death of Isaac Maynard," *Utica Morning Herald and Daily Gazette,* 24 February 1885.

269   Thomas Hopper, *The Utica Water Works: A Paper Read before the Oneida Historical Society, January, 1886* (New York?, n.p. 1886), 6.

270   Hopper, *The Utica Water Works,* 14, 16–18.

271   Hopper, *The Utica Water Works,* 14, 16–18.

272   Forest Hill Cemetery Office, "Record of Interments, 1849 to 1901," Isaac Maynard, 239. "Death of
      Isaac Maynard," *Utica Morning Herald and Daily Gazette*, 24 February 1885.

273   Henry J. Cookingham, *History of Oneida County, New York From 1700 to the Present Time* (Chicago:
      S. J. Clarke Publishing Company, 1912), 2 vols., 1:276, 1:553. Bagg, *Memorial History of Utica*, 32
      (biographical section).

274   "Utica, Clinton and Binghamton Railroad," *Utica Morning Herald and Daily Gazette*, 19 January 1881,
      p. 2.

275   "Death of Isaac Maynard," *Utica Morning Herald and Daily Gazette*, 24 February 1885.

276   "Isaac Maynard," editorial, *Utica Morning Herald and Daily Gazette*, 24 February 1885.

277   "Isaac Maynard," *The New York Times*, 24 February 1885.

278   Oneida County Wills, Book E, p. 49, Will of Isaac Maynard, Oneida County Surrogate's Office,
      Utica, New York. The will was executed on 5 May 1878.

279   "Village Treat at Ruishton," *The Taunton Courier*, 21 July 1886.

280   "Seven Per Cent. Guaranteed," *The New York Times*, 15 April 1886, p. 5. Hungerford, *The Story of the
      Rome, Watertown, and Ogdensburg Railroad*, 169. The Utica & Black River Railroad had absorbed the
      Ogdensburg & Morristown and the Clayton & Theresa railroads just a month earlier ("Railroad
      Consolidated," *Buffalo* [New York] *Morning Express and Illustrated Buffalo Express*, 20 March 1886, p.
      5). "Utica and Black River," *Utica Morning Herald and Daily Gazette*, 16 April 1886, p. 4.

281   *The Utica City Directory for the Year 1890* . . . (Utica: L. C. Childs, 1890), 540. Edwin and Jennie also
      had no children.

282   "The Late Mr. John Thorn," *The Courier for Taunton and Western Counties*, 16 January 1895. "Death of
      Mrs. John Thorn," *Utica Daily Observer*, 24 April 1891, p. 5.

283   "Mrs. John Thorn," *Utica Morning Herald and Daily Gazette*, 25 April 1891. Minor additions to
      punctuation have been added for clarity.

284   "Mrs. John Thorn," *Utica Morning Herald and Daily Gazette*, 25 April 1891. Charles Wesley Brooks, *A
      Century of Missions in the Empire State* . . . (Philadelphia: American Baptist Publication Society, 1909),
      247.

285   Passenger manifest for the *Aurania,* arriving 12 September 1892, lines 406–8, Jno. Thorn, Edwin
      Thorn, and Mrs. Thorn, viewed on Ancestry.com, citing "Passenger and Crew Lists of Vessels
      Arriving at New York, New York, 1820–1897," NARA, RG 36, microfilm publication M237, 675
      rolls, roll 597.

286   "Death of John Thorn," *Utica Morning Herald and Daily Gazette*, 1 January 1895, p. 4.

287   "Death of Mr. Thorn," *The Courier for Taunton and Western Counties*, 9 January 1895.

288   "John Thorn's Generosity," *Watertown Daily Times*, 1 May 1895, p. 5.

289   Clarke, *Utica: For a Century and a Half,* 238.

290   Edwin died there in 1912 ("Sudden Death of Edwin Thorn," *Utica Herald-Dispatch*, 19 July 1912, p.
      3). Jennie eventually moved to Pasadena, California, where she died in 1928 ("Mrs. Edwin Thorn
      Dies in California," *Watertown* [New York] *Daily Standard,* 1 March 1928, p. 16).

291   "Death of Mrs. Isaac Maynard," *Utica Morning Herald and Daily Gazette*, 3 December 1896.

292   The surname DeForest has many variations in spelling, often varying within nuclear families and for
      the same individual on different records. Sometimes the name is written as two words, sometimes
      as one. DeForest, Deforest, deForest, De Forest, and de Forest, as well as versions employing a
      "double-r," are all common. The spelling of DeForest is used here unless a particular variation is
      specifically indicated.

293   Riverside Cemetery Office, "Internments [*sic*], 1855–1910," Joseph B. Hubbard, 107.

294   *Oswego City Directory . . . for 1888* (Oswego: Oliphant & Boyd, 1888), 258.

295   "Oswego," marriage notice for George DeForest and Sara C. North, *The Syracuse* [New York]
      Standard, 10 April 1885, p. 6.

296   1865 New York State Census, southern 4th Ward, City of Oswego, p. 45, dwelling 270, family 296, Charles North household, viewed on Ancestry.com. 1875 New York State Census, 8th Ward, Oswego, p. 35, dwelling 308, family 312, Charles North household, viewed on Ancestry.com.

297   Forest Hill Cemetery Office, "Record of Interments, 1927 to 1961," George DeForest, 90. "Death Removes George De Forest," *Utica Daily Press*, 7 October 1929, p. 3.

298   1860 U.S. Census, Woodbury, Litchfield County, Connecticut, p. 50 (penned), dwelling 423, family 4438, George DeForrest household. Also in the household was the Cady family: Lewis, 38, Mary J., 30, and their son John, an infant. Lewis was working as a butcher, in addition to Robert [Smith?], 71, a laborer. Neither the Cadys, nor Robert [Smith?] were of obvious immediate relation to the DeForests. 1870 U.S. Census, Woodbury, Litchfield County, Connecticut, p. 21, dwelling 202, family 209, George DeForest household, viewed on Ancestry.com.

299   "Woodbury," *Waterbury* [Connecticut] *Daily American*, 9 December 1870, p. [4]. Minor additions to punctuation have been added for clarity. Wesleyan Academy was sometimes referred to colloquially as "the Wilbraham Academy."

300   "Wesleyan Academy, Wilbraham, Mass.," classified ad, *Rutland* [Vermont] *Weekly Herald*, 28 August 1873, p. 8.

301   "Woodbury," *Waterbury Daily American*, 12 April 1871, p. [2]. Age at death calculated from dates of birth and death. Minor additions to punctuation have been added for clarity. See the DeForest Family section of Chapter Five.

302   "Woodbury," *Waterbury Daily American,* 30 October 1873, p. 1. Minor changes to punctuation and capitalization have been added for clarity.

303   Mary Ann DeForest declined administration of her husband's intestate estate, and George B. Lewis was appointed as young George's guardian (Guardianship Bond dated 3 May 1871, Estate of George DeForest, Woodbury Probate District, 1871, No. 1243, viewed on Ancestry.com, "Connecticut, Wills and Probate Records, 1609–1999," probate place: Hartford, Connecticut. The use of the middle initial "L." here is the only instance in which George Sr. was named with one. His son George used the middle initial "L" consistently). Mr. Lewis, apparently unrelated to the DeForests, had a long career in banking and trust estates ("Woodbury: George B. Lewis," *Newtown* [Connecticut] *Bee*, 18 October 1889, p. 1. According to the obituary, "No man among us in the last 100 years has been more widely trusted in fiduciary affairs." In addition to this qualification, in 1870, he also lived next door to George's aunt and uncle Lucy and David Bull, who were providing a home to George's grandfather, Marcus DeForest [1870 U.S. Census, Woodbury, p. 15, dwelling 149, family 153, David S. Bull household, viewed on Ancestry.com]).

304   *1875–'76 Benham's New Haven City Directory and Annual Advertiser* (New Haven: J. H. Benham, 1875), 135. By 1877, the name of the firm was J. N. Adam & Co. (*Benham's New Haven Directory: 1877* [New Haven, Connecticut: Price, Lee & Co., 1877], 77). Although there were many other DeForests in New Haven at the time, George does not seem to have garnered their support directly—at least by living with them. During the years that he worked in the city, he boarded with others who were of no obvious relation to him (*1875-'76: Benham's New Haven City Directory and Annual Advertiser*, 135; George was boarding at 38 Academy Street. *Benham's New Haven Directory: 1877*, 77; George was boarding at 17 Court Street. *Benham's New Haven Directory: 1878* (New Haven, Connecticut: Price, Lee & Co., 1878), 77-78; George was boarding at 91 Olive Street). The proprietor of Adam & Taylor, and later J. N. Adam & Co., was James Nobel Adam, who had come to the United States from Scotland in 1872, at first working for his brother in a dry goods store in Buffalo, New York. ("James Nobel Adam, Friend of Buffalo, Died This Morning," *Evening Times* [Buffalo, New York], 9 February 1912, p. 1; and "City Loses Foremost Citizen," p. 4.) According to his 1912 obituary, James Adam stayed in New Haven until 1881, when he left to return to Buffalo. He established a business there, retired in 1904, then devoted his energies to politics. He was mayor of Buffalo from 1905 to 1909. He died in 1912, "one of the most prominent citizens of Buffalo . . . and a strong favorite with the city at large." ("James Nobel Adam, Friend of Buffalo Died This Morning," and "City Loses Foremost Citizen," *Evening Times,* 9 February 1912).

305   *Benham's New Haven Directory: 1879* (New Haven, Connecticut: Price, Lee & Co., 1879), 78, where George would have been listed.

306   *Oswego City Directory for 1880* (Oswego: Oliphant & Pool, 1880), 108, 135, 242.

307   "Changes To Occur," *Oswego Daily Palladium*, 20 March 1894, p. 5.

308   *Oswego City Directory for 1880* (Oswego, New York: Oliphant & Pool, 1880), 145.

309   "Oswego Officials," *Oswego Palladium*, 1 April 1891, p. 6. *Oswego City Directory . . . for 1888*, 140, 258.

310   "Oswego Officials," *Oswego Palladium*, 1 April 1891.

311   "A Card Party," *Oswego Daily Palladium*, 14 December 1895, p. 5. "Donations Acknowledged," *Oswego Daily Palladium*, 4 June 1895, p. 5.

312   "Personal Mention," [Oswego] *Daily Palladium*, 30 September 1893, p. 5.

313   "Obituary: Charles North," *Oswego Daily Palladium*, 15 February 1892. Riverside Cemetery Office, "Internments [*sic*], Riverside Cemetery, 1855–1910," 146. Riverside Cemetery Office, "Interment Record B," interment record for Section T, Lot 10, "Charles North & Hubbard," 692. "Death Removes George De Forest," *Utica Daily Press*, 7 October 1929, 3.

314   M. M. Bagg, M.D., *Memorial History of Utica, N.Y. from Its Settlement to the Present Time* (Syracuse, New York: D. Mason, 1892), 353–56. T. Wood Clarke, *Utica: For a Century and a Half* (Utica: Widtman Press, 1952), 57–60.

315   From *Picturesque Utica* (Utica: W.A. Semple, 1898).

316   Clarke, *Utica for a Century and a Half*, 73. The shoe industry never recovered, however.

317   Clarke, *Utica for a Century and a Half*, 73, 75–76, 78, 80. The automobile came through Utica on 25 May 1899.

318   Clarke, *Utica for a Century and a Half*, 73, 57–60.

319   Clarke, *Utica for a Century and a Half*, 67.

320   *Utica City Directory 1896* (Utica: Utica Directory Publishing, 1896), 392. The directory lists George's middle initial as "E," and his address as "2 Comstock Place," which was the name of their brick building containing several residences and located on Plant Street (*Steber Directory of Utica, Oneida County, New York State, 1913* [Utica: Utica Directory Publishing, 1913], 153). *Insurance Co. Map [of] Utica, New York, including Deerfield and Deerfield Corners* (New York: Sanborn Map and Publishing Co., 1888), map, 31 pages, p. 26, viewed online at Library of Congress, www.loc.gov., "Sanborn Fire Insurance Map from Utica, Oneida County, New York." Author's visit, 2020.

321   "To Succeed John M. Crouse," *Utica Herald-Dispatch*, 1 August 1906, p. 3. Transactions of the New England Cotton Manufacturers' Association, No. 60, Annual Meeting (Waltham, Massachusetts: E. L. Barry, 1896), 17.

322   *Oswego City Directory for 1880* (Oswego, New York: Oliphant & Pool, 1880), 145.

323   "A new, beautiful, useful Gift-," display advertisement, *Chicago* [Illinois] *Sunday Tribune*, 10 November 1929, picture section, p. 12.

324   Peter Eisenstadt, *The Encyclopedia of New York State* (Syracuse, New York: Syracuse University Press, 2005), 1546. Carding is the "process of separating individual fibres, using a series of dividing and redividing steps, that causes many of the fibres to lie parallel to one another while also removing most of the remaining impurities" (*Encyclopedia Britannica*, online edition, www.britannica.com, "Carding: Textile Production").

325   Sonia G. Benson, *Development of the Industrial U.S. Almanac* (Detroit: Thomson Gale, 2006), 10. Kevin Hillstrom and Laurie Collier Hillstrom, eds., *Industrial Revolution in America: Textiles* (Santa Barbara, California: ABC-CLIO, 2006), 2, 10.

326   Benson, *Development of the Industrial U.S. Almanac*, 10. Hillstrom and Hillstrom, *Industrial Revolution in America: Textiles*, 4–5.

327   Henry J. Cookingham, *History of Oneida County, New York: from 1700 to the Present Time* (Chicago: S. J. Clarke Publishing Company, 1912), 2 vols., 1:434.

328   Hillstrom and Hillstrom, *Industrial Revolution in America: Textiles*, 12.

329   Eisenstadt, *The Encyclopedia of New York State*, 1546–47.

330   Clarke, *Utica: For a Century and a Half*, p. 47. Cookingham, *History of Oneida County*, 1:442.

331   "Our State Institutions—XXXIII: The Cotton and Woolen Mills in and Around Utica," *New York Times*, 11 May 1872, p. 1.

332   "Our State Institutions," *New York Times*, 11 May 1872.

333   "Death Removes George De Forest," *Utica Daily Press*, 7 October 1929, p. 3. "Geo. DeForest, Retired Mill Manager Dies," *Utica Observer-Dispatch*, 7 October 1929, p. 12. Cookingham, *History of Oneida County*, 1:442.

334   Forest Hill Cemetery Office, "Record of Interments, 1927 to 1961," John F. Maynard, 239. Passport application of John F. Maynard, 6 April 1922, issued 11 April 1922, #143397 (penned), viewed on Ancestry.com, citing "Passport Applications, 1795–1905," NARA RG 59, microfilm publication M1372, 694 rolls, roll 295. 1855 New York State Census, Utica, Oneida County, New York, p. 14, dwelling 78, family 120, Isaac Maynard household.

335   1855 New York State Census, Utica, Isaac Maynard household. 1855 New York State Census, Utica, p. 14, dwelling 79, families 121 and 122, John E. Bult and Joshua Tavender households, viewed on Ancestry.com.

336   In 1859, Isaac lived at 22 Whitesboro Street (*The Utica City Directory, for 1859–60* [Utica: Joseph Arnott, 1859], 134) and in 1860, at 283 Genesee (*The Utica City Directory, for 1860–1* [Utica: Joseph Arnott, 1860], 122). The house was brick (1865 New York State Census, 7th Ward, Utica, Oneida County, New York, p. 1, dwelling 1, family 1, Isaac Maynard household, viewed on Ancestry.com).

337   *Utica City Directory 1870* (Utica: John H. Francis, 1870), 182. Although he was treasurer of the railroad, the 1870 census shows Isaac's primary occupation as a wool dealer (1870 U.S. Census, Utica, Ward 7, Oneida County, New York, p. 1, dwelling 6, family 7, Isaac Maynard household).

338   Edward Hungerford, *The Story of the Rome, Watertown and Ogdensburgh Railroad* (New York: Robert M. McBride & Company, 1922), 162.

339   "Personal," *Utica Morning Herald and Daily Gazette*, 7 September 1876, p. 2.

340   *Biographical Directory of the American Congress 1774–1971; the Continental Congress September 5, 1774, to October 21, 1788; and the Congress of the United States from the First through the Ninety-first Congress March 4, 1789, to January 3, 1971, inclusive* (Washington, D.C.: United States Government Printing Office, 1971), 569.

341   From the collection of Maynard Kirk Davis.

342   "Hon. A. M. Beardsley Dead," *Rome* [New York] *Daily Sentinel*, 1 November 1905, p. 2.

343   "Hon. A. M. Beardsley Dead," *Rome Daily Sentinel*, 1 November 1905. Minor additions in punctuation have been added for clarity.

344   "Forest Hill Cemetery, Record of Interments, 1927 to 1961," John F. Maynard Jr., p. 239. See Maynard Family section of Chapter Five for a discussion of Arthur's birthdate.

345   Original letter in the possession of the author.

346   Edward Hungerford, *The Story of the Rome, Watertown and Ogdensburgh Railroad* (New York: Robert M. McBride, 1922), 165. "Utica and Black River," *Utica Morning Herald and Daily Gazette*, 16 April 1886.

347   *The Story of the Rome, Watertown and Ogdensburgh Railroad* (New York: Robert M. McBride, 1922), 162, 169. "Utica and Black River," *Utica Morning Herald and Daily Gazette*, 16 April 1886.

348   Passenger manifest for the R.M.S. *Aurania*, arriving 15 October 1888, passenger nos. 587–592, J. F. Maynard, Mrs. Maynard, Arthur Maynard, and J. F. Maynard Jr., viewed on Ancestry.com, citing "Passenger and Crew Lists of Vessels Arriving at New York, New York, 1820–1897," NARA RG 36, microfilm publication M237, 675 rolls, roll 526.

349 J. F. Maynard, "1st Book Diary: Diary for the year 1896–7," handwritten manuscript, from the collection of Holbrook R. Davis. J. F. Maynard, untitled journal, 17 May–22 August 1898, handwritten manuscript, from the collection of Holbrook R. Davis, [p. 1–27].

350 *Catalogue of Yale University, CXCVIII Year, 1897–98* (New Haven, Connecticut: Tuttle, Morehouse & Taylor, 1897), 384. *Catalogue of Yale University, 1898–99* (New Haven, Connecticut: Tuttle, Morehouse & Taylor Press, 1898), 156, 403.

351 New York Supreme Court, Appellate Division—Fourth Department, *Globe Woolen Company, Plaintiff-Respondent, against Utica Gas & Electric Company, Defendant-Appellant,* Case and Exceptions, #792 (inked), (Utica: Press of Thomas J. Griffiths, [1910]), testimony by John F. Maynard Sr., pp. 170–71.

352 Clarke, *Utica: For a Century and a Half,* 43–47.

353 New York Supreme Court, Globe Woolen Company, Plaintiff-Respondent, against Utica Gas & Electric Company, Defendant-Appellant, pp. 170–71.

354 Clarke, *Utica, For a Century and a Half,* 85–87.

355 "From $25.00 to $18.00 and $15.00," display advertisement, *Philadelphia* [Pennsylvania] *Inquirer,* 20 November 1894, p. 10.

356 "From $25.00 to $18.00 and $15.00," *Philadelphia* [Pennsylvania] *Inquirer,* 20 November 1894. "Woolens and Worsted Mfrs, Importers," classified ad, *Fall River* [Massachusetts] *Daily Evening News,* 6 February 1897, p. 55.

357 *Globe vs. Utica Gas & Electric,* testimony by John F. Maynard Sr., pp. 171–72. Worsted is a firm, tightly twisted, wool yarn (*The American Heritage Dictionary,* 4th ed. [Boston and New York: Houghton Mifflin, 2000], 1984).

358 *Bulletin of the National Association of Wool Manufacturers for 1895,* vol. XXV, (Boston: n.p. 1895), p. 4.

359 "To Succeed John M. Crouse, *Utica Herald-Dispatch,* 1 August 1906, p. 3. "Death Removes George De Forest," *Utica Daily Press,* 7 October 1929. *Globe Woolen Company vs. Utica Gas & Electric Company,* testimony by John F. Maynard Sr., pp. 170–71.

360 "To Succeed John M. Crouse, *Utica Herald-Dispatch,* 1 August 1906, p. 3. "Death Removes George De Forest," *Utica Daily Press,* 7 October 1929. See the Maynard Family section of Chapter Five.

361 "Death Removes George De Forest," *Utica Daily Press,* 7 October 1929, p. 3.

362 "J. Fred Maynard, 78, Claimed by Death at Summer Home," *Utica Observer-Dispatch,* 5 September 1929, p. 27.

363 "Daughters of the Revolution," *Rome Daily Sentinel,* 5 June 1896, p. 4.

364 "The Bachelors Danced," *Utica Observer,* 30 December 1902, p. 4.

365 "Fete a Success," *Utica Herald-Dispatch,* 18 July 1902, p. 4. Minor additions to punctuation in the quotation have been added for clarity.

366 "Golf Match Drew Crowd," *Utica Journal,* 12 June 1904, p. 2.

367 Edwin F. Bacon, Ph. B., *Otsego County, New York: Geographical and Historical* (Oneonta, New York: Oneonta Herald, 1902), 72–74.

368 "Automobiling . . . ," *Brooklyn* [New York] *Life,* 28 July 1906, p. 11, using an alternative spelling of DeForest.

369 From the Collection of Holbrook R. Davis.

370 "The June Weddings," *Utica Observer,* 20 June 1907, p. 8.

371 See the Maynard Family section of Chapter Five.

372 Passport application of John F. Maynard [Sr.], no. 19023, issued 8 June 1888, viewed on Ancestry.com, citing "Passport Applications, 1795–1905," NARA RG 59, microfilm publication M1372, 694 rolls, roll 307, mentioning "nurse" Mary A. Murphy. Passenger manifest for the R.M.S. *Aurania,* arriving 15 October 1888, passenger nos. 587–593, J. F. Maynard, Mrs. Maynard, Arthur Maynard, J. F. Maynard Jr., Miss Maynard, Miss Murphy ("governess"), and Miss Williams, viewed on Ancestry.com,

citing *Passenger and Crew Lists of Vessels Arriving at New York, New York, 1820–1897*, NARA RG 36, microfilm publication M237, 675 rolls, roll 526. J. F. Maynard, "1st Book Diary: Diary for the year 1896–7," handwritten manuscript, from the collection of Holbrook R. Davis, p. 47. Page numbers, some perhaps added at a later time, are indicated through page 53; subsequent page numbers, indicated in brackets, are the author's.

373 Passenger manifest for the R.M.S. *Aurania*, J. F. Maynard, Mrs. Maynard, Arthur Maynard, and J. F. Maynard Jr.

374 Maynard, "1st Book Diary 1896–7." John F. Maynard, "2nd Book Diary: Diary for the year 1897," handwritten manuscript, from the collection of Holbrook R. Davis.

375 Maynard, "1st Book Diary: Diary for the year 1896–7," p. 1.

376 This was likely another boat or an error. John's 2 March 1897 entry, made after several months of travel on land in Europe, describes traveling aboard the *Columbia* and having the "same stateroom that we had coming over. No. 29" (Maynard, "1st Book Diary 1896–7," p. 106), and in his 28 March entry, he writes, "Just 4 months ago today we sailed out of New York harbor on the 'Columbia'" (Maynard, "2nd Book Diary: Diary for the year 1897," pp. [5–6]. Page numbers are the author's). In addition, according to the *Brooklyn Daily Eagle*, the famous publisher Joseph Pulitzer was aboard the boat when the Maynards made their voyage from New York ("Sailed by the Columbia," *Brooklyn Daily Eagle*, 28 November 1896, p. 1), which was noted in John's diary on 30 November (Maynard, "1st Book Diary 1896–7," p. 3).

377 Maynard, "1st Book Diary 1896–7," p. 1. "Uncle Sam" was probably J. Fred's brother, Samuel Richard Maynard.

378 Photograph by the author.

379 J. Kent Layton, *Transatlantic Liners* (Oxford, England: Shire Publications, 2012), online version (Shire Book 660), 17.

380 *Across the Atlantic: Hamburg-American Line* (n.l.: Wohlfeld, 1900), promotional pamphlet, 67–68. Layton, *Transatlantic Liners*, 50.

381 Cabin number from Maynard, "1st Book Diary 1896–7," p. 106. *Across the Atlantic*, 16, 67–68.

382 *Across the Atlantic*, 64–65.

383 *Across the Atlantic*, 39.

384 Maynard, "1st Book Diary 1896–7," p. 12.

385 Maynard, "1st Book Diary 1896–7," p. 14.

386 Maynard, "1st Book Diary 1896–7," pp. 13, 17–18.

387 Maynard, "1st Book Diary 1896–7," pp. 17–53.

388 Maynard, "1st Book Diary 1896–7," pp. 26, 48: "I studied in the morning as usual." Presumably, study took place on "regular" school days, as John noted on New Year's Day "we had breakfast later than usual, because Art and I don't have to study" (Maynard, "1st Book Diary 1896–7," p. 37).

389 Maynard, "1st Book Diary 1896–7," pp. 32, 34.

390 Maynard, "1st Book Diary 1896–7," pp. 42, [55]. See the Maynard Family section of Chapter Five. After Ogden Backus's death in 1906, Hattie married John Waters McLean's brother, Thomas Chalmers McLean. Neither Grace nor Hattie had children. Domino whist is a domino game for four players (*Britannica* online encyclopedia, www.britannica.com, "Domino whist").

391 Maynard, "1st Book Diary 1896–7," pp. 9, 14, [55–60], [66–67], [72], [81–99], [108].

392 Maynard, "1st Book Diary 1896–7," p. [121].

393 Maynard, "2nd Book Diary 1896–7," pp. [15–17].

394 Maynard, "2nd Book Diary 1896–7," p. [21].

395 Maynard, "2nd Book Diary 1896–7," pp. [27–44], [52–64], [69].

396 Maynard, "2nd Book Diary 1896–7," p. [93], [99].

397   Maynard, "1st Book Diary 1896–7," pp. [103], [106]. They presumably kept their plans to return
       on the *Etruria,* which arrived in New York 4 September. "Ocean Steamers," *Buffalo* [New York]
       Commercial, 4 September 1897. "*Etruria* Still a Flier," *New York Times,* 8 August 1897, p. 10. Maynard,
       "2nd Book Diary 1897," p. [93], in which John wrote that rooms had been purchased for the passage
       home aboard the *Etruria,* and p. 121, in which John commented on the arrival of the *Etruria* in
       Queenstown, Ireland, that evening. In his 22 August entry, John indicated that there were six days
       left of the trip.

398   J. F. Maynard, untitled journal, 17 May–22 August 1898, handwritten manuscript, from the collection
       of Holbrook R. Davis, unpaginated. Page numbers, indicated in brackets, are the author's. p. [1],
       [4–15], [19–27].

399   J. F. Maynard, untitled journal, 17 May–22 August 1898, pp. [28–29].

400   "Across the Atlantic: Hamburg-American Line," promotional pamphlet, (n.l.: Wohlfeld, 1900), 29.

401   J. F. Maynard, untitled journal, 17 May–22 August 1898, p. [27].

402   J. F. Maynard, untitled journal, 17 May–22 August 1898, pp. [10], [24], [41].

403   J. F. Maynard, untitled journal, 17 May–22 August 1898, pp. [37–40].

404   Passenger List for the *Auguste-Victoria,* departing Hamburg, Germany 25 August 1898, passenger
       nos. 131–134, J. F. Maynard (age 47), J. Maynard, Arthur B. Maynard, and J. F. Maynard (age 13),
       viewed on Ancestry.com, citing Staatsarchiv Hamburg, Hamburg, Germany, volume no. 373–7 I,VIII
       (Immigration Office), microfilm no. K-1758, p. 687. "Steamer Movements," *Democrat and Chronicle*
       [Rochester, New York], 3 September 1898, p. 5.

405   "Returned Home," *Utica Sunday Journal,* 30 December 1900, p. 11. *A Handbook of The Best Private
       Schools of the United States and Canada* (Boston, Massachusetts: Porter E. Sargent, 1915), 40–41.

406   Pomfret School gradebook for 1900–1901, p. 209, and gradebook for 1901–1902, p. 9, both courtesy
       of Pomfret School Archives. Walter Hinchman, Pomfret School Archivist, "John Frederick Maynard—
       Pomfret 1902," email to the author, dated 24 August 2020.

407   William B. Boulton, "1894–1903," in *The Pomfret Years: A collection of reminscences in commemoration of
       Pomfret School's 75th anniversary* (Pomfret, Connecticut: Pomfret School [1970]), unpaginated.

408   Boulton, "1894–1903," *The Pomfret Years.*

409   "Social Happenings," *Utica Sunday Journal,* 29 December 1901, p. 11.

410   From the collection of Maynard Kirk Davis.

411   "Social Happenings," *Utica Sunday Journal,* 29 December 1901, p. 11.

412   "Social Happenings," *Utica Sunday Journal,* 28 December 1902, p. 11.

413   Mrs. Sara B. Maxwell, *Manners and Customs of To-Day* (Des Moines, Iowa: Cline, 1890), 421, 383.

414   Mrs. Burton Kingsland, *Etiquette for All Occasions* (New York: Doubleday, Page, 1901), 174–179, 183.

415   "Social Happenings," *Utica Journal,* 18 December 1904, p. 8.

416   "J. F. Maynard Rites Today," *Utica Daily Press,* 24 November 1945, p. 6. Yale University, *Directory of
       Living Graduates of Yale University, Issue of 1912* (New Haven: The University, 1912), p. 198. Arthur
       graduated in the class of 1900.

417   *Catalogue of Yale University, 1902–1903* (New Haven: Tuttle, Morehouse & Taylor, 1902), 604, 631.
       Yale University, *The Yale Banner,* December 1905, 64 ([New Haven, Connecticut]: The University,
       1905), 306. William McK. Barber, *Five Year Record: Class of Nineteen Hundred and Five, Sheffield Scientific
       School, Yale University* (New Haven, Connecticut: Tuttle, Morehouse & Taylor, 1910), 92.

418   *Utica City Directory 1896* (Utica: Utica Directory Publishing, 1896), 392.

419   Anne Gibson Moffett, "Anne's Book," bound typescript, 1980, unpaginated, Oneida Square section,
       author's collection.

420   Moffett, "Anne's Book," Oneida Square section. "General Social Events," *Utica Sunday Tribune,* 25
       December 1898. Margaret's name is spelled in the variant "Marguerite" here. "Who Is My Neighbor?"
       Utica Daily Press, 18 December 1899, p. 3. 1900 U.S. Census, Utica, enumeration district no. 76, sheet

no. 5, dwelling nos. 76 (crossed out)/75 (corrected); and 77 (crossed out), 76 (corrected); family nos. 102 (crossed out), 101 (corrected); and 103 (crossed out), 102 (corrected); George DeForrest and Hattie Chamberlain households, showing the DeForests at 11 Plant Street and the Chamberlains at 9 Plant Street. Priscilla's name appears as "Percetta" here, owing to the inversion of the second and third letters of her name and the erroneous crossing of the double "Ls" to appear as double "Ts."

421   "An Enjoyable Recital," *Utica Sunday Journal*, 26 March 1899, p. 16.

422   "Summer Play Grounds for Children," *Utica Daily Press*, 28 May 1900, p. 5. "Vacation Schools," *Utica Herald-Dispatch*, 25 May 1900, p. 5. "The New Century Club," *Utica Morning Herald*, 6 September 1900.

423   Kingsland, *Etiquette for All Occasions,* 122.

424   Maxwell, *Manners and Customs of To-Day*, 182.

425   "Social Happenings," *Utica Journal*, 8 January 1905, p. 8.

426   The Baldwin School, *The Baldwin Annual*, 1906 (Bryn Mawr, Pennsylvania: Baldwin School, 1906), courtesy of the Baldwin School Archives. The name of the school changed from "Miss Baldwin's School" to "The Baldwin School" in Mary's graduation year of 1906 ("Baldwin," Mission and History, online at www.baldwinschool.org/about/mission-and-history).

427   Courtesy of the Baldwin School, Bryn Mawr, Pennsylvania.

428   "Baldwin," Mission and History. "The Baldwin School for Girls," classified ad, *The Churchman*, 49, 24 April 1909, p. 582.

429   "Seminary Girls Taking Holiday," unsourced newspaper clipping, collection of Holbrook R. Davis.

430   Maxwell, *Manners and Customs of To-Day*, 348–349.

431   From the collection of Holbrook R. Davis.

432   Maxwell, *Manners and Customs of To-Day*, 348–349.

433   Kingsland, *Etiquette for All Occasions*, 85, 99.

434   Kingsland, *Etiquette for All Occasions*, 85, 87, 95–97, 99.

435   "Personals," *Utica Herald-Dispatch*, 31 December 1906, p. 3.

436   "Society Wedding at Christ Church," *Utica Herald-Dispatch*, 25 June 1907, p. 3.

437   *Steber Directory of Utica, Oneida County, New York State, 1908* (Utica: Utica Directory Publishing, 1908), 562. "The June Weddings," *Utica Observer*, 20 June 1907, p. 8.

438   *Steber Directory of Utica, 1911*, 562. "J. F. Maynard Rites Today," *Utica Daily Press*, 24 November 1945.

439   *Steber Directory of Utica, County of Oneida, State of New York, 1918* (Utica: Utica Directory Publishing, 1918), 602, entry for Maynard & Woodward, Inc.

440   New York Supreme Court, Appellate Division—Fourth Department, *Globe Woolen Company, Plaintiff-Respondent, against Utica Gas & Electric Company, Defendant-Appellant,* Case and Exceptions, #792 (inked) (Utica: Press of Thomas J. Griffiths, [1910]), testimony by John F. Maynard Sr., 171.

441   "Wedded in Ohio," *Utica Observer*, 25 September 1909, p. 7.

442   Maxwell, *Manners and Customs of To-Day*, 262–263.

443   Passenger List for the S.S. *Shawnee*, arriving 14 February 1929, p. 13, lines 9–12; John F. Maynard Jr., Mary De F. Maynard, Mary Louise Maynard, and George De F. Maynard; viewed on Ancestry.com, citing NARA RG 85, microfilm publication A3621, "U.S. Citizen Passenger Lists of Vessels Arriving at Miami, Florida, 1899–1948," roll 8, listing birthdates for four Maynard passengers.

444   From the collection of Maynard Kirk Davis.

445   T. Wood Clarke, *Utica: For a Century and a Half* (Utica, New York: Widtman, 1952), 93. "Callan Law Registration," [New York, New York] *Evening Post*, 8 September 1910, p. 7.

446   *Cycle and Automobile Trade Journal*, vol. X, no. 4 (1 October 1905): 66B.

447   Clarke, *Utica, For a Century and a Half*, 103. The plane had been scheduled to make a landing in Utica but got lost *en route*.

448 From the collection of Maynard Kirk Davis.

449 Clarke, *Utica, For a Century and a Half,* 114.

450 *Steber Directory of Utica, County of Oneida, State of New York, 1918* (Utica: Utica Directory Publishing, 1918), 415, 602. Clarke, *Utica, For a Century and a Half,* 111.

451 "Epidemic Still Serious in Utica," *Utica Herald-Dispatch,* 21 October 1918, p. 2.

452 Moffett, "Anne's Book," unpaginated, "The First Flu Epidemic."

453 *Proceedings of the Common Council 1918, City of Utica, N.Y.* (Utica: Dodge-Graphic Press, [1918]), 158.

454 *Proceedings of the Common Council 1918, City of Utica,* 4–6, 8–9.

455 *Proceedings of the Common Council 1918, City of Utica,* 158.

456 "Epidemic Still Serious in Utica," *Utica Herald-Dispatch,* 21 October 1918. "Italians Help in Fighting Epidemic," *Utica Herald-Dispatch,* 21 October 1918, p. 2. Moffett, "Anne's Book," unpaginated, "The First Flu Epidemic."

457 Common Council of Utica, *Official Proceedings [1918],* 158.

458 "Caroline Shultas Crouse," *Hartford* [Connecticut] *Courant,* 6 January 1913, p. 9. "Sweet Young Life Closed," *Utica Observer,* 4 January 1913, p. 8. She was a student at Westover School in Connecticut.

459 "Roadmen Scout Theory Blaming Engineer Doyle," [Albany, New York] *Argus,* 11 June 1920, p. 1.

460 "Uticans Die in Wreck on Central!: Family of N. M. Crouse Meet Terrible Death in Wreck of Pullman Car," *Utica Herald-Dispatch,* 9 June 1920, pp. 1, 8. Initial reports featured in other newspapers contained incorrect information concerning the death of Nellis's children, including one by the *Ithaca* [New York] *Journal* which erroneously listed a 20-month-old female named Marion Crouse among the dead ("Eleven Are Killed, Many Injured When Central Engineer Runs by Warning Signals at Schenectady," *Ithaca* [New York] *Journal,* 9 June 1920, p. 1). The gravestone inscriptions of the Crouse boys confirm their deaths (Photograph of gravestone at FindaGrave.com, memorial #156440423 and #156440579, Daniel Nellis Crouse and Watson Bowne Crouse, Forest Hill Cemetery. The boys share a stone).

461 "Family of N. M. Crouse Meet Terrible Death," *Utica Herald-Dispatch* 9 June 1920. Baptism of Helen Boune [*sic*] Crouse, born 11 June 1920, Baptisms, St. Peter's Church, New York, New York (1920), p. 153, viewed on Ancestry.com, "Episcopal Diocese of New York Church Records, 1767–1970."

462 Clarke, *Utica, for a Century and a Half,* 125–130.

463 Memorial Service program, Sarah Maynard Davis, St. Peter's Episcopal Church, Osterville, Mass., 1 June 2016, author's files.

464 From the collection of Maynard Kirk Davis.

465 U.S. Senate, Seventieth Congress, First Session, *Cotton Prices: Hearings before a Subcommittee of the Committee on Agriculture and Forestry . . . Pursuant to S. Res. 142, A Resolution to Investigate the Recent Decline in Cotton Prices* (Washington, D.C.: United States Government Printing Office, 1928), 878. Clarke, *Utica, for a Century and a Half,* 125.

466 Kevin Hillstrom and Laurie Collier Hillstrom, *Industrial Revolution in America: Textiles* (Santa Barbara, California: ABC-CLIO, 2006), 204.

467 Alexander R. Thomas, *In Gotham's Shadow: Globalization and Community Change in Central New York* (Albany, New York: State University of New York Press, 2003), 39. Hillstrom and Hillstrom, *Industrial Revolution in America: Textiles,* 249.

468 Hillstrom and Hillstrom, *Industrial Revolution in America: Textiles,* 249.

469 Clarke, *Utica, For a Century and a Half,* 102.

470 "Death Removes George De Forest," *Utica Daily Press,* 7 October 1929, p. 3.

471 "Death Removes George De Forest," *Utica Daily Press,* 7 October 1929, p. 3. "Geo. DeForest, Retired Mill Manager," *The Utica Observer-Dispatch,* 7 October 1929, p. 12.

472 "J. Fred Maynard, 78, Claimed by Death at Summer Home," *Utica Observer-Dispatch,* 5 September 1929, p. 27.

473 "Faxton Trustees Hear Report on Plans for Dance," *Utica Observer-Dispatch*, 6 January 1927, p. 25. "Anti-Suffrage Women Convene Here Today," *Washington* [D.C.] *Herald*, 7 December 1916, p. 3.

474 Steven M. Beuchler, *Women's Movements in the United States: Woman Suffrage, Equal Rights, and Beyond* (New Brunswick, New Jersey: Rutgers University Press, 1990), 179.

475 From the collection of Holbrook R. Davis.

476 "Anti-Suffragists at Card Party," *Rome Daily Sentinel*, 31 January 1917, p. 2.

477 Passport application of John F. Maynard, 6 April 1922, issued 11 April 1922, #143397 (penned), viewed on Ancestry.com, citing "Passport Applications, 1795–1905," NARA RG 59, microfilm publication M1372, 694 rolls, roll 295.

478 Passport application, John F. Maynard, 6 April 1922. Holbrook R. Davis, telephone conversation with the author, 6 August 2020.

479 From the collection of Holbrook R. Davis.

480 From the collection of Maynard Kirk Davis.

481 From the collection of Maynard Kirk Davis.

482 "Golf Links at Ormond Busy as Arrivals Fill Hotels at the Beach," *New York* [New York] *Tribune*, 9 February 1919, p. 7. Various letters to George DeForest, dated 1924–1925, "Resorts & Travel" folder, ref. no. II UCRA MM 5.2-4, George DeForest Papers, Utica College Library, Utica, New York.

483 Letter to George F. Murray from George DeForest, dated 6 February 1925, "Clubs," folder, ref. no. II UCRAM 6.3, George DeForest Papers.

484 Letter to George F. Murray from George DeForest, dated 6 February 1925. Receipt from Frederic B. Weed of Packard Motor Cars & Trucks to Mr. Geo. DeForest, dated 7 December 1923 and letter from H. B. Vigneron of Automobile Mutual Insurance Company of America to Mr. George DeForest, dated 24 December 1923, "Automobile" folder, George DeForest Papers Utica College Library, describing the car as Mrs. Sarah N. DeForest's.

485 Courtesy of the National Automotive History Collection, Detroit Public Library.

486 "J. Fred Maynard, 78, Claimed by Death at Summer Home," *Utica Observer-Dispatch*, 5 September 1929. Letter from John A. McGregor to Mr. George DeForest, dated 26 July 1923 (and other similar letters addressed to George at Eastern Point), manila folder, George DeForest papers, Utica College Library, Utica. Preservation Connecticut, Local Historic District and Property Commissions in Connecticut, Eastern Point Historic District, online at http://lhdct.org/district/eastern-point -historic-district, accessed 20 August 2020.

487 "Obituary: Mrs. George De Forest, *Oswego Palladium-Times*, 21 November 1927.

488 Forest Hill Cemetery Office, Utica, "Record of Interments, 1927 to 1961," p. 239.

489 "J. Fred Maynard, 78, Claimed by Death at Summer Home," *Utica Observer-Dispatch*, 5 September 1929, p. 27.

490 "J. Fred Maynard, 78, Claimed by Death at Summer Home," *Utica Observer-Dispatch*, 5 September 1929.

491 "Death Removes George De Forest," *Utica Daily Press*, 7 October 1929.

492 To add to the toll, earlier that summer, John's uncle Isaac suffered the loss of his wife, Margaret Field Maynard, who died in Utica on 7 August (Forest Hill Cemetery, Utica, New York, Record of Interments, 1849 to 1901, 239.). Isaac, Margaret, and their son Richard had joined the Maynards briefly during their European tour in 1897.

493 "Achievement and Outlook," display advertisement, *Utica Observer-Dispatch*, 6 November 1929, p. 13.

494 "Mrs. B. M. Crouse Missing from Home; Offer $500 Reward," *Utica Observer-Dispatch*, 16 November 1929, p. 1.

495 "Kin Confident Local Woman Is Still Alive," *Utica Observer-Dispatch*, 11 December 1929.

496 "Kin Confident Local Woman Is Still Alive," *Utica Observer-Dispatch*, 11 December 1929.

497   "Kin Confident Local Woman Is Still Alive," *Utica Observer-Dispatch*, 11 December 1929. "Notes Written By Mrs. Crouse Offer Problem," *Utica Observer-Dispatch*, 26 November 1929, pp. 1, 21.

498   "Find Body of Long Missing Mrs. Crouse," *Hartford* [Connecticut] *Courant,* 16 March 1930, p. 1.

499   "Find Body of Long Missing Mrs. Crouse," *Hartford* [Connecticut] *Courant,* 16 March 1930, p. 1.

500   "Herman W. Hamilton, Plaintiff-Respondent, against Utica Products, Inc., Defendant-Appellant," #318 (stamped), in *State of New York Supreme Court, Appellate Division—Fourth Department, Record on Appeal,* (Batavia, New York: Batavia Times Law Printers, [1928]), 108. The original suit and subsequent appeal was made regarding a dispute over payment to an employee of Utica Products, Inc. who had been engaged under a verbal agreement.

501   "Herman W. Hamilton vs. Utica Products," 130.

502   "Herman W. Hamilton vs. Utica Products," 129.

503   "J. F. Maynard Rites Today," *Utica Daily Press,* 24 November 1945, p. 6.

504   *Steber's Utica City Directory, 1938* (Utica: R. L. Polk, 1938), 339.

505   "Committee of 100 Has Large Party at Miami Beach," *New York Sun*, 25 February 1931, p. 28.

506   "The marriage of . . . ," *Utica Observer-Dispatch*, 5 May 1935, Section III (C), p. 1.

507   "George Maynard," *Utica Observer-Dispatch,* 15 November 1963, p. 24.

508   "George Maynard," *Utica Observer-Dispatch,* 15 November 1963, p. 24. *Steber's Utica City Directory, 1938*, 339.

509   "Sarah Maynard to Become Bride," *New York Times*, 4 November 1945, p. 40.

510   "Vassar Alumna Bride of H. R. Davis," *Poughkeepsie* [New York] *Journal*, 26 March 1946, p. 8.

511   From the collection of Holbrook R. Davis.

512   Forest Hill Cemetery Office, Utica, "Record of Interments, 1927 to 1961," p. 239. Sally's engagement was announced on 4 November ("Sarah Maynard to Become Bride," *New York Times*, 4 November 1945, p. 40).

513   "John F. Maynard Jr.," *New York Times*, 24 November 1945. "J. F. Maynard Rites Today," *Utica Daily Press,* 24 November 1945.

514   "Announcements," [Utica] *Daily Press,* 8 July 1959, p. 16.

515   Unlike George, Lee spelled his surname as two words. Several uncited histories and genealogies provide the probable connections between Lee De Forest and David DeForest, through Lee's father, Henry Swift[7] DeForest (*Lee[6], Gideon[5], Joseph[4], Samuel[3], David[2], Isaac[1]*). See Samuel Orcutt, *A History of the Old Town of Stratford and the City of Bridgeport, Connecticut,* 2 vols. (n.l.: Fairfield County Historical Society, 1886), 2:1191–3; *A Walloon Family in America: Lockwood de Forest and his Forbears 1500– 1848,* 2 vols. (Boston and New York: Houghton Mifflin Company, 1914), 2:298–299; and William Cothren, *History of Ancient Woodbury, Connecticut, from the First Indian Deed in 1659 to 1872, Including the Present Towns of Washington, Southbury, Bethlehem, Roxbury, and a part of Oxford and Middlebury,* 2 vols. (Woodbury, Connecticut: the author, 1872), 2:1491.

516   "Dr. Lee DeForest Dies in California," *Miami* [Florida] *Herald Sun*, 2 July 1961, p. 64.

517   "Lee De Forest, 87, Radio Pioneer, Dies," *New York Times*, 2 July 1961, p. 1.

518   Judith Schiff, "The man who invented radio," *Yale Alumni Magazine*, vol. 72, no. 2 (Nov/Dec 2008), unpaginated version online at https://yalealumnimagazine.com/articles/2285-the-man-who -invented-radio, viewed 21 July 2020.

519   Samuel Lubell, "Magnificent Failure," *Saturday Evening Post*, vol. 214, no. 29, 17 January 1942, 75. "Lee De Forest, 87, Radio Pioneer, Dies," *New York Times*, 2 July 1961.

520   Lubell, "Magnificent Failure," *Saturday Evening Post*, 17 January 1942, 76.

521   "Lee De Forest, 87, Radio Pioneer, Dies," *New York Times*, 2 July 1961.

522   Lubell, "Magnificent Failure," *Saturday Evening Post*, 17 January 1942, p. 78. For a biography of David, see J. W. De Forest, *The deForests of Avesnes (and of New Netherland): A Hugenot Thread in American Colonial History, 1494 to the Present Time, with Three Heraldic Illustrations* (New Haven, Connecticut:

Tuttle, Morehouse & Taylor, 1900), 112–60. Yale University, *Yale Endowments: A Description of the Various Gifts and Bequests Establishing Permanent University Funds* (New Haven, Connecticut: The University, 1917), 88. David Curtis[5] DeForest (*Benjamin*[4-3], *David*[2], *Isaac*[1]), Lee De Forest, and George DeForest were all descendants of David[2] (De Forest, *The deForests of Avesnes*, p. 233–34, and Note 524).

523　Yale University, *Yale Endowments,* 88. Scholarship documentation uses the "DeForest" spelling of the surname.

524　"Lee De Forest, 87, Radio Pioneer, Dies," *New York Times*, 2 July 1961.

525　Lubell, "Magnificent Failure," *Saturday Evening Post*, 17 January 1942, p. 78.

526　Beecher M. Crouse was a member of Yale's Class of 1893 (Noah H. Swayne 2d, *Twenty-Five Year Record: Class of Ninety-Three, Yale College* [New Haven, Connecticut: Tuttle, Morehouse & Taylor, 1918], 185). "Lee De Forest, 87, Radio Pioneer, Dies," *New York Times*, 2 July 1961.

527　Yale University, *Directory of Living Graduates of Yale University*, Issue of 1912 (New Haven: The University, 1912), 198.

528　"Lee De Forest, 87, Radio Pioneer, Dies," *New York Times*, 2 July 1961.

529　"Guglielmo Marconi," in "World of Invention: Biography," 2006, *Gale in Context*, https://link.gale .com/apps/doc/K1647000240/BIC?u=mlin_c_worfree&sid=BIC&xid=7b7ac96a, viewed 23 July 2020.

530　Clarke, *Utica: For a Century and a Half*, 49.

531　"Lee De Forest, 87, Radio Pioneer, Dies," *New York Times*, 2 July 1961.

532　Alamy stock photo.

533　"Lee De Forest, 87, Radio Pioneer, Dies," *New York Times*, 2 July 1961.

534　"Lee De Forest, 87, Radio Pioneer, Dies," *New York Times*, 2 July 1961. Schiff, "The man who invented radio," *Yale Alumni Magazine*, Nov/Dec 2008. "Out of De Forest and Onto the Air Came Music," *New York Times*, 14 January 1990, 219. "Dr. Lee DeForest [*sic*] Dies in California," *Miami* [Florida] *Herald Sun*, 2 July 1961.

535　"Lee De Forest, 87, Radio Pioneer, Dies," *New York Times*, 2 July 1961. Schiff, "The man who invented radio," *Yale Alumni Magazine*, Nov/Dec 2008. "Dr. Lee DeForest [*sic*] Dies in California," *Miami* [Florida] *Herald Sun*, 2 July 1961.

536　"Lee De Forest, 87, Radio Pioneer, Dies," *New York Times*, 2 July 1961.

537　"Dr. Lee DeForest [*sic*] Dies in California," *Miami* [Florida] *Herald Sun*, 2 July 1961, p. 64. "Lee De Forest, 87, Radio Pioneer, Dies," *New York Times*, 2 July 1961.

538　"Lee De Forest, 87, Radio Pioneer, Dies," *New York Times*, 2 July 1961.

539　"Lee De Forest, 87, Radio Pioneer, Dies," *New York Times*, 2 July 1961. Samuel Lubell, "Magnificent Failure," *Saturday Evening Post*, vol. 214, no. 31 (31 January 1942): 48.

540　"Lee De Forest, 87, Radio Pioneer, Dies," *New York Times*, 2 July 1961.

541　"Lee De Forest, 87, Radio Pioneer, Dies," *New York Times*, 2 July 1961. Samuel Lubell, "Magnificent Failure," *Saturday Evening Post*, vol. 214, nos. 29, 30, and 31 (17, 24, and 31 January 1942). Schiff, "The man who invented radio," *Yale Alumni Magazine*, Nov/Dec 2008. *This Is Your Life: Dr. Lee DeForest* [*sic*]," episode aired 22 May 1957, *Internet Movie Database* [IMDb], https://www.imdb.com/title /tt11859828/, viewed 23 July 2020.

542　"Dr. Lee DeForest [*sic*] Dies in California," *Miami* [Florida] *Herald Sun*, 2 July 1961.

543　Samuel Lubell, "Magnificent Failure," *Saturday Evening Post*, 31 January 1942, p. 48.

544　"Lee De Forest, 87, Radio Pioneer, Dies," *New York Times*, 2 July 1961.

545　"Lee De Forest," *New York Times,* 4 July 1961, p. 18.

546　Marriage Settlement between Joseph and William North, and Ann Elizabeth and Margaret Whitestone; Dublin, Ireland, Registry of Deeds, Book 566, p. 410, Item 384183, FHL Film #007,905,952, "Transcripts of memorials of deeds, conveyances and wills," Deeds, vols. 565–566

1804–1805. The agreement, dated 5 October 1804, concerns the impending marriage of William North and Margaret Whitestone.

547   Dublin, Ireland, Registry of Deeds, Book 21, No. 83, Deed, "Pilkington, etc." dated 21 October 1839; FHL Film #008,094,462, "Transcripts of memorials of deeds, conveyances and wills," Deeds, etc., vols. 21–24 1839, describing William's wife as a widow.

548   North-Whitestone Marriage Settlement, 5 October 1804. The document was witnessed 19 May 1805, which may have been their actual wedding date or closer to it. Letter from Alicia M. North to Charles North, dated September 1852, postmarked Liverpool 25 September 1852, "Eight letters of Mrs. Anne Pilkington, Kingstown, Co. Dublin, to her brother Charles North, Oswego, N.Y., on family affairs, 1840–1853," National Library of Ireland, Ms. 13,093, photostat copy of original letters (contrary to the manuscript title listing at NLI, not all of the letters in this collection were written by Anne). See also the discussion of varied reports of Samuel's birth year in Note 580.

549   Letter from Alicia M. North to Charles North, dated September 1852, mentioning that their mother died one day shy of her 72nd birthday.

550   "Deaths," *Cork* [Ireland] *Examiner*, 22 September 1852, p. 3. "September 16 at Kingstown, Margaret Anne, relict of William North, of Northbrook, in the county of Galway, esq." Letter from Alicia M. North to Charles North, dated September 1852.

551   North-Whitestone Marriage Settlement, Registry of Deeds, 5 October 1804. "Deaths," *Cork Examiner*, 22 September 1852.

552   1880 U.S. Census, Onalaska Village, La Crosse County, Wisconsin, p. 8, dwelling 61, family 64, Samuel W. North household, viewed on Ancestry.com and 1900 U.S. Census, Baraboo, Sauk County, Wisconsin, enumeration district 125, sheet no. 2, dwelling 27, family 29, Harry North household, viewed on Ancestry.com. *The Circus Kings: Our Ringling Family Story* (Garden City, New York: Doubleday & Company, 1960), 155.

553   The story may have been fueled by the fact that Samuel's older brother Joseph did marry a woman named Letitia (although she was not of obvious Spanish descent) (see Joseph North sketch [#A.1.i]).

      Other information informed by and regarding Samuel Wade North is suspect and may indicate that he was an inveterate storyteller. For instance, according to his grandson Henry Ringling North, Samuel claimed to have never worked (North, *Circus Kings*, 155–56), yet the 1860 and 1870 U.S. censuses listed him as a laborer (1860 U.S. Census, Onalaska, La Crosse County, Wisconsin, p. 236, dwelling 2008, family 1717, Samuel North household, and 1870 U.S. Census, Onalaska, p. 2, dwelling 8, family 8, Samuel North household). In addition, the location of his marriage was implied to be in Montreal in *Circus Kings* (North, *Circus Kings*, 155) and reported as Albany in Samuel's obituary (Obituary of Samuel Wade North, *La Crosse County Record*, 11 July 1895, p. 3, courtesy of the La Crosse Public Library, La Crosse, Wisconsin), but his marriage certificate was issued in Wisconsin (Registration of Marriage for Samuel W. North and Mary Fahey, uncertified copy provided by the Wisconsin State Vital Records Office, issued 17 January 2020, author's file).

554   "Obituary: Charles North," *Oswego Daily Palladium*, 15 February 1892, p. 5. North, *Circus Kings*, 155. The Napoleonic Wars took place from 1796 to 1815 (*Encyclopaedia Britannica*, online version, "Napoleonic Wars," accessed 17 October 2020).

555   "Deaths," *Cork Examiner*, 22 September 1852, reads "William North, of Northbrook, in the county of Galway, esq."

556   "Obituary: Charles North," *Oswego Daily Palladium*, 15 February 1892, p. 5.

557   Letter from Anne E. Pilkington to Charles North, dated 1 May 1850, "Eight letters of Mrs. Anne Pilkington, Kingstown, Co. Dublin. . . ."

558   County Galway, Ballinasloe, register of deaths for 1886, p. 12 (stamped), no. 137, Joseph North, viewed on Irishgenealogy.ie 3 September 2020, birth year calculated from his age at death. His widow was listed as Arabella.

559   For their marriage: Dublin, Ireland, Registry of Deeds, book 21, no. 83, deed, "Pilkington, etc." dated 21 October 1839; FHL Film #008,094,462, "Transcripts of memorials of deeds, conveyances and

wills," Deeds, etc., vols. 21–24 1839. The deed mentions "Joseph North and Letitia his wife," and Letitia is also referred to a "Letitia Lambert now Letitia North." Also mentioned in the deed is a marriage settlement between Joseph and Letitia, dated 5 December 1835, which has not been found. For Letitia's parentage: Dublin, Ireland, Registry of Deeds, book 13, no. 197, Deed, "Burke to Frend," dated 1 June 1837, FHL Film # 008093128, "Transcripts of memorials of deeds, conveyances and wills," Deeds, etc., vols. 13–15 1837. The deed, although incorrectly naming her husband as William North, mentions Letitia Lambert North as the daughter of the late Henry Lambert of Aggard, County Galway.

560 Burial/Death Record Abstract, Letitia Sophia North, date of death 13 February 1856, "near Ballinasloe," County Galway, online at www.rootsireland.ie., East Galway Family History Society.

561 General Valuation of Ireland ("Griffith's Valuation"), 1855, Parish of Kilcloony, Clonmacnowen, County Galway, p. 34, "Tobergrellan," viewed on Ancestry.com, "Ireland, Griffith's Valuation, 1847–1864."

562 St. Mary's Church, Dublin, marriages (1857), p. 12, no. 23, Joseph A. North and Arabella Selina Naghton, viewed on Irishgenealogy.ie, 3 September 2020.

563 Declaration of Intention of Henry W. North, 2 November 1867, viewed on FamilySearch.org, citing State Historical Society of Wisconsin, Madison, La Crosse County, Declarations of intention 1851—1880, vol. B, p. 529. "Obituary" [Henry W. North], *La Crosse County Record*, 10 May 1894, p. 3, listing his age at death as 83.

564 "Obituary" [Henry W. North], *La Crosse County Record*, 10 May 1894.

565 Parish of Lickerrig, Loughrea, County Galway, civil marriage registrations, p. 289, Henry W. North and Mary Boulger, viewed on Irishgenealogy.ie. Persse was listed as deceased on the registration.

566 Roderick Hamilton Burgoyne, *Historical Records of the 93rd Sutherland Highlanders* (London: Richard Bentley and Son, 1883), 366. "Captain in the regiment, 2nd of April, 1807; brevet-major, 4th of June 1814 (1819). Served at New Orleans, and was severely wounded on the 8th of January."

567 Parish of Lickerrig, civil marriage registrations, Henry W. North and Mary Boulger.

568 Declaration of Intention of Henry W. North, 2 November 1867.

569 1900 U.S. Census, Adams, Jefferson County, New York, enumeration district no. 2, sheet no. 7A, dwelling 181, family 194, Rufus P. White household, viewed on Ancestry.com. The 1910 Census shows 1864, however (1910 U.S. Census, Adams Township, Jefferson County, New York, enumeration district no. 1, sheet no. 4A, dwelling 6, family 6, Annie White household, viewed on Ancestry.com).

570 Passenger and Crew List for the *City of London*, arriving in New York 10 July 1866, p. 9, lines 17–19; Mary North, Margaret Boulger, and William North; viewed on Ancestry.com, citing "Passenger and Crew Lists of Vessels Arriving at New York, New York, 1820–1897," NARA RG 36, microfilm publication M237, 675 rolls, roll 268. They traveled with Mary Boulger, 30, perhaps a cousin of Mary's.

571 "Obituary" [Henry W. North], *La Crosse County Record*, 10 May 1894. "Obituary" [Mrs. Henry W. North], *La Crosse County Record*, 6 September 1888, p. 3.

572 Declaration of Intention, Henry W. North, 2 November 1867.

573 1900 U.S. Census, Adams, Jefferson County, New York, enumeration district 6, p. 31A, dwelling 181, family 194, Rufus P. White household, viewed on Ancestry.com, reads March 1850; her gravestone reads 1847 (Photograph of gravestone at FindaGrave.com, memorial #206828653, Anna North White, Elmwood Cemetery, Adams).

574 Photograph of gravestone at FindaGrave.com, memorial #206828653, Anna North White, buried at Elmwood Cemetery, Adams, Jefferson County, New York, viewed 23 September 2020.

575 "Marriages: White and Tracy," *Irish Times* [Dublin, Ireland], 12 June 1889, p. 1. The announcement describes Anna as being the widow of Dr. Tracy, and the "only daughter of Henry W. North, Esq., late of Northbrook, County Galway, Ireland, and granddaughter of Major P. O. K. Boulger, late 93rd Highlanders." The year given appears to be printed as 1890, but the newspaper was published in

1889; Ancestry.com, "New York, New York, Extracted Marriage Index, 1866–1937," database online, confirms the date as 21 May 1889.

576   1870 U.S. Census, Onalaska, La Crosse County, Wisconsin, p. 4, dwelling 26, family 27, Henry North household, viewed on Ancestry.com, showing William's birthplace to be Wisconsin, in error, given his birth and immigration years. 1900 U.S. Census, La Crosse City, La Crosse County, Wisconsin, enumeration district 86, sheet 4B, dwelling 79, family 84, William N. North household, viewed on Ancestry.com.

577   1900 U.S. Census, La Crosse County, Wisconsin, William N. North household, listing the couple as having been married 20 years.

578   Letter from Anne E. Pilkington to Charles North, dated 1 May 1850. Public Record Office of Ireland, Marriage License Bonds, Diocese of Meath, Anna E. North and Henry Pilkington, viewed on FindMyPast.com 7 September 2020, "Ireland Diocesan and Prerogative Marriage License Bonds indexes 1623-1866," which gives only the year of marriage.

579   North, *Circus Kings*, 154.

580   The 1850, 1860, 1870, and 1880 censuses (1850 U.S. Census, District No. 21—Turtle, Rock County, Wisconsin, the page following page 861 [penned], 113 [also penned], 431 [stamped], dwelling 753, family 827, John Hopkins household; 1860 U.S. Census, Onalaska, La Crosse County, Wisconsin, p. 236, dwelling 2008, family 1717, Samuel North household; 1870 U.S. Census, Onalaska, p. 2, dwelling 8, family 8, Samuel North household; and 1880 U.S. Census, Onalaska, p. 8, dwelling 61, family 63, Samuel W. North household; all viewed on Ancestry.com) all imply an approximate birth year of 1820 for Samuel; however, his gravestone reads 1812 (Photograph of gravestone at FindaGrave.com, memorial #32197273, Samuel Wade North), and his obituary claims 1810 (Obituary of Samuel Wade North, *La Crosse County Record*, 11 July 1895).

581   Photo of gravestone at FindaGrave.com, memorial #32197273, Samuel Wade North.

582   Registration of Marriage for Samuel W. North and Mary Fahey. Henry Ringling North erroneously implies that the marriage took place in Montreal (North, *Circus Kings*, 155), and Samuel Wade North's obituary claims that the couple was married in Albany, New York (Obituary of Samuel Wade North, *La Crosse County Record*, 11 July 1895).

583   Obituary of Samuel Wade North, *La Crosse County Record*, 11 July 1895 reads Montreal. 1880 U.S. Census, Onalaska, Samuel W. North household reads Quebec. 1870 U.S. Census, Onalaska, Samuel North household reads New York. 1860 U.S. Census, Onalaska, Samuel North household reads Ireland and gives her age erroneously as 36, rather than 22.

584   Photograph of gravestone at FindaGrave.com, memorial #32197272, Mary Fahey North. Obituary of Samuel Wade North, *La Crosse County Record*, 11 July 1895.

585   Photograph of gravestone at FindaGrave.com, memorial #32197272, Mary Fahey North.

586   1860 U.S. Census, Onalaska, La Crosse, Wisconsin, p. 236, dwelling 2008, family 1717, Samuel North household, viewed on Ancestry.com 1 December 2019; 1880 U.S. Census, Onalaska (Village), La Crosse, Wisconsin, p. 8, Samuel W. North household and Joseph North household, viewed on Ancestry.com 1 December 2019.

587   1870 U.S. Census, Onalaska, Samuel North household. 1880 U.S. Census, Onalaska, Joseph North household.

588   "Harry North Dies Early Sat. Morning," *Baraboo* [Wisconsin] *Weekly News*, 24 February 1921, p. 1.

589   1880 U.S. Census, Onalaska, Joseph North household.

590   1880 U.S. Census, Onalaska, Samuel North household.

591   1880 U.S. Census, Onalaska, Samuel North household.

592   1880 U.S. Census, Onalaska, Samuel North household.

593   1870 U.S. Census, Onalaska, Samuel North household. 1880 U.S. Census, Onalaska, Samuel North household. 1905 Wisconsin State Census, Harry North household.

594 Obituary of Samuel Wade North, *La Crosse County Record,* 11 July 1895.

595 1870 U.S. Census, Onalaska, Samuel North household; 1880 U.S. Census, Onalaska, Samuel North household.

596 Obituary of Samuel Wade North, *La Crosse County Record*, 11 July 1895.

597 "Harry North Dies Early Sat. Morning," *Baraboo* [Wisconsin] *Weekly News*, 24 February 1921, p. 1.

598 Obituary of Samuel Wade North, *La Crosse County Record*, 11 July 1895.

599 Letter from Alica M. North to Charles North, dated September 1852, signing "your affectionate and attached sister."

600 *Calendar of All Grants of Probate and Letters of Administration Made in The Principal Probate Registry . . . of Ireland . . . during the Year 1903* (Dublin, Ireland: Alex. Thom and Co., 1905), 416.

601 *Thom's Official Directory of the United Kingdom of Great Britain and Ireland, for the Year 1883* (Dublin, Ireland: Alexander Thom & Co., 1883), [318]–319, "Gormanston." Charles was uncle to Jenico William Joseph Preston, Viscount Gormanston of Ireland. Alicia is described as the "daughter of William North, [E]sq. Late of Northbrook."

602 Richard A. North, naturalization, filed 11 September 1844, Montgomery County, New York, viewed on FamilySearch.org, "New York, County Naturalization Records, 1791–1980," Montgomery Petition evidence 1820–1882, L–P. "Obituary: George A. F. North," *Brooklyn Daily Eagle*, 5 November 1910. Gravestone of Richard A. North and Joseph Palmateer, et al., Hagaman Mills Cemetery, Hagaman, Montgomery County, New York, Section B, Lot 34, photographed by the author 5 October 2020, "Richard A. North, Died April 26, 1858, Aged 38 yrs."

603 Gravestone of Richard A. North and Joseph Palmateer, et al., Hagaman Mills Cemetery, Montgomery County, New York, Letters of Administration, vol. 5, p. 121, viewed on FamilySearch.org, "New York, Wills and Probate Records, 1659–1999," Letters of Administration, vol. 0003–0005, 1821–1869.

604 Gravestone of Richard A. North and Joseph Palmateer, et al., Hagaman Mills Cemetery, "Ellen A. [wife of] R. North, Died March 29, 1858, Aged [29?] yrs." While the stone is badly worn and difficult to read, it does describe Ellen as Richard's wife. The four-sided monument is shared with other members of the Palmateer family, including Joseph Palmateer ([1794]–1874), William M. Palmateer ([1841]–1917), and Sara A. Palmateer ([1831]–1883), all of whom correspond to family members listed with Ellen on the 1850 census in the adjacent town of Perth, Fulton County—Joseph as her apparent father and William and Sara as apparent siblings (1850 U.S. Census, Perth, Fulton County, New York, p. 35 [penciled], dwelling 2678, family 1782, Joseph Palmateer household, listing [all with surname Palmateer]: Joseph, 54; Ellen, 22; Sarah, 19; Adaline, 13; William, 10; Jeremiah, 8; and Henry, 2).

605 1855 New York State Census, Amsterdam, Montgomery County, family 129, Richard North household, listing Ellen's age as 26. 1850 U.S. Census, Perth, Joseph Palmateer household, listing Ellen's age as 22.

606 Gravestone of Richard A. North and Joseph Palmateer, et al., Hagaman Mills Cemetery, "Ellen A. [wife of] R. North, Died March 29, 1858, Aged [29] yrs."

607 Envelope for letter from Alicia M. North to Richard [and Charles] North, dated 29 March [18]40, "Eight letters of Mrs. Anne Pilkington, Kingstown, Co. Dublin."

608 Envelope for letter from Mrs. H. Pilkington to Charles North, dated 24 September 1841 (postmarked Kingstown 13 October 1841), "Eight letters of Mrs. Anne Pilkington, Kingstown, Co. Dublin."

609 Richard A. North, naturalization, filed 11 September 1844.

610 1850 U.S. Census, St. Johnsville, Montgomery County, New York, p. 538 (penciled), dwelling 84, family 91, Benjamin Richardson household. Richard's age is off by several years, and his birthplace is given incorrectly as Scotland, making it almost certain that his enumeration was provided by a member of the Richardson family and not by Richard himself. Richard's occupation as a teacher connects him to his subsequent listing on the 1855 census. (The 1850 listing also includes a real estate value of $1,500 that likely belongs to the household of Mary Lasher on the following line).

611 Montgomery County, New York, Deeds, vol. 70, pp. 331–32, viewed on FamilySearch.org. Both deeds were recorded on 19 August 1858, after Richard's death in April that year.

612 1855 New York State Census, Amsterdam, Richard North household.

613 Montgomery County, New York, Letters of Administration, vol. 5, p. 121. Gravestone of Richard A. North and Joseph Palmateer, et al., Hagaman Mills Cemetery.

614 1860 U.S. Census, Fulton County, Joseph Palmateer household.

615 Footstone of Anna A. North, Hagaman Mills Cemetery. Gravestone of Richard A. North and Joseph Palmateer, et al., Hagaman Mills Cemetery.

616 Footstone of Anna A. North, Hagaman Mills Cemetery. Gravestone of Richard A. North and Joseph Palmateer, et al., Hagaman Mills Cemetery. 1855 New York State Census, Amsterdam, Richard North household.

617 "Obituary: George A. F. North," *Brooklyn Daily Eagle*, 5 November 1910. 1850 U.S. Census, Turtle, John Hopkins household. 1900 U.S. Census, Brooklyn, Kings County, New York, enumeration district 462, sheet 10A, dwelling 123, family 228/230, George A. F. North household.

618 "Obituary: George A. F. North," *Brooklyn Daily Eagle*, 5 November 1910.

619 1850 U.S. Census, Rock County, Wisconsin, John Hopkins household. 1855 New York State Census, New Lots, Kings County, dwelling 212, family 354, George North household. 1900 U.S. Census, Brooklyn, George A. F. North household, showing George and Sarah to have been married 51 years.

620 "Obituary: George A. F. North," *Brooklyn Daily Eagle*, 5 November 1910. Letter from Alicia M. North to Richard and Charles North, postmarked Kingstown, Ireland, 18 March [18]42, "Eight letters of Mrs. Anne Pilkington, Kingstown, Co. Dublin." 1855 New York State Census, Brooklyn, New York, George North household.

621 1850 U.S. Census, Rock County, Wisconsin, John Hopkins household. 1855 New York State Census, Brooklyn, New York, George North household.

622 1855 New York State Census, Brooklyn, New York, George North household.

623 1900 U.S. Census, Brooklyn, Kings County, New York, enumeration district 462, sheet 10A, dwelling 123, family 227/229, George A. F. North Jr. household.

624 1865 New York State Census, New Lots, Kings County, New York, p. 11, family 59, viewed on Ancestry.com.

625 "Obituary: George A. F. North," *Brooklyn Daily Eagle*, 5 November 1910.

626 1900 U.S. Census, Brooklyn, George A. F. North household.

627 Letter from Alicia M. North to Richard and Charles North, postmarked Kingstown, Ireland, 18 March [18]42, "Eight letters of Mrs. Anne Pilkington, Kingstown, Co. Dublin." He had been ill for two years and lived with his brother Joseph for the final year of his life.

628 "Obituary: Charles North," *Oswego Daily Palladium*, 15 February 1892. "Obituary: George A. F. North," *Brooklyn Daily Eagle*, 5 November 1910.

629 Riverside Cemetery Office, "Internments [*sic*], Riverside Cemetery, 1855–1910: Records of 4th & 5th Ward Cemeteries," Charles North, 146. Naturalization Card, Charles North, Oswego County Naturalization Records, Oswego County Records Center, Oswego, citing #724, Second Papers 1829–1878, showing his birth year as 1819.

630 "Obituary: Charles North," *Oswego Daily Palladium*, 15 February 1892. Riverside Cemetery Office, Oswego, "Internments [*sic*], Riverside Cemetery, 1855–1910," Charles North, 146. Riverside Cemetery Office "Interment Record B," interment record for Section T, Lot 10, "Charles North & Hubbard," p. 692.

631 Cummington, Massachusetts, 1845 marriages, p. 160, item 12, Charles North and Harriet N. Mitchell, viewed on AmericanAncestors.org 19 July 2019, "Massachusetts: Vital Records, 1841–1910"; the marriage took place in 1844, despite the page header.

632 Cummington, Massachusetts, 1845 marriages, p. 160, item 12, Charles North and Harriet N. Mitchell; viewed on www.AmericanAncestors.org, "Massachusetts: Vital Records, 1841–1910," listing Harriet's parents as Capt. Chester and Venila Mitchell.

633 "Obituary: Mrs. Harriet Mitchell North," [1901], unsourced newspaper clipping from the collection of Holbrook R. Davis. Riverside Cemetery, Harriet Mitchell (North) gravestone, photograph taken by the author, 2019.

634 Riverside Cemetery Office, "Internments [*sic*], Riverside Cemetery, 1855–1910," Harriet North, 146. Riverside Cemetery, Harriet Mitchell gravestone, photograph taken by the author, 2019.

635 Riverside Cemetery Office, "Interment Record B," "Charles North & Hubbard," p. 692. Riverside Cemetery Office, "Internments [*sic*], Riverside Cemetery, 1855–1910," William Lorenzo North, 146. Riverside Cemetery, William L. North gravestone, photograph taken by the author, 2019.

636 Riverside Cemetery Office, "Internments [*sic*], Riverside Cemetery, 1855–1910," Alicia M. North, 146.

637 Photograph of gravestone at FindaGrave.com, memorial #141752082, Alicia M. North, Riverside Cemetery. Riverside Cemetery Office, "Internments [*sic*], Riverside Cemetery, 1855–1910," Alicia M. North, 146. Her grave was moved from the East Cemetery and was reinterred 16 June 1859.

638 Riverside Cemetery Office, "Internments [*sic*], Riverside Cemetery, 1855–1910," Venelia M. North, 146, which reads 16 August. Photo of gravestone taken by the author (which includes only the year of death), 2019. Riverside Cemetery Office, "Interment Record B," interment record for Section T, Lot 10, "Charles North & Hubbard," p. 692, which reads 13 August. Her grave was moved from the East Cemetery and was reinterred 16 June 1859 (Interment Book B reads 1856 in error).

639 1900 U.S. Census, First District, Sixth Ward, Oswego, enumeration district 130, Sheet 135A, 156 (crossed out)/165 (corrected), 181 (crossed out)/176 (corrected), Walter H. Pulver household; viewed on Ancestry.com.

640 Photograph of gravestone at FindaGrave.com, memorial #159122011, Laura W. North Pulver, Riverside Cemetery. "Deaths in the County," *Fulton* [New York] *Patriot*, 27 October 1938, p. 17.

641 1900 U.S. Census, Oswego, Walter H. Pulver household.

642 *The Oswego Directory: 1931* (Syracuse, New York: Sampson & Murdock, [1931]), 245.

643 1900 U.S. Census, Oswego, Walter H. Pulver household, listing William W. Pulver, 76, as Walter's father.

644 1900 U.S. Census, Oswego, Walter H. Pulver household. Laura was listed as the mother of four children, three of whom were living.

645 Riverside Cemetery Office, "Internments [*sic*], Riverside Cemetery, 1855–1910," Chester M. North, 146. Photo of gravestone taken by the author, 2019.

646 "Oswego," *Syracuse* [New York] *Standard*, 10 April 1885, p. 6. Forest Hill Cemetery, "Record of Interments, 1902 to 1926," Sarah N. DeForest, 90. (This volume includes several post-1926 deaths.)

647 "Oswego," *Syracuse* [New York] *Standard*, 10 April 1885, p. 6.

648 Riverside Cemetery Office, "Internments [*sic*], Riverside Cemetery, 1855–1910," Hattie N. North, 146. Riverside Cemetery, Hattie N. North gravestone, photograph taken by the author, 2019.

649 1900 U.S. Census, Glen Ridge, Essex, New Jersey, enumeration district 213, sheet 14 B, Frederick C. Osterhout household. Photograph of gravestone at FindaGrave.com, memorial #179563012, Louise N. Osterhout, viewed 6 September 2020. "Obituary: Mrs. Frederick C. Osterhout," [Oswego] *Palladium-Times*, 28 May 1960, p. 5.

650 Photograph of gravestone at FindaGrave.com, memorial #179563012, Louise N. Osterhout, Riverside Cemetery. "Obituary: Mrs. Frederick C. Osterhout," [Oswego] *Palladium-Times*, 28 May 1960.

651 "Frederick C. Osterhout: Director of Rogers Peet Company Dies of Pneumonia," *New York Times*, 6 October 1930.

652 "Obituary: Mrs. Frederick C. Osterhout," [Oswego] *Palladium-Times*, 28 May 1960.

653   "Obituary: Charles North," *Oswego Daily Palladium*, 15 February 1892. 1900 U.S. Census, Essex
       County, New Jersey, Frederick C. Osterhout household, showing Louisa as the mother of zero
       children. "Obituary: Mrs. Frederick C. Osterhout," [Oswego] *Palladium-Times*, 28 May 1960.

654   George and his father Marcus's probable lineage is based on the description of the family given in
       the uncited family history by William Cothren: *History of Ancient Woodbury, Connecticut, from the First
       Indian Deed in 1659 to 1872, Including the Present Towns of Washington, Southbury, Bethlehem, Roxbury,
       and a part of Oxford and Middlebury,* 2 vols. (Woodbury, Connecticut: the author, 1872), 2:1491–93.

655   1850 U.S. Census, Woodbury, Litchfield County, Connecticut, p. 734 (in sequence with other
       penciled numbers)/p. 368 (stamped on folios), dwelling 235, family 235, Geo. DeForest household.

656   North Cemetery, Woodbury, Connecticut, George DeForest and Mary A. Linsley gravestone,
       photograph taken by the author, 2020.

657   1850 U.S. Census, Woodbury, Litchfield, Connecticut, page 734 (in sequence with other penciled
       numbers)/page 368 (stamped on folios), dwelling 232, family 232, Marcus DeForest household;
       viewed on Ancestry.com. Will of Marcus De Forest, dated 17 December 1875, Litchfield County,
       Connecticut, Wills, vol. 32, p. 386–390 at 387, mentioning "George L. son of my deceased son
       George," viewed on Ancestry.com.

658   Cothren, *History of Ancient Woodbury*, 1480. 1850 U.S. Census for Woodbury, Litchfield County,
       Connecticut, p. 735 (in sequence with other penciled numbers)/p. 368 (stamped on folios), dwelling
       235, family 235, George DeForest household, shows George, 25, and Mary, 26, as married.

659   North Cemetery, Woodbury, Connecticut, George DeForest and Mary A. Linsley gravestone,
       photograph taken by the author, 2020.

660   Woodbury Probate District, Estate of Harvey J. Linsley, Town of Woodbury, Litchfield County,
       Connecticut, 1853, no. 2754, viewed on Ancestry.com, "Connecticut, U.S., Wills and Probate
       Records, 1609–1999." The will, dated 2 January 1852, lists wife Mary Linsley; children James Linsley,
       Mary Ann DeForest, Laura Bassett, and Jane Linsley; and executors Eli Summers and Thomas Bull.

661   The 1850 U.S. Census for Woodbury, Connecticut, shows George and Mary Ann living with Emily
       E. DeForest, age 6. Emily is not listed with the family in any subsequent census. If Cothren's marriage
       date of 3 October 1849 is correct for George and Mary, this is likely a niece or other relative. Emily
       is a name that is used often in this family during this time period (for instance, George's niece Emily
       DeForest, 6 months, listed two households away on the same census [1850 U.S. Census, George [L.]
       DeForest household]). It is also possible that this Emily was a daughter of George's from an unknown
       previous marriage, born when he was 19.

662   Guardianship Bond dated 3 May 1871, Estate of George DeForest, Woodbury Probate District,
       Connecticut, 1871, no. 1243, viewed on Ancestry.com, "Connecticut, Wills and Probate Records,
       1609–1999," probate place: Hartford, Connecticut. Forest Hill Cemetery Office, "Record of
       Interments, 1927 to 1961," George DeForest, 90. "Death Removes George De Forest," *Utica Daily
       Press*, 7 October 1929, p. 3. Although the headline for this obituary reads "De Forest," the subsequent
       article spells the surname "DeForest."

663   "Death Removes George De Forest," *Utica Daily Press*, 7 October 1929. Forest Hill Cemetery Office,
       "Record of Interments, 1927 to 1961," George DeForest, 90.

664   "Oswego," marriage notice for George DeForest and Sara C. North, *The Syracuse* [New York]
       Standard, 10 April 1885, p. 6. "Death Removes George De Forest," *Utica Daily Press*, 7 October 1929.
       Forest Hill Cemetery Office, "Record of Interments, 1902 to 1926," Sarah N. DeForest, 90.

665   Forest Hill Cemetery Office, "Record of Interments, 1902 to 1926," Sarah N. DeForest, 90.

666   Forest Hill Cemetery Office, "Record of Interments, 1927 to 1961," Mary L. Maynard, p. 239.

667   Richard was "of the Parish of Ruishton" when he married Sarah Farthing in 1801 (Kingston St. Mary,
       Somerset, parish registers [1801], Richard Maynard and Sarah Farthing, viewed on Ancestry.com,
       "Somerset, England, Marriage Registers, Bonds and Allegations, 1754–1812").

668   Ruishton, Somerset, marriage registers (1779), Richard Maynard and Sarah Lyssant. Witnesses were
       Henry Maynard and Hannah Maynard. Paul Street, Taunton, Somerset, parish registers (1782), p.

146, "Baptisms by Tho.ˢ Reader, A.D. 1782," viewed on Ancestry.com, "England & Wales, Non-Conformist and Non-Parochial Registers, 1567–1970," citing Public Record Office RG4/1567. The entry describes Richard's baptism in April 1781, along with baptisms of two other siblings in 1780 and 1782. Richard's age at baptism is given as "about a month old." The date of baptism in April was written as a single illegible digit, followed by a superscript "th," hence either the 4ᵗʰ, 5ᵗʰ, 6ᵗʰ, 7ᵗʰ, 8ᵗʰ, or 9ᵗʰ.

669   Paul Street, Taunton, Somerset, parish registers (1782), p. 146.

670   1841 Census of England, St. Magdalena, Taunton, Somerset, p. 36, Sarah Maynard household.

671   Kingston St. Mary, Somerset, parish registers (1801), Richard Maynard and Sarah Farthing, witnessed by Thomas Hawkins and Sarah Maynard. "Abstract Will of Robert Farthing, Gentleman of Kingston, Somerset," digital copy, National Archives, Kew, London, England, IR 26/293/100, Item 381/12: listing daughter Sally Maynard. Although Robert's wife was mentioned in the abstract, she was not named.

672   1851 Census of England, St. Magdalena, Taunton, Somerset, p. 36, Sarah Maynard household.

673   "Abstract Will of Robert Farthing, National Archives, Kew.

674   Mary Maynard Thorn's 1891 obituary describes her as a sister of Alfred Maynard and aunt of Howard Maynard, suggesting that Alfred was another child of Richard and Sarah (Farthing) Maynard. This is likely in error, and instead refers to her *nephew* Alfred Maynard and Alfred's son, her *great-nephew*, Howard. See "Death of Mrs. John Thorn," *Taunton Courier*, 13 May 1891, p. 2, and the sketch for her brother Richard Maynard (#1. iv) and his children. See also: Silver Street (Baptist) Church register, births of Sarah, Maria, Mary, Richard, Sarah (again), Robert, James, and Isaac Maynard, viewed on Ancestry.com; "England & Wales, Non-Conformist and Non-Parochial Registers, 1567–1970"; RG4: Registers of Births, Marriages and Deaths, Somerset Baptist Piece 3219: and Taunton, Silver Street (Baptist), 1782–1837. Eight children of Richard and Sarah Maynard had births recorded into this register on 4 July 1820 by Rev. Richard Horsey. Below these entries reads: "All of the above was entered at the particular request of the parties concerned and according to their information of the time of the births of each—all of which being before the Establishment of this Interest." Each registration lists the parents as "Richard Maynard and Sarah his Wife of the Parish of Ruishton in the County of Somerset." The birthdates of both Isaac and Mary match the birthdates recorded at their deaths at Forest Hill Cemetery in Utica.

675   Paul Street, Taunton, Baptisms (1801), p. 62 (penned), 74 (stamped), Sarah Farthing Maynard, PRO Ref. RG4/1567, viewed on Ancestry.com, "England & Wales, Non-Conformist and Non-Parochial Registers, 1567–1970," Taunton, Paul Street (Independent), 1699–1837. Silver Street (Baptist) Church register, birth of Sarah Maynard (1801).

676   Silver Street (Baptist) Church register, birth of Sarah Maynard (1809).

677   Silver Street (Baptist) Church register, birth of Maria Maynard (1803).

678   "Utica," death notice for Mrs. John E. Bult, *Rome Daily Sentinel*, 17 November 1883, p. 2, indicating death on 16 November. Forest Hill Cemetery Office, "Record of Interments, 1849 to 1901," Maria Bult, 46, showing death as 15 November.

679   Ruishton, Taunton, Somerset, England, marriage registers, p. 14 (1831), no. 27, John Eland Bult and Maria Maynard, viewed on Ancestry.com, "Somerset, England, Marriage Registers, Bonds and Allegations, 1754–1914, Marriage Registers Ruishton 1824–1894." John was described as a "sojourner of this parish," while Maria was a member of it. It was a first marriage for both. Also "Mrs. John Thorn," *Utica Morning Herald*, 25 April 1891, mentioning Mrs. John E. Bult as a sister.

680   Forest Hill Cemetery Office, "Record of Interments, 1849 to 1901," John E. Bult, 46.

681   "Utica," death notice for Mrs. John E. Bult, *Rome Daily Sentinel*, 17 November 1883. "Tabernacle Baptist Church," *Utica Morning Herald*, 1 September 1875, p. 2.

682   Photograph of gravestone at FindAGrave.com, memorial #207750429, Hannah Maria Bult, viewed 12 October 2020. She and her sister Mary share a stone. 1855 New York State Census, Utica, p. 14, dwelling 79, family 121, John E. Bult household, listing her as "Hannah"; 1860 U.S. Census,

2nd Ward of the City of Utica, Oneida, New York, p. 41, dwelling 262, family 326, John E. Bult household, viewed on Ancestry.com, listing her as "Anna M." 1865 New York State Census, Second Ward in the City of Utica, John E. Bult household, listing her as "Hannah M."

683   Photograph of gravestone at FindaGrave.com, memorial #207750411, Mary E. Bult Johnson, "wife of Newell Johnson," viewed 12 October 2020. She and her sister Hannah share a stone. 1855 New York State Census, Utica, John E. Bult household.

684   1865 New York State Census, Utica, John E. Bult household, listing Maria as the mother of five children.

685   Silver Street (Baptist) Church register, birth of Mary Maynard. Forest Hill Cemetery Office, "Record of Interments, 1849 to 1901," Mary M. Thorn, 433.

686   Forest Hill Cemetery Office, "Record of Interments, 1849 to 1901," Mary M. Thorn, 433. "Mrs. John Thorn," *Utica Morning Herald*, 25 April 1891.

687   "Mrs. John Thorn," *Utica Morning Herald,* 25 April 1891.

688   "Death of John Thorn," *Utica Morning Herald and Daily Gazette*, 1 January 1895, p. 4. Forest Hill Cemetery Office, "Record of Interments, 1849 to 1901," John Thorn, 342.

689   "Death of John Thorn: A Well Known and Highly Respected Citizen Passes Away," *Utica Morning Herald*, 1 January 1895.

690   Silver Street (Baptist) Church register, birth of Richard Maynard.

691   Calendar of the Grants of Probate and Letters of Administration made in the Probate Registers of the High Court of Justice in England, London, England, Wills, 1865, Richard Maynard, p. 131, viewed on Ancestry.com, "England & Wales, National Probate Calendar (Index of Wills and Administrations, 1858–1995)."

692   1851 Census of England, St. James, Taunton, Somerset, p. 24/72, Richard Maynard household. When Richard's son Richard's delayed birth certificate was recorded in 1837, it gave his 1829 birth date, his mother's maiden name as Harriet Goodland Jennings, and her parents as Robert and Harriet Jennings of Cannington, Somerset (Silver Street [Baptist] Church Registers [1837], Taunton, delayed [25 January 1837] birth certification for Richard Maynard [Jr.], p. 14, "England & Wales, Non-Conformist and Non-Parochial Registers, 1567–1970," RG4: Registers of Births, Marriages and Deaths, Somerset Baptist, Piece 3219: Taunton, Silver Street (Baptist), 1782–1837.

693   "Marriages," *Taunton Courier*, 11 August 1858, p. 8. *Calendar of Probate*, Wills, 1865, Richard Maynard, p. 131.

694   "Awfully Sudden Deaths," *Taunton Courier*, 25 January 1865, p. 5.

695   Silver Street (Baptist) Church Registers (1837), Taunton, delayed birth certification for Richard Maynard. Maria Bult and Sarah Maynard signed as witnesses to his 1829 birth.

696   Silver Street (Baptist) Church Registers (1837), Taunton, delayed (25 January 1837) birth certification for Alfred Maynard, p. 14. Sarah Maynard and Mary Dunston signed as witnesses to the 1831 birth.

697   "Taunton," *West Somerset Free Press,* 4 August 1900, p. 5.

698   "Death of Mrs. John Thorn," *Taunton Courier*, 13 May 1891.

699   "Death of Mr. H. Maynard: Prominent Tauntonian: Tributes at Funeral," *Somerset County Herald*, 5 September 1936, p. 3, listing his age at death as 76.

700   Silver Street (Baptist) Church Registers (1837), Taunton, delayed (25 January 1837) birth certification for Harriet Maynard, p. 14. Mary Dunston and Mary Leusmore made marks as witnesses to the 1833 birth.

701   Silver Street (Baptist) Church Registers (1837), Taunton, delayed (25 January 1837) birth certification for Walter Maynard, p. 14. Maria Bult and Anne Wolfe Gibson signed as witnesses to the 1834 birth.

702   Silver Street (Baptist) Church register, birth of Sarah Maynard (1809).

703   Silver Street (Baptist) Church register, birth of Robert Maynard (1811).

704   Silver Street (Baptist) Church register, birth of James Maynard (1813).

705   Silver Street Baptist Church Registers, birth of Charlotte Maynard (1817). 1851 Census of England, St. Magdalena, Taunton, Somerset, p. 36, Sarah Maynard household.

706   St. Mary Magdalen, Taunton, Somerset, Marriage registers, p. 179 (1858), item 358, John David Woolen and Charlotte Maynard, viewed on Ancestry.com. John David was listed as a hairdresser, his father as a cabinet maker. See also "Joshua Tavender, an Old and Respected Utican," *Utica Morning Herald*, 11 October 1895.

707   Passenger manifest for the ship *Wellington*, arriving 6 September 1839, viewed on Ancestry.com, citing NARA RG 36, "Passenger Lists of Vessels Arriving at New York, New York, 1820–1897," microfilm publication M237, 675 rolls, roll 040. 1851 Census of England, St. Magdalena, Taunton, Sarah Maynard household.

708   Forest Hill Cemetery Office, "Record of Interments, 1849 to 1901," Harriet M. Tavender, 368. Harriet was described in her husband's obituary as being a sister of Mrs. John Thorn of Utica ("Joshua Tavender, an Old and Respected Utican," *Utica Morning Herald*, 11 October 1895). Silver Street Baptist Church Registers, birth of Harriet Maynard (1819).

709   "Joshua Tavender, an Old and Respected Utican," *Utica Morning Herald*, 11 October 1895.

710   1841 Census of England, St. Mary Magdalen, Taunton, Somerset, Sarah Maynard household.

711   1855 New York State Census, City of Utica, Oneida County, p. 14, dwelling 79, family 122, Joshua Tavender household.

712   1860 U.S. Census, 2nd Ward, Utica, Oneida County, New York, p. 41, dwelling 263, family 327, Joshua Tavender household.

713   Forest Hill Cemetery Office, "Record of Interments, 1849 to 1901," Mary Emma Tavender, 368. She was not listed in the 1870 census with her family (1870 U.S. Census, Sixth Ward City of Utica, Oneida County, New York, p. 8, dwelling 23, family 61, Joshua Tavender household) or in any censuses afterward.

714   1860 U.S. Census, Utica, Joshua Tavender household, where Mary Jane is listed as "Mary J." 1870 U.S. Census, Utica, Joshua Tavender household, where Mary is listed as "Jane M." 1880 U.S. Census, Utica, Oneida County, New York, enumeration district 132, p. 28, dwelling 173, family 221, Joshua Tavender household, where she is listed as "Jennie."

715   1860 U.S. Census, Utica, Joshua Tavender household.

716   1870 U.S. Census, Utica, Joshua Tavender household.

717   Forest Hill Cemetery Office, "Record of Interments, 1849 to 1901," Thomas Maynard, 239.

718   Forest Hill Cemetery Office, "Record of Interments, 1849 to 1901," Thomas Maynard, 239. 1860 U.S. Census, 7th Ward, Utica, mortality schedule, line 13, Thomas Maynard, viewed on Ancestry.com.

719   1855 New York State Census, First Ward, Utica, Oneida County, p. 8, dwelling 58, family 74, Thomas Maynard household. Georgiana was born in about 1833 in "Hindostan" (India), and her younger sister Juliana in Bombay, India, two years later. Both are listed with the surname "Sampson" in the 1850 U.S. Census for Augusta, New York (1850 U.S. Census, Town of Augusta, Oneida County, New York, pp. 17–18, dwelling 130, family 138, Hiram S. Hamilton household), along with their aunt Elizabeth Barker, in the household of clergyman Hiram S. Hamilton. In 1860, both Juliana and Elizabeth resided with Georgiana and Thomas (1860 U.S. Census, Utica, Thomas Maynard household).

720   1855 New York State Census, Utica, Thomas Maynard household. Queens County [New York] Surrogate's Court, Estate of Georgiana Hastings Sampson Maynard, proved 17 October 1917, Liber 104, p. 7, 1983, Filing Case A224, Deposition of Harry V. Hoyt, 17 October 1917, viewed on Ancestry.com, "New York, Wills and Probate Records, 1659–1999," Queens, Mixed Proceedings, Case #0393-0402, 1917.

721   M. M. Bagg, M.D., *Memorial History of Utica, N.Y., from Its Settlement to the Present Time* (Syracuse, New York: D. Mason, 1892), 279. William Richards, *The Utica City Directory for 1843–'44* (Utica: Roberts & Curtiss, 1843), 71.

722   1860 U.S. Census, 7th Ward, Utica, Oneida County, New York, mortality schedule, p. 687 (stamped),
       line 13, Thomas Maynard. According to M. M. Bagg, Thomas had moved to Cleveland (Bagg,
       Memorial History of Utica, 279). However, Thomas's listing on the 1860 mortality schedule for Utica,
       the fact that he was buried there, and that his wife and children were residents of Utica in 1860 and
       afterward, makes it likely that he was visiting Cleveland but perhaps intended to relocate.

723   1875 New York State Census, Utica, Oneida County, p. 1, dwelling 1, family 1, Georgiana H. S.
       Maynard household.

724   1865 New York State Census, Utica, Georgiana Maynard household.

725   1865 New York State Census, Utica, Georgiana Maynard household. Will of John Thorn, Oneida
       County, New York Wills, vol. 48, p. 497, viewed on FamilySearch.org.

726   "Notice of Hearing of Petition for Probate of Will No. P-2867," *Pasadena* [California] *Post,* 21
       December 1937, p. 10, describing her as deceased.

727   "Utica," *Rome* [New York] *Daily Sentinel*, 24 April 1884, p. 2. Will of John Thorn.

728   1865 New York State Census, Utica, Georgiana Maynard household. 1880 U.S. Census, Excelsior,
       Hennepin County, Minnesota, enumeration district 219, p. 1 (penned), 136 (stamped), dwelling 8,
       family 9, Georgiana Maynard household. Queens County [New York] Surrogate's Court, Estate of
       Georgiana Hastings Sampson Maynard.

729   Forest Hill Cemetery Office, "Record of Interments, 1849 to 1901," Isaac Maynard, 239. His
       obituary reads 1805 ("Death of Isaac Maynard," *Utica Morning Herald*, 24 February 1885); however,
       census information more closely corroborates the 1815 date: he was listed as 50 in 1865 (1865
       New York State Census, 7th Ward, Utica, p. 1, dwelling 1, family 1, Isaac Maynard household), as 54
       in 1870 (1870 U.S. Census, Utica, p. 1, dwelling 6, family 7, Isaac Maynard household, viewed on
       Ancestry.com), and as 63 in 1880 (1880 U.S. Census, Utica, enumeration district 133, p. 21, dwelling
       154, family 215, Isaac Maynard household, viewed on Ancestry.com). In 1855, his recorded age was
       35, approximating a birth year of 1820 (1855 New York State Census, Utica, Oneida County, New
       York, p. 14, dwelling 78, family 120, Isaac Maynard household), and in 1840, if he was one of the four
       males in John Thorn's household, he was listed as being age 20–30, placing his year of birth before
       1820 (1840 U.S. Census, Ward 2, Utica, p. 11, John Thorn household, viewed on Ancestry.com,
       showing four white males between the ages of 20 and 30, and one female between the ages of 30 and
       40, which would be consistent with John, his wife, and three boarders, including Isaac).

730   "Death of Isaac Maynard," *Utica Morning Herald*, 24 February 1885. Forest Hill Cemetery Office,
       "Record of Interments, 1849 to 1901," Isaac Maynard, 239.

731   "Married," *Utica Daily Gazette*, 26 August 1844. Isaac's obituary gives their year of marriage
       incorrectly as 1846 ("Death of Isaac Maynard," *Utica Morning Herald*, 24 February 1885).

732   Three Utica sources offer information as to the date of birth, location, and parents for Margaret
       Aitken, who was implied as being born in 1827–28 on the 1850 U.S. Census (1850 U.S. Census, p. 787
       (penned), 394 (stamped), dwelling 154, family 165, Isaac Maynard household, viewed on Ancestry.com):
       first, her gravestone (Forest Hill Cemetery, Utica, gravestone of Isaac Maynard and Margaret Aitken,
       photograph by the author, 2019), which gives her date of birth as 27 March 1826; second, the record
       of interments at Forest Hill Cemetery (Forest Hill Cemetery Office, "Record of Interments, 1849 to
       1901," Margaret Aitken Maynard, 239), which gives her date of birth as 27 April 1825, the location
       as Falkirk, Scotland, and her parents as Thomas and Mary Aitken; third, her newspaper obituary
       ("Death of Mrs. Isaac Maynard," *Utica Morning Herald,* 3 December 1896, p. 5), which gives her
       date of birth as 27 of April 1825, and the location as Falkirk, Scotland. Baptism records for Falkirk
       show two possibilities, each of which corresponds to this conflicting information in part: one for
       Margaret Aitken, daughter of Thomas Aitken and Mary Falconer, born 12 February 1826 (National
       Records of Scotland, Edinburgh, Old Parish Registers, Falkirk, Stirlingshire, p. 479, Margaret Aitken
       baptism, 1826, vol. 100, p. 126, viewed on ScotlandsPeople.gov.uk 23 January 2020, image 255 of
       592, witnessed by John Kincaid and James Manuel); and one for Margaret Aitken, daughter of James
       Aitken and Mary Henderson, born 27 March 1826 (National Records of Scotland, Edinburgh, Old
       Parish Registers, Falkirk, Stirlingshire, 479, Margaret Aitken baptism, 1826, vol. 100, p. 255, viewed

on ScotlandsPeople.gov.uk 20 January 2020, image 198 of 592, witnessed by James Mickle and William Scott). The latter seems most likely, given that the birthdate matches the information on her gravestone exactly and the other records in part. However, the first could be correct. It is possible that a distraught informant may have given her date of birth and parents' names incorrectly for her burial record and obituary, but that this information was corrected later on her gravestone. James Aitken, a seaman, and Mary Henderson were married at Old Machar, Aberdeenshire, Scotland, 25 June 1820 (National Records of Scotland, Edinburgh, Old Parish Registers, Old Machar, Aberdeenshire, 168/B, James Aiken and Mary Henderson marriage, 1820, vol. 16, p. 5 [original] 8 [corrected]), viewed on scotlandspeople.gov.uk 23 January 2020).

733   Forest Hill Cemetery Office, "Record of Interments, 1849 to 1901," Margaret Aitken Maynard, 239.

734   Sources differ as to Mary's year of birth. Forest Hill Cemetery, Record of Interments, 1849 to 1901, p. 81, gives it as 1849. Her gravestone shows it as 1847 (Photograph of gravestone at FindaGrave.com, memorial #209903295, Mary L. Crouse, Forest Hill Cemetery, Utica, viewed 17 October 2020). The censuses of 1850, 1855, 1860, and 1865 all show her estimated birth year as 1845 or 1846, and each shows her three-years-older brother Isaac, whose birth year of 1849 has been confirmed by other sources (1850 U.S. Census, Utica, Isaac Maynard household; 1855 New York State Census, Utica, Isaac Maynard household; 1860 U.S. Census, Utica, Isaac Maynard household; 1865 New York State Census, Utica, Isaac Maynard household). Her middle name is from the Will of Isaac Maynard, proved 18 March 1885, viewed at Oneida County Surrogate's Office, Utica, 2019.

735   Forest Hill Cemetery, Record of Interments, 1849 to 1901, p. 81. "Obituary: Death of Mrs. John M. Crouse, of Utica, This Morning," *Utica Daily Observer*, 29 June 1893, p. 5. "Utica," *Rome* [New York] *Semi-Weekly Citizen*, 20 March 1896, p. 8.

736   "Death Record of a Week," *Utica Sunday Tribune*, 18 July 1906. The 1865 New York State Census shows Mary L. Maynard, 19, living with her parents, Isaac and Mary Maynard (1865 New York State Census, Utica, Isaac Maynard household); the 1870 U.S. Census shows her as Mary Crouse, living with John's parents (1870 U.S. Census, Utica, Oneida County, New York, p. 6, dwelling 40, family 43, Daniel Crouse household).

737   "Death of Mrs. John M. Crouse, of Utica, This Morning," *Utica Daily Observer*, 29 June 1893.

738   "Death Record of a Week," *Utica Sunday Tribune*, 18 July 1906; according to the obituary, John's father, Daniel, was in the general store business in Canastota before moving to Utica. John was survived by his brother, Daniel Nellis Crouse. The 1850 U.S. Census shows the brothers living together in the household of Daniel and C. Jane Crouse (1850 U.S. Census, Lenox, Madison, County, New York, p. 503 (penned), 252 (stamped), dwelling 1344, family 1345, Daniel Crouse household, viewed on Ancestry.com). For Catherine's full name, see photograph of gravestone at FindaGrave.com, memorial #156959073, Catherine Jane Beecher Crouse, Forest Hill Cemetery, viewed 27 November 2020.

739   "Death Record of a Week," *Utica Sunday Tribune*, 18 July 1906. U.S. Passport Application of John M. Crouse, issued 31 May 1904 (stamped), no. 88346, viewed on Ancestry.com, citing NARA RG 59, "Passport Applications, 1795–1905," microfilm publication M1372, 694 rolls, roll 653.

740   "Death Record of a Week," *Utica Sunday Tribune*, 18 July 1906. "Utica," *Rome* [New York] *Semi-Weekly Citizen*, 20 March 1896, p. 8.

741   U.S. Passport Application, John M. Crouse, 31 May 1904.

742   "Utica," *Rome* [New York] *Semi-Weekly Citizen*, 20 March 1896, p. 8.

743   "Death of Mrs. John M. Crouse, of Utica, This Morning," *Utica Daily Observer*, 29 June 1893.

744   "Death Record of a Week," *Utica Sunday Tribune*, 15 July 1906.

745   "Death Record of a Week," *Utica Sunday Tribune*, 18 July 1906. U.S. Passport Application of Beecher Maynard Crouse, issued 17 July 1922 (stamped), no. 205244, viewed on Ancestry.com, citing NARA RG 59, "U.S. Passport Applications, 1795–1925," microfilm publication M1490, 2740 rolls, roll 2063. Forest Hill Cemetery Office, "Record of Interments, 1927–1961," Beecher M. Crouse, 81. "Utica Textile Leader Dead," *New York* [New York] *Sun*, 2 October 1934, p. 25.

746   "A Country Wedding: A Hartford Girl Married at Guilford," *Hartford* [Connecticut] *Courant*, 6 September 1894, p. 3.

747   U.S. Passport Application, Beecher Maynard Crouse, 17 July 1922. Forest Hill Cemetery Office, "Record of Interments, 1927–1961," Louise S. K. Crouse, 81.

748   Forest Hill Cemetery Office, "Record of Interments, 1927–1961," Louise S. K. Crouse, 81.

749   "A Country Wedding: A Hartford Girl Married at Guilford," *Hartford* [Connecticut] *Courant*, 6 September 1894, p. 3. Forest Hill Cemetery Office, "Record of Interments, 1927–1961," Louise S. K. Crouse, 81.

750   "Beecher Crouse is Married to Miss Wheeler," *Utica Observer-Dispatch*, 29 March 1931, Section C, p. 1.

751   "Invitations have been sent . . ." *Hartford* [Connecticut] *Courant*, 25 August 1894, p. 5.

752   "Utica Textile Leader Dead," *New York Sun*, 2 October 1934.

753   "Death Record of a Week," *Utica Sunday Tribune*, 18 July 1906. Passport application of John M. Crouse, 31 May 1904. Forest Hill Cemetery Office, "Record of Interments, 1962 [to Present]," Mary Gordon, 149.

754   Utica, Oneida County, marriage certificate no. 2818, Beirne Gordon Jr. and Mary Louise Crouse, viewed on FamilySearch.org, "New York, County Marriages, 1847–1848; 1908–1936," Oneida Licenses, 1911, nos. 4279–4797, image 1562 of 1618.

755   Forest Hill Cemetery Office, "Record of Interments, 1927 to 1961," Isaac N. Maynard, 239. U.S. Passport Application of Isaac N. Maynard, issued 26 June 1897, no. 6193, viewed on Ancestry.com, citing NARA RG 59, "U.S. Passport Applications, 1795–1925," microfilm publication M1372, 694 rolls, roll 491F. Middle name from Will of Isaac Maynard, Oneida County. "Maynard "Isaac Maynard Is Dead after Brief Illness," *Utica Observer-Dispatch*, 11 February 1936, p. 29. "Mated: A Chicago Man Finds a Blooming Bride in Dull St. Louis," *Chicago* [Illinois] *Post*, 8 March 1873, p. 4. Forest Hill Cemetery Office, "Record of Interments, 1927 to 1961," Margaret F. Maynard, 239.

756   Forest Hill Cemetery Office, "Record of Interments, 1927 to 1961," Margaret F. Maynard, 239.

757   "Isaac Maynard Is Dead after Brief Illness," *Utica Observer-Dispatch*, 11 February 1936. *Edwards' Sixteenth Annual Directory of the . . . City of Chicago for 1873* (Chicago: Richard Edwards, 1873), p. 768, listing for Platt, Thorn & Maynard: "Platt, Thorn & Maynard (Nathan Platt, Edwin Thorn and Isaac M. [sic] Maynard), pig iron, 9 and 11 N. Canal." Isaac was also listed on p. 660 of the directory, with no address.

758   "Isaac Maynard Is Dead after Brief Illness," *Utica Observer-Dispatch*, 11 February 1936.

759   "Isaac Maynard Is Dead after Brief Illness," *Utica Observer-Dispatch*, 11 February 1936.

760   U.S. Passport Application of Richard Field Maynard, no. 6194, issued 26 June 1897 (stamped), viewed on Ancestry.com, citing NARA RG 59, "U.S. Passport Applications, 1795–1925," microfilm publication M1372, 694 rolls, roll 491F.

761   "Deaths," *New York Times*, 4 March 1964, 37.

762   "North Bennington," *Rutland* [Vermont] *Daily Herald*, 10 January 1917, p. 8.

763   "Died," *Stamford* [Connecticut] *Advocate,* 30 November 1971, p. 6.

764   "Richard F. Maynard," *Stamford* [Connecticut] *Advocate,* 4 March 1964, p. 6.

765   Finding aid for "Papers of Lorraine Maynard, 1850–2013 (inclusive), 1897–1930 (bulk)," Harvard University, Schlesinger Library, Radcliffe Institute, Archive/Manuscript, history note, viewed online at hollis.harvard.edu 27 November 2020.

766   Photograph of gravestone at FindaGrave.com, memorial #156314775, Sophia Margaret Maynard Crouse, Forest Hill Cemetery, Utica. U.S. Passport Application of Sophia M. Crouse, issued 28 February 1916 (stamped), no. 18777 (stamped), viewed on Ancestry.com, citing NARA RG 59, "Passport Applications, January 2, 1906–March 31, 1925," Microfilm Publication M1490, 2740 rolls, roll 0295.

767   "Society Chit-Chat," *Utica Sunday Tribune*, 2 January 1881, p. 4. The article preceded the actual ceremony by four days, which was slated to be "witnessed only by the relatives of the contracting

parties," with a reception following at the home of the bride's parents. Presumably, the event, "momentous to Utica society," took place on the day and in the fashion that was planned. Grace Maynard was listed as a bridesmaid. Daniel was first married to Charlotte Gray Beckwith of Hartford, Connecticut, with whom he had two children. She died in 1876. They had two sons, Clarence B. Crouse and Harry P. Crouse, both of whom predeceased him. ("Was a Well Known Utican: Daniel N. Crouse Dies Following Attack of Heart Trouble—Prominent in Many Ways," [Rome, New York] *Daily Sentinel*, 20 February 1919, p. 5).

768   Commonwealth of Virginia, Certificate of Death, Irvington, Lancaster County (1957), State File No. 12595, Registered No. 18, Registration District No. 510-B, Nellis Maynard Crouse, viewed on Ancestry.com, "Virginia, Death Records, 1912–2014," 1957, 12284–12599. "Was a Well Known Utican," *Daily Sentinel*, 20 February 1919, p. 5.

769   "Was a Well Known Utican," *Daily Sentinel*, 20 February 1919, describing him as the son of the late Daniel Crouse. See also, "Death Record of a Week," the obituary of John Miles Crouse, *Utica Sunday Tribune*, 18 July 1906, describing Daniel as the brother of John. The 1850 U.S. Census shows the brothers living together in the household of Daniel and C. Jane Crouse (1850 U.S. Census, Lenox, Madison, County, New York, p. 503 (penned), 252 (stamped), dwelling 1344, family 1345, Daniel Crouse household, viewed on Ancestry.com). For Catherine's full name, see photograph of gravestone at FindaGrave.com, memorial #156959073, Catherine Jane Beecher Crouse, Forest Hill Cemetery, viewed 27 November 2020.

770   U.S. Passport Application of Daniel N. Crouse, issued 1 March 1910 (stamped), no. 21033 (stamped), viewed on Ancestry.com, citing NARA RG 59, "U.S. Passport Applications, 1795–1925," microfilm publication M1372, 694 rolls, roll 102.

771   "Was a Well Known Utican," *Daily Sentinel*, 20 February 1919.

772   Irvington, Lancaster County, Virginia, Certificate of Death (1957), Registration District 510-B, State File no. 12595, Registered no. 18, Nellis Maynard Crouse, viewed on Ancestry.com, "Virginia, Death Records, 1912–2011." Forest Hill Cemetery Office, "Record of Interments, 1927–1961," Nellis M. Crouse, 81.

773   State of New York, Affidavit for License to Marry, City of Utica, Oneida County, No. 1547 (stamped), 836 (penned), 310 (penned) (1909), Nellis M. Crouse and Rebecca L. Bowne, viewed on Ancestry.com. New York State Department of Health and Vital Statistics, Certificate and Record of Marriage, Utica, Registered no. 836 (1909), Nellis M. Crouse and Rebecca L. Bowne, viewed on Ancestry.com, "New York County Marriage Records, 1847–1849, 1907–1936," Oneida 1904–1909.

774   "N. M. Crouse Dies in Sleep," *Ithaca* [New York] *Journal*, 13 May 1957, p. 2.

775   Photograph of gravestone at FindaGrave.com, memorial #213980405, Margaret Crouse Hart, viewed 22 September 2020. Forest Hill Cemetery Office, "Record of Interments, 1927–1961," Margaret K. Hart, 162.

776   Affidavit for License to Marry, Merwin K. Hart and K. Margaret Crouse, dated 17 November 1909, filed 15 December 1909, no. 2326 (stamped), no. 466 (penned), and no. 1319 (penned), viewed on Ancestry.com, "New York, County Marriage Records, 1847–1849, 1907–1936." "Was a Well Known Utican," *Daily Sentinel*, 20 February 1919.

777   1900 U.S. Census, Utica Town, Ward 7, Oneida County, New York, enumeration district 60, sheet 1B, dwelling 11, family 11, John W. MacLean household. Will of Isaac Maynard, Oneida County. "Mrs. John W. MacLean Dies Unexpectedly," *Utica Observer-Dispatch*, 9 November 1931, p. 16.

778   Utica, Christ Church, Members, Baptisms, Marriages, 1830–1893 (1886–1888), "U.S., Dutch Reformed Church Records in Selected States, 1639–1898," New York, viewed on Ancestry.com, which lists his middle name as Walter; all other records reviewed show his middle name to be his mother's maiden name of Waters. Photograph of gravestone at FindaGrave.com, memorial #156487564, John Waters MacLean, Forest Hill Cemetery.

779   "Death of Mrs. Charles McLean," *Utica Daily Observer*, 4 October 1900, describing Mrs. McLean as the mother of both "Chalmers" McLean of the U.S. Navy and John W. McLean of Utica.

780   1900 U.S. Census, Utica Town, John W. MacLean household.

781   Photograph of gravestone at FindAGrave.com, memorial #156487564, John Waters MacLean [*sic*], Forest Hill Cemetery.

782   "Mrs. John W. MacLean Dies Unexpectedly," *Utica Observer-Dispatch*, 9 November 1931. She was called "Julia" in 1860 (1860 U.S. Census, 7th Ward, City of Utica, Oneida County, New York, p. 85, family and dwelling 681, Isaac Maynard household).

783   "Mrs. John W. MacLean Dies Unexpectedly," *Utica Observer-Dispatch*, 9 November 1931.

784   1910 U.S. Census, Utica, Oneida County, New York, enumeration district 119, sheet 5B, dwelling 151, family 198, J. W. MacLean household, showing Sarah Grace as the mother of zero children. Also "Mrs. John W. MacLean Dies Unexpectedly," *Utica Observer-Dispatch*, 9 November 1931, p. 16, mentioning no children.

785   Forest Hill Cemetery Office, "Record of Interments, 1927–1961," Harriet Maynard McLean, 251. "Mrs. Harriet McLean," *Utica Observer-Dispatch*, 24 August 1937, p. 22.

786   Forest Hill Cemetery, "Record of Interments, 1927–1961," Harriet Maynard McLean, 251. "Mrs. Harriet McLean," *Utica Observer-Dispatch*, 24 August 1937, p. 22.

787   "Dr. Ogden Backus," *Rome* [New York] *Daily Sentinel*, 12 February 1906, p. 6. His first wife was Jeannie L. Lasell, whom he married 23 June 1891 in Whitinsville, Worcester County, Massachusetts (Northbridge, Worcester County, Massachusetts marriages (1891), no. 16, Ogden Backus and Jeannie L. Lasell, listing Ogden's parents). Whitinsville is a village in Northbridge.

788   Photograph of his gravestone at FindAGrave.com, memorial #20456124, Mount Hope Cemetery, Rochester, Monroe, New York.

789   "Dr. Ogden Backus," *Rome* [New York] *Daily Sentinel*, 12 February 1906.

790   "Dr. Ogden Backus," [Rochester, New York] *Democrat and Chronicle*, 11 February 1906, p. 8.

791   His first wife, Emily Gordon, whom he married 29 December 1875, died in 1901, leaving three children (*The National Cyclopedia of American Biography*, ongoing series, [New York: James T. White, 1922], vol. 18, pp. 343–44, listing for Thomas Chalmers McLean).

792   "Death of Mrs. Charles McLean," *Utica Daily Observer*, 4 October 1900, describing Mrs. McLean as the mother of both "Chalmers" McLean of the U.S. Navy and John W. McLean of Utica. *The National Cyclopedia of American Biography*, vol. 18, 343–44.

793   Oneida County Marriages (1909), p. 416, no. 2078, Thos. Chalmers McLean and Harriet Maynard Backus, viewed on FamilySearch.org, "New York, County Marriages, 1847–1848; 1908–1936[;] Oneida Marriage Records, 1908–1911," vol. 1, p. 416. *The National Cyclopedia of American Biography*, vol. 18, 343–44. FindAGrave.com, memorial #57195558, Adm. Thomas Chalmers McLean, Arlington National Cemetery, Arlington, Arlington County, Virginia, viewed 27 November 2020.

794   "Mrs. Harriet McLean," *Utica Observer-Dispatch*, 24 August 1937.

795   "Dr. Ogden Backus," [Rochester, New York] *Democrat and Chronicle*, 11 February 1906.

796   *The National Cyclopedia of American Biography*, vol. 18, 343–44.

797   Samuel's date of birth was given as 17 September on passport application, Samuel R. Maynard, issued 29 October 1888, no. 22993, viewed on Ancestry.com, citing NARA RG 59, "Passport Applications, 1795–1905," microfilm publication M1372, 694 rolls, roll 315. It was given as 12 September on passport application, Samuel Richard Maynard, issued 17 May 1897 (stamped), no. 4096, viewed on Ancestry.com, citing "Passport Applications, 1795–1905," NARA RG 59, microfilm publication M1372, 694 rolls, roll 315. His year of birth only is provided in Forest Hill Cemetery Office, "Record of Interments, 1927 to 1961," Samuel R. Maynard, 239.

798   Forest Hill Cemetery Office, "Record of Interments, 1927 to 1961," Samuel R. Maynard, 239.

799   "A Notable Utica Wedding," *Rome* [New York] *Daily Sentinel*, 26 September 1894, p. 2. "Death and Funeral Record of the Day in Utica," *Utica Observer-Dispatch*, 8 February 1932, p. 18.

800 Forest Hill Cemetery Office, "Record of Interments, 1902–1926," Marion W. Maynard, 239. Photograph of gravestone at FindaGrave.com, memorial #156488121, Marion Starr Wadhams Maynard, viewed 29 August 2020.

801 Passport application of Marion S. Wadhams, 19 November 1891, no. 33892, viewed on Ancestry.com, citing "U.S. Passport Applications, 1795–1925," NARA RG 59, Microfilm Publication M1372, 694 rolls, roll 382. Forest Hill Cemetery Office, "Record of Interments, 1902–1926," Marion W. Maynard, 239. Photograph of gravestone at FindaGrave.com, memorial #156488121, Marion Starr Wadhams Maynard, showing Marion's middle name. Her birthdate was erroneously listed as 15 September 1867 on her husband's 1897 passport (passport application, Samuel Richard Maynard, 1897).

802 "Samuel R. Maynard," *Utica Observer-Dispatch*, 8 February 1932, p. 18. "Death of Mrs. Marian W. Maynard," *Wilkes-Barre* [Pennsylvania] *Times Leader, the Evening News, Wilkes-Barre Record*, 19 October 1907, p. 6.

803 New York City, New York, Certificate and Record of Marriage (1915), no. 23016 (penned), 20021 (stamped), Samuel R. Maynard and Marion W. Bawtinheimer, author's files. The certificate shows Samuel's place of residence as Thomasville, [Thomas County], Georgia. Passenger List for the S.S. *Santa Paula*, arriving 15 May 1934, no. 104, p. 6 (stamped), line 6, Marion Maynard, viewed on Ancestry.com, citing NARA RG 85, "Passenger and Crew Lists of Vessels Arriving at New York, New York, 1897–1957," microfilm publication T715, showing Marion's U.S. citizenship having been established "thru marriage September 22, 1915."

804 Blenheim, Oxford County, Ontario, Canada, Births, Schedule A, p. 201, no. 73, Marion Bawtinheimer, viewed on Ancestry.com, "Ontario, Canada Births, 1832–1914." Forest Hill Cemetery Office, "Record of Interments, 1927 to 1961," Marion Maynard, 239. Photograph of gravestone at FindaGrave.com, memorial #131758751, Chrysler Bawtinheimer, Wolverton Cemetery, Wolverton, Oxford County, Ontario, Canada, viewed 18 September 2020. The surname has also appeared as "Bawtenheimer" and "Bawtenheiner." Her headstone shows her death year as 1960 (Photograph of gravestone at FindaGrave.com, memorial #152040618, Samuel R. Maynard, Forest Hill Cemetery).

805 "Samuel R. Maynard," *Utica Observer-Dispatch*, 8 February 1932, p. 18.

806 *The Phillips Bulletin*, vol. XVI, no. 2, January 1922 (Andover, Massachusetts: Phillips Academy, 1922), 43.

807 "Samuel R. Maynard," *Utica Observer-Dispatch*, 8 February 1932, p. 18. *Alumni Directory of Yale University: Living Graduates & Non-Graduates* (New Haven: The University, 1926), 275. He was a member of the Class of 1890.

808 Passport application, Samuel Richard Maynard, 1897.

809 1930 U.S. Census, Utica City, Oneida County, New York, Ward 7, enumeration district 33-90, sheet 11B, dwelling 214, family 341, Samuel R. Maynard household.

810 New York City, New York, Certificate and Record of Marriage (1915), Samuel R. Maynard and Marion W. Bawtinheimer.

811 Passenger List for the S.S. *Santa Paula,* arriving in New York 18 April 1934, p. 6 (stamped) no. 104, line 7, Grace Maynard, viewed on Ancestry.com, citing NARA microfilm publication T715, 8892 rolls, roll 5475. "Grace Maynard Nunes, 79," online obituary, GenealogyBank.com, citing *Greenwich* [Connecticut] *Citizen*, 9 May 2003, giving her birthplace as the Brookline section of Boston.

812 "New York, New York, Index to Marriage Licenses, 1908–1910, 1938–1940, database online, Grace Maynard and Edward Vernon Nunes.

813 Forest Hill Cemetery Office, "Record of Interments, 1927 to 1961," John F. Maynard Sr., 239. Passport application, John F. Maynard, 6 April 1922, issued 11 April 1922 (stamped) #143397 (penned), viewed on Ancestry.com, citing "Passport Applications, January 2, 1906–March 31, 1925," NARA RG 59, microfilm publication M1490, 2740 rolls, roll 1898.

814 Forest Hill Cemetery Office, "Record of Interments, 1927 to 1961," John Frederick Maynard, 239.

815 "Personal," *Utica Morning Herald*, 7 September 1876, p. 2.

816 Forest Hill Cemetery Office, "Record of Interments, 1927 to 1961," Mary A. B. Maynard, 239.

817 Passport application, Arthur B. Maynard, issued 28 November 1922, no. 236944 (penned), viewed on Ancestry.com, citing NARA RG 59, Microfilm Publication M1490, "Passport Applications, January 2, 1906–March 31, 1925," 2740 rolls, roll 2148. Passenger manifest for the S.S. *Aquitania*, arriving 2 August 1937, Arthur B. Maynard, p. 58, line 20, viewed on Ancestry.com, citing NARA RG 85, "Passenger and Crew Lists of Vessels Arriving at New York, 1897–1957," microfilm publication T715, 8892 rolls, roll 6017. 1909 Marriage License Application, Arthur Beardsley Maynard and Anne Garretson Lee, Columbiana County, Ohio, Marriage Record (1909), p. 154, viewed on FamilySearch.org, "Ohio, County Marriage Records, 1774–1993," Columbiana 1842–1910 (stating that Arthur would be 32 years of age on 28 August 1909). N. Gray and Company Funeral Home, San Francisco, San Francisco County, California, Funeral Records, book 37, p. 272, Arthur Beardsley Maynard, viewed on Ancestry.com. An 1898 passport application erroneously gives Arthur's birth year as 1878, overwritten as 1888 (Emergency Passport Application for John F. Maynard, 1 August 1898 in Stockholm, Sweden, no. 23, viewed on Ancestry.com, citing NARA RG 59, "Emergency Passport Applications [Passports Issued Abroad], 1877–1907," microfilm publication M1834, 57 rolls, roll 9).

818 N. Gray and Company Funeral Home, Funeral Records, book 37, p. 272.

819 Columbiana County, Ohio, Marriage Records (1909), p. 54, Arthur Beardsley Maynard to Anne Garretson Lee.

820 Forest Hill Cemetery Office, "Record of Interments, 1927 to 1961," John F. Maynard, Jr., 239.

821 "The June Weddings," *Utica Observer*, 20 June 1907, p. 8.

822 Forest Hill Cemetery Office, "Record of Interments, 1927 to 1961," Mary L. Maynard, p. 239.

823 Passenger List for the S.S. *Shawnee*, arriving 14 February 1929, page 13, line 11, Mary Louise Maynard, viewed on Ancestry.com, citing NARA RG 85, microfilm publication A3621, "U.S. Citizen Passenger Lists of Vessels Arriving at Miami, Florida, 1899–1948," roll 8.

824 "Mrs. Parsons," *The Item of Millburn and Short Hills* [New Jersey], 25 December 1952, p. 2.

825 "The marriage of . . ." *Utica Observer-Dispatch*, 5 May 1935, Section III (C), p. 1.

826 "Mrs. Parsons," *The Item of Millburn and Short Hills* [New Jersey], 25 December 1952.

827 Passenger List for the S.S. *Shawnee*, arriving 14 February 1929, George de F. Maynard.

828 "George Maynard," *Utica Observer-Dispatch,* 15 November 1963, p. 24.

829 Jackson County, Missouri, marriage license no. A68318 (1937), George deForest Maynard and Martha Wiles, viewed on Ancestry.com, "Missouri, Jackson County Marriage Records, 1840–1985"; the license was issued 3 September 1937.

830 Divorce & Annulment Index, p. 191, George D. Maynard and Martha W. Maynard, viewed on Ancestry.com, "Florida, Divorce Index, 1927–2001."

831 "Patricia Burton Maynard," *High Point* [North Carolina] *Enterprise*, 16 September 2011, p. 2B.

832 Photograph of gravestone at FindaGrave.com, memorial #156488457, Patricia Burton Maynard, Forest Hill Cemetery. "Patricia Burton Maynard," *High Point* [North Carolina] *Enterprise*, 16 September 2011.

833 Photograph of gravestone at FindaGrave.com, Patricia Burton Maynard. "Patricia Burton Maynard," online obituary, 16 September 2011. The city of High Point stretches over several counties.

834 Jenifer Kahn Bakkala, *An American Family: Four Centuries of Labor, Love, and Reward* (Boston, Massachusetts: Newbury Street Press, 2018), 111.

835 "Vassar Alumna Bride of H. R. Davis," *Poughkeepsie* [New York] *Journal*, 26 March 1946, p. 8.

Index

Numbers in *italics* refer to pages with images.
Numbers in **bold** refer to family tree charts.

CPSIA information can be obtained
at www.ICGtesting.com
Printed in the USA
BVHW020710110122
624248BV00002B/8

9 781887 043922